D0908346

Intellect and Public Life

Intellect and Public Life

Essays on the Social History
of Academic Intellectuals in the United States

Thomas Bender

The Johns Hopkins University Press
Baltimore and London

The Johns Hopkins University Press
2715 North Charles Street
Baltimore, Maryland 21218-4319
The Johns Hopkins Press Ltd., London

Bender, Thomas.
    Intellect and public life : essays on the social history of academic intellectuals in the United States / Thomas Bender.
        p.   cm.
    Includes bibliographical references and index.
    ISBN 0-8018-4433-9 (alk. paper)
    1. Intellectuals—United States—Attitudes—History.   2. Intellectuals—United States—Political activity—History.   3. Political participation—United States—History.   4. Community development, Urban—United States—History.   5. Urban policy—United States—Citizen participation—History.   6. United States—Intellectual life.   I. Title.
HT690.U6B46   1992
001.1'0973—dc20   92-11393

In gratitude to two teachers
WILSON SMITH
CARL E. SCHORSKE

Contents

Preface

I WAS ONCE INTRODUCED AT A SESSION OF THE AMERICAN HISTORICAL Association as the only American urban historian who is an intellectual historian. It got a laugh, but it also pointed to a persistent preoccupation in my work, a preoccupation that is manifest in and even central to these essays on intellect and public life. I have explored the borderland between or, phrased more optimistically, at the intersection of urban and intellectual history. These studies of the academic professions and academic intellectuals in the United States derive their distinctive strengths and insights from that particular fascination. Their weaknesses and lacunae are no doubt inherited from the same source.

In the 1970s, when I began my career as a historian, to be a historian of both cities and intellectuals was to struggle against the current, even two currents. Urban history was defined as the study of social problems and social mobility, of plumbing and pavements, of ethnic relations and machine politics. If nearly everyone was willing to give lip service to the notion of cities as centers of art, intellect, and high culture, neither traditional urban historians nor the so-called new urban historians were inclined to incorporate intellectual and cultural subjects into the domain of urban history.[1]

Intellectual historians had their own limitations. They were in the 1970s quite on the defensive, challenged by social historians and suffering the consequences of their overbroad claims for the field in the previous generation.[2] The field was nearly buried by a surging and relentlessly ambitious social history. The social historians were committed to greater descriptive precision (at least in its quantitative branch) and to the history of ordinary people, of nonelite people, very distinctly and with reason not artists and intellectuals or the highly educated generally. With only a couple of notable exceptions, historians still practicing intellectual and cultural history seemed strangely (to me) inattentive to the site of intellectual production and reception. But the exceptions inspired me, and I learned from their examples. In American history, Neil Harris linked urban development to cultural development in the United States in a brief but rich essay published in 1971.[3] Carl Schorske's work on Vienna provided what I thought might be a model for work on New York, though when I tried to use it thus I ended up with my own model, one that stressed more than did Schorske the importance of long-term changes and continuities.[4]

There was then a sense of isolation that is no more. The city has, if anything, become a preferred site for the pursuit of modern cultural history. This observation may mark me as the optimist, but I think it is well grounded. A more pessimistic survey of the state of things was recently offered by Donald Olsen, author of *The City as a Work of Art*.[5] In a paper prepared for a session on the metropolis at the International Congress of Historical Sciences held in Madrid in August 1990, Olsen argued that "students of cities have had remarkably little to say about culture, and students of culture even less to say about cities." In his view, things were not changing. There was still a troubling "diffidence" about exploring the cultural history of the city. My own contribution to the same session emphasized recent changes, noting work, mostly by cultural as opposed to urban historians, that was using the city as a site to explicate both the experience of urban life and the making and reception of high-culture forms.[6]

Insofar as cultural historians have led the way, one might inquire into the possible reasons for the reluctance of urban historians to embrace the study of opera houses and art galleries as they have that of sewers and slums. I suspect that urban historians are (unknowingly) very much in the tradition of the early sociological study of the city. They are students of urban pathology, even as they more often than not attack the Victorian assumptions that largely structure that perception of the city.

The association of cities with social problems rather than with culture is particularly pronounced in American culture.[7] It may be a legacy of American misunderstanding of Matthew Arnold, but I think it has deeper roots, deriving from an eighteenth-century assumption. It is an assumption held by Jean-Jacques Rousseau but *few* other European intellectuals and held by Thomas Jefferson and *many* American intellectuals: the notion is that there is some inherent conflict between cultural advance and social advance. One must choose between cultural achievements and social and political justice.[8]

If urban history, a field marked by deep decline in historiographical significance at the moment, is to realize its rich possibilities for historical inquiry, it must transcend this great schism. In fact, the intercourse among culture, society, and politics in the modern city is quite promiscuous and extraordinarily complex. None of these vectors of urban life can be grasped independent of the others. Any historian of metropolitan culture must begin, I think, with this understanding. High culture cannot be isolated, as some modernists proposed, from other levels of culture— or from social and political life.[9] There is, of course, an internal history of cultural fields—whether of science or the opera—but it is only when that internal history is brought into relation with external contingencies, including place, economy, social relations, and politics, that one begins to write an urban history of culture.

For good reason, recent work in cultural history has been self-conscious about the boundaries of high and popular culture, even the boundaries of culture and society. The sort of autonomy sought by the New Critics in literature or a formalist like Clement Greenberg in painting leaves no nexus of attachment to the metropolis. Nor can high culture be adequately studied outside the complex patterns of relation to more popular forms of culture: high and popular, sacralized and commercial, elite and more general cultural forms are deeply entangled with each other in ways that mutually define them and that establish their metropolitan identity and role.[10] If there is to be a history of urban culture, the object of inquiry must be the culture *of* the city, not simply culture *in* the city.

There are some recent disciplinary tendencies that bear importantly on the writing of the cultural history of the city. The ambition to be global, to write *l'histoire totale*, the impulse toward ethnographic density of description, and the exploration of interrelationships has encouraged historians to think about a canvas smaller than the nation-state but large enough to sustain rich analysis and important enough to justify study. This has encouraged a focus on the local and particular, legitimating what Clifford Geertz called "local knowledge."[11] This shift in historical practice promises to draw more scholars, especially cultural historians, to the study of cities.

Donald Olsen, in the paper already mentioned, worried that much of this new work tends to ignore established institutions and elites generally, focusing instead upon marginal groups, those excluded from public culture in the past because of race, gender, class, illiteracy, and the like. Yet this is not cause for alarm. If much recent scholarship on urban culture has tended to show more interest in workers' entertainments than in avant-garde art, we should not complain. This newly won understanding of popular forms of social life and culture is valuable in its own right. And it is increasingly understood to be indispensable to the understanding of elite culture. Elizabeth Kendall, for example, showed the popular theatrical and women's culture roots for the emergence of modern dance in America, while Peter Jelavich's recent study of modernism in Munich revealed how deeply the avant garde was entangled with and dependent upon popular art forms. We need to know more than the history of painting to write the cultural history of an artistic production and reception in cities. We must understand, in the phrase of Svetlana Alpers, the "visual culture" of a time and place in order to interpret elite pictorial and architectural forms.[12]

It is possible, as Donald Olsen worried, that those who call themselves urban historians will not do the work of writing this history. Perhaps. Yet the work will be done. If not by urban historians, then it will be by cultural historians who have found in the city a milieu of scale that allows one to track the actual working of cultural production and reception, the social relations and formal borrowings involved in both the production and the reception of culture, in sufficient richness to meet the demanding standards of current historiographical practice.

The essays in this volume are less concerned with the arts of the city than with the relation of urban patterns of intellectual life and academic forms of higher learning. My focus is more on production than reception, and my mode of investigation is institutional. Having been encouraged by my teachers to think about the institutional context of ideas, my urban interests directed me to examine those urban institutions that sustained intellectual life, including some fairly popular forms.[13] Here, it seemed to me, and it still does so seem, is a way to solve the problem of the insufficient social specificity in traditional intellectual history. It offered a way of being precise about the nature of the connection between intellectual and social history, fields once comfortably linked. That is the argument I made at a conference, a somewhat panicky conference, on the future of intellectual history held in 1977. My contribution to that conference appears here as chapter 1.

At least since the fifteenth or sixteenth century, cities have been nodal points for societies, a point where the interplay of politics, culture, and society is intensified and clarified. The history of intellect (and of universities) has been interwoven into this history.[14] One of the themes of these essays is that this centrality of the city is being eroded, being replaced by translocal institutions (professions and corporations, for example).[15] But the analytical usefulness of such a conception of the city's role in society survives that historical trend.

The recovery of the city from behind the structures of the modern academic disciplines (a work infused, especially in some of the earlier essays, by what now seems a bit too much nostalgia) also provided me with leverage on the problem that was central to the study of the professions in the 1970s: resistance to the self-promoting whiggism evident in so much writing about the history of the professions. Too often historians had accepted the darkness and light version of the relation of what preceded professionalization, a version purveyed in the sources by the very interested parties who advocated reform and eventually displaced older structures with the ones in which we work.[16]

For many historians of the academic disciplines, the work of Thomas Kuhn, notably his *Structure of Scientific Revolutions*, provided an escape route from the progressivist fallacy that I have designated here as whiggism.[17] Kuhn shifted the discussion from inherent quality to the sociological issue of evaluating and legitimating scientific work. In his scholarship, science became at least in part a social process, with work conducted in communities of scientists who shared common scientific paradigms. The historian of science became less a chronicler of progressive triumph of truth and more an analyst of how successive structures of perception are adopted and used within the social organization of science. Part of the appeal of Kuhn for historians was his radical contextualism. Historians welcomed it, no doubt, as David A. Hollinger pointed out, because Kuhn's work was very much in the tradition of historical scholarship. His having applied historicist methods to the study of science made them all the more appealing when we brought them home again.[18] What most appealed to me, however, was his sociology, much of it implicit in the book. Scientific work was structured and validated by communities of scientists. Obviously, Kuhn had in mind highly organized disciplines, working in the context of paradigms. Yet I wondered: might the historian of more general ideas benefit by inquiring into the structure of more ordinary validating communities?[19] It seemed helpful to think in terms of sequences of structures (social and perceptual) as a way of understanding the development of academic culture. One system, in this way of looking at things, would be replaced by another when the earlier could not work, whether not working was defined socially or intellectually.[20] Instead of a story of a movement from nothing to something, the emergence of the modern academic professions rep-

resented a reorganization of intellectual culture—from a civic foundation to a professional and academic one. From my point of view, this
understanding was liberating. It meant that one could respect what
preceded the modern structure of intellectual life and inquire—in a
rather detailed way—into its real and perceived deficiencies without
losing sight of its strengths. The earlier structure, like the Aristotelian
science that concerned Kuhn, could be understood on its own terms,
not only in relation to a successive structure into which I had myself
been socialized.

The collapse of the older organization of culture was neither inherent nor determined. It was a historical event. There were, presum-
ably, historically specifiable problems, perhaps precipitated by new social
and intellectual circumstances. The new academic culture also had attractions that were not available in the older patterns of higher learning,
but these might be quite various, not simply the inherent logic of intellectual development. By thus loosely linking Kuhn's implicit sociology
with the question of the interplay of cities and professions, I was able
to free myself from the common—but disturbingly ahistorical—tendency, even in historical works, to treat professionalization as a dependent
variable of the modernization process.[21]

I cannot say that I propose or even exemplify a *method* in these
essays. Yet I had a way of framing the object of inquiry. With what was
really a spatial metaphor of a field of action overlaid with social frameworks that structured patterns of interaction on that field, I was able to
clarify my analytical task.[22] Assimilating these structured frameworks
and patterns of interaction into what I called "cultures of intellectual
life," I asked how one culture related to another, whether a predecessor
or a successor culture. I asked as well: How tightly bounded are they?
How did this boundedness change over time? What differentiated the
civic culture from the culture of professionalism that succeeded it? What
difference was made by the social closeness of intellectual interchange
(direct and pesonal rather than mediated by print alone)? What were
the different meanings for the "text" or a cultural object in these two
social settings?[23] But most important to me, at least in these essays, was
that, by spatializing my approach to the question of institutional development, I was able to reinforce my resistance to the whiggish and
modernization models of professionalization.

There are many critical vantages that different historians have assumed in approaching the development of the academic disciplines.
Several distinguished studies recently focused upon the question of objectivity.[24] Some emphasized authority, and others focused on class

ambition and definition.[25] Most recently of all, Samuel Haber tracked the persistence of premodern notions of honor into the modern formation of the professions.[26] My fixed point has been a concern with the fate of our public culture. What are the implications of different structures of intellectual life and, as I suggest in the last essay, different theories of knowledge for the quality of civic discourse, for the vitality of public culture in an era when our higher intellectual culture is so heavily academicized?

Several themes of a general sort run through the essays. The most important two are linked in an unfortunate way: the increasing incorporation of academic culture into the center of American life, socially and intellectually, is accompanied and causally related to a progressive impoverishment of the public sphere. There is also an argument that intellectuals turned to academic culture as a hedge against the market—whether to insist upon the superiority of honor to market values, or for a sanctuary from intellectual chaos and competitiveness, or to purify and clarify discourse, even at the risk of social irrelevance.

These essays cumulatively tell the story of the rise of expert authority. It is, of course, a partial history, one particularly concerned for the fate of public culture. And that perspective produces a counternarrative, a growing difficulty of relations between academic culture and civic culture. Even in its triumph, it seems, professional social science inquiry is problematic, particularly in relation to democratic practice.

In the last essay, therefore, I attempt to address this issue directly, raising not only political and social questions but epistemological ones as well. One could argue, I realize, that my solicitude for public culture produced a distorted reading of the history of American academic culture. I do not, of course, rule out that possibility. Yet I am not convinced that the drift of these chapters is idiosyncratic. I find sustenance for my perspective in the recent work of Charles Lindblom, one of the most distinguished social scientists in the United States. In two books published during the past decade, *Usable Knowledge* (1979), co-authored with David Cohen, and *Inquiry and Change* (1990), he asked some very hard questions about the capacity of professional social inquiry. What kind of knowledge? What use is it? He answered that the harvest is less full and less useful than most social scientists acknowledge. And that recognition impelled him to elevate the significance of the intelligence of democracy, the give-and-take of political and social life. The product of such social experience is, he averred, knowledge, and it is useful social knowledge. We define these issues differently and look to different solutions, but for both Lindblom and me it is important to recognize the limits of social science. The best prospects for democracy reside within those limits.[27]

The partial dissolution of the project of professional social inquiry, what some might call the abandonment of the strong program for the social sciences, complements democracy in important ways. For me, though not for Lindblom, this perspective gives a new relevance to John Dewey's considerations of the relations of academic social inquiry, the public, and democracy, a theme I develop in the last chapter.

Although I call these studies essays in social history, I would not want that phrasing to be misunderstood. I do not offer a social explanation for the transformation that I am here exploring. I am sure a critic more acute than I have been will notice places where I have slipped into such simple and one-sided explanations of change, but I have tried throughout to make the point that any explanation of change in intellectual institutions must link the social and the intellectual. One cannot find purely social causes for changes in the conduct of intellectual life. Nor is an idealistic explanation sufficient. The two must be related, even if sometimes one cannot get more precise than identifying elective affinities between intellectual and social formations. Social changes (I speak even of crisis in the pages that follow) provided the motivation for new structures of authority for social inquiry, yet it was an intellectual problem, a perceptual need for a new kind of social representation and explanation, that supplied the circumstance for the establishment of professional sociology.[28]

So much of our intellectual history has been explicitly or implicitly grounded in the history of Boston and New England that it is a matter of interpretive importance that much of my work has been developed from my study of New York's history. The New England–centered interpretation of American culture that Peter Dobkin Hall has written, to take only one recent and important study, portrays a culture marked by purity and class solidarity that is hard to find in New York or, I would argue, in the United States generally.[29] What Lee Benson and many colonial historians have said about New York remains compelling: New York may be unique among the states, but in the very diversity that makes it unique it best represents the United States as a whole.[30]

When I began these essays, my view was from the provincial America that understood New York to be the metropolis. I was curious to understand provincial intellectual and cultural forms, and the first two chapters, the first two essays written, reveal this perspective. By chapter 3 my perspective is changing. The issues are the same, but now my historiographical location is in the metropolis iself. The reasons are rather obviously biographical. I moved to New York in 1974, and by the late 1970s I was becoming more and more curious about New York both as a place for my own work and as a possible subject for my work, something I realized with the publication of *New York Intellect* in 1987. The shift is not abrupt, and I think the whole book benefits by the presence of both perspectives.

These essays with three exceptions were written in the 1980s. Chapters 1 and 2 were written and published in the 1970s, whereas the last chapter was written as a lecture in 1990 and revised into the present form in 1991. My perspective held rather firmly through these years, and the essays have a consistency of style, purpose, and interpretive stance, save for the last, which is explicitly revisionist in intention. Indeed, there is so much consistency that it occasionally manifests itself in repeated phrases and the same example in successive essays. A discipline provides a structure for thinking through questions, and an individual working within a disciplinary field is liable to return again and again to the same ideas in the interest of pushing a bit farther, eventually to a new idea. Whether any genuinely new ideas emerge over the course of these essays I leave to the reader's judgment. But I urge forebearance of the reader when essays written for different purposes and different times have, when pulled together between two covers, an occasional echo. I might have removed these embarrassments, but except for one case I have decided to leave stand all the discomfiting phrases. The one change is because I liked a quotation from Alfred North Whitehead so much that I used it to end two different essays. I have, therefore, excised the last paragraph of chapter 3. But the others I leave. The last essay, I should say, intentionally echoes the earlier ones with the aim of pressing an alternative interpretation.

I have one final embarrassment to report. These essays all attach themselves to the issue of and the fate of what I call public culture. What is absent, however, is a single, systematic statement of what I mean by that notion. I had hoped to provide a brief essay in definition, but that essay has itself grown into a book. I had further hoped that the book-length study of the term would be published at the same time as these essays. Unfortunately, that work, *History and Public Culture*, continues to expand. Rather than holding up the publication of these essays any longer, waiting for the other volume, I am publishing them now. The two books will speak to each other, but they do not depend upon each other.

Acknowledgments

SEVERAL FRIENDS ENCOURAGED MY WORK IN THIS LINE, AND I THANK ESPE-
cially Thomas L. Haskell, David A. Hollinger, Peter Dobkin Hall, William
R. Taylor, John Higham, the late Herbert G. Gutman, the late John
William Ward, and Gwendolyn Wright, who is also my wife. Perhaps
it is the latter circumstance that enabled her so many times to persuade
me that what I wrote was wonderful, even though it required a complete
rewriting. To Henry Tom, my editor and friend, I owe much. I am
especially thankful for that rich combination of patience and the knack
for solving the problems (usually of the delaying kind) that authors
bring to editors. I met Henry when I was just beginning to work on this
theme; he maintained his interest in it and his faith in me for longer
than I might fairly have expected. Tracy Tullis, a graduate student in
History at New York University, assisted in the tedious task of checking
the quotes and footnotes, for which I am thankful.

I am taking the occasion of this book to express my gratitude, by
way of dedication, to two teachers. They are very different men, very
different scholars. And my relations with them have been quite different—at different stages in my continuing education as a historian. Wilson Smith was formally my teacher; he was my dissertation adviser.
Carl E. Schorske has been an informal teacher for more than a decade.
Both are very special friends. Both have supported, sustained, and prod-
ded a young scholar who was trying to grow, but who was not quite
sure how to do it. Both are deeply concerned about the subject of these
studies: the vocation of academic intellect. Finally, and perhaps most
important of all, both have continually impressed upon me the need for
clarity about a practical task very important to me: living a life of honest
scholarship and ethical commitment.

PART I.
NINETEENTH-CENTURY ORIGINS OF ACADEMIC CULTURE

❧[1]❧ The Cultures of Intellectual Life: The City and the Professions

The basic terms for the essays that follow are established here. I outline the value of attending to the spatial structuring of intellectual life and develop it into an analytical distinction between civic culture *and* professional culture. *These terms, sometimes phrased differently, have proven enormously fruitful to my work and, if citations mean anything, to other historians as well.*

This essay was first prepared as my contribution to a conference organized by John Higham and Paul Conkin to commemorate the eightieth birthday of Merle Curti. That conference, held at the Wingspread Conference Center in Wisconsin, in 1977, was devoted to the future of intellectual history. For many of the participants the future was bleak indeed, but several of us who were classified as younger historians were not prepared for such a pessimistic outlook on our future. Like some of the others of my generation at the conference, I proposed a way to proceed with an intellectual history, perhaps chastened by its confrontation with social history but enriched as well. My paper was published with this title in John Higham and Paul Conkin, eds., New Directions in American Intellectual History *(Baltimore: Johns Hopkins University Press, 1979), 181–95.*

MEN AND WOMEN OF IDEAS WORK WITHIN A SOCIAL MATRIX THAT CONSTI-tutes an audience or public for them. Within this context they seek legitimacy and are supplied with the collective concepts, the vocabulary of motives, and the key questions that give shape to their work. These communities of discourse, which I am here calling *cultures of intellectual life,* are historically constructed and are held together by mutual attachment to a cluster of shared meanings and intellectual purposes. They socialize the life of the mind and give institutional force to the paradigms that guide the creative intellect.[1]

A consideration of the historical development of these cultures of intellectual life brings us to an insufficiently studied but vital point where intellectual history and social history touch. To discern the character of these networks of intellectual discourse, to assess their relative significance over time, and to discover their pattern of interaction promise to illuminate the social foundations of intellectual life in America.

The public culture that intellectual historians seek to explicate and understand is the product of an exceedingly complex interaction between speakers and hearers, writers and readers. Reality is created out of this dynamic interplay.[2] "Men of knowledge," writes Robert Merton, "do not orient themselves exclusively toward their data nor toward the total society, but to special segments of that society with their special demands, criteria of validity, of significant knowledge, of pertinent problems, etc. It is through anticipation of these demands and expectations of particular audiences, which can be effectively located in the social structure, that men of knowledge organize their own work, define their own data, seize upon problems."[3]

Merton obviously has in mind the disciplinary peers so prominent in contemporary intellectual life, but his point can be applied to earlier periods, when the social organization of knowledge took different forms. Before the rise of modern professionalism, there were identifiable audiences that judged and affected the work of American thinkers. Until the middle of the nineteenth century, in fact, the city provided the primary context for the life of the mind. Since the "social frameworks of knowledge" that give shape to relationships between thinker, audience, and that which is to be explained are historically variable, they are properly the subject of sociological and historical inquiry, as is the interaction between these particular cultures of intellectual life and the larger society.[4]

Intellectual historians are beginning to consider the professions as a context for intellectual life, but neither they nor urban historians have so far devoted much attention to the importance of the local community as a context and audience for intellectual life.[5] If the modern professions can be described as community without locality, it is important to recall that before 1850 locality provided an important sense of "we-ness" to intellectual life. I aim in what follows to suggest the changing significance of two fundamental and contrasting foundations of intellectual community: the city and the professions.

Questions of legitimacy and hegemony apply to intellectual life as well as to politics. Different cultures of intellectual life may succeed each other; they may also vie for hegemony within a given society. An adequate account of the life of the mind in America requires an understanding of why and how one or another of these cultures achieves hegemony. The way in which the scientific professionals founded disciplinary associations and ensconced themselves in research universities at the end of the nineteenth century provides an example of the kind of problem that must be resolved. They succeeded in appropriating and institutionalizing science within the context of a culture of professionalism. They persuaded many of their contemporaries (and historians since) that they stood for the advent of "real" science in America. Yet they actually represented a particular kind of scientific inquiry. They were able to achieve hegemony by discrediting an alternative pattern of science based upon different assumptions about the nature of reality and rooted in civic, as opposed to disciplinary, institutions.[6]

Several obvious questions flow from the perspective suggested here. We must ask what failures in the older organization of intellectual life (and what new intellectual needs) prepared the way for such shifts in intellectual hegemony. How did the differing social organizations of knowledge affect or relate to the way "reality" was perceived? Did particular frameworks of knowledge, whether because of their structural characteristics or their acquired traditions, emphasize mystical over rational knowledge, positive over reflective approaches, symbolic over concrete understanding?[7] How did different patterns of social relationships within particular cultures of intellectual life affect intellectual style and strategies? Felix Gilbert rightly notes that "whether a manuscript [was] circulated among a small number of people with education and interests similar to those of the writer, or whether a manuscript might be read by a great number of people unknown to the author creates necessarily a great difference in the attitude of an author."[8] Does it make a difference that locally-based intellectual life was overwhelmingly face-to-face interchange, while in the modern professions communication is mediated by the printed word?[9] What analytical capacities were strengthened (or weakened) by a shift from one culture of intellectual life to another? How was society's need for general explanatory ideas affected? What was the effect on the prospects for a shared public culture and for a socially responsible intelligentsia?

Professionalism in the eighteenth and early nineteenth centuries differed profoundly from what emerged in association with the graduate school. The scientific professionals who led the way in defining the new professionalism did not take the traditional professions as their model. They created something original.[10] In stressing this discontinuity in the history of the professions, I make a conceptual distinction between what I call *civic professionalism* and *disciplinary professionalism*. The former pattern has a historic association with the commercial city and the Florentine tradition of civic humanism, while the latter coincides with the emergence of industrial and corporate capitalism.[11] During the course of the nineteenth century in America, civic professionalism declined in significance and even the traditional professions of law, medicine, and the ministry began to associate themselves with the model provided by the rising disciplinary professions.

The outlines of the change can be sketched in a quick comparison of professionalism revealed in the careers of two men remembered for their contributions to the development of medical training: Samuel Bard and William H. Welch.[12] Bard's reputation rests on his advocacy of a hospital that could be made part of the medical instruction offered at Kings College. His campaign led to the founding of the New York Hospital in 1771, and most commentators have assumed that he thus anticipated "the modern structure of academic medicine."[13] But a superficial similarity with the Johns Hopkins idea of a university hospital should not be allowed to obscure a profound difference between eighteenth- and twentieth-century medical professionalism. Early American professionals were essentially community oriented. Entry to the professions was usually through local elite sponsorship, and professionals won public trust within this established social context rather than through certification. While specialisms were recognized, disciplinary professions did not exist. Medicine, like other professions and learned avocations, represented an emphasis within a shared and relatively accessible public culture that was nurtured by general associations of cognoscenti.

Although eighteenth-century professionals were cosmopolitan in their interests, this did not compromise their attachment to localities. They participated avidly in the transatlantic "Republic of Letters," but this union was decentralized and federalized, and not, to use the eighteenth-century political term, consolidated. The cosmopolitanism of intellectuals and professionals often took the form of city boosting. Bard, who studied in Edinburgh, wanted New York City to have the medical institutions that major European cities had. His advocacy of a hospital was linked to his work on behalf of a whole network of civic institutions. He was active in the effort to rebuild Trinity Church after it was damaged in the Revolutionary War, he was a leader in the reorganization that transformed Kings College into Columbia, and he was one of the initiators of the New York Society Library, the New York Historical Society, and the New York Society for Promoting Useful Knowledge. These efforts in civic improvement were the product of the combined energies of the educated and powerful in the city, and they integrated and gave shape to its intellectual life.[14]

In contrast, the Johns Hopkins of Daniel Coit Gilman and Welch was a product of professional, disciplinary communities. To that extent it was an alien presence in Baltimore. It was created, President Eliot of Harvard stiffly observed, not because of any civic ambition in Baltimore, but because one man, a bachelor Quaker, willed it. The original faculty of philosophy included no Baltimoreans, and no major appointments in the medical school went to members of the local medical community. William Welch, who moved from New York to Johns Hopkins, identified with his profession in a new way; it was a branch of science—a discipline—not a civic role. Bard had been involved, as Welch was not, in a civic culture reminiscent of the traditional role of cities in directing intellectual life.

Other examples of early American civic culture come easily to mind as further illustrations. In antebellum Boston, the intellectual leadership provided by George Ticknor did not depend upon his disciplinary accomplishments or his Harvard professorship. For all of his cosmopolitan awareness and interest in the German model of academic life, Ticknor was enmeshed, socially and intellectually, in the life of the city. He wanted most to be a gentleman of Boston whose civic activities included being a Harvard professor and promoter of the public library. Hence, he took his intellectual cues from his fellow citizens, and their respect made him a preeminent and influential intellectual.[15]

This embrace of civic culture was not merely an eastern seaboard phenomenon. One of the most striking facts of the movement of people and institutions west during the first half of the nineteenth century, at least in the North, was the replication of this civic institution pattern of urban culture in locality after locality. Because intellectual and cultural historians have been careless about specifying the setting for intellectual activity, they have failed to note the surprisingly dense networks of institutions supporting intellectual life in nineteenth-century provincial towns and cities.[16] Even places with small populations aspired to a full intellectual life and established a full complement of urban institutions to nourish it.[17]

Western towns organized their intellectual life on the "principle of mutual instruction."[18] Within the context of this broadly inclusive culture of intellectual life, townspeople discussed the leading scientific and literary publications of the day. In larger towns and cities the key institution giving form to this culture might be a local institute of arts and science; the structure of discourse might, however, be quite informal in small towns. William Dean Howells recalled that, in his father's printing office in a small Ohio town about 1850,

> there was always a good deal of talk going on. . . . When it was not mere banter, it was mostly literary; we disputed about authors among ourselves and with the village wits who dropped in. There were several of these who were readers, and they liked to stand with their back to our stove and challenge opinion concerning Holmes and Poe, Irving and Macaulay, Pope and Byron, Dickens and Shakespeare. Any author who made an effect in the East became promptly known in that small village of the Western reserve. . . . Literature was so commonly accepted as a real interest, that I do not think I was accounted altogether queer in my devotion to it.[19]

If Howells emphasized literary interests, other commentators, from Tocqueville, to Martineau, to Lyell, remarked upon the extent of scientific activity they found in American towns. Lyell also noticed how remarkably inclusive intellectual life was. In Cincinnati, he commented, the joining of literary and scientific men, lawyers, clergymen, physicians, "and principal merchants of the place forms a society of a superior kind."[20]

While these townspeople were certainly aware of the greater accomplishments of the metropolises of the East and of Europe, they were not intimidated. In an address before a local literary society in 1814, Daniel Drake of Cincinnati observed:

> Learning, philosophy and taste, are yet in early infancy, and the standards of excellence in literature and science is proportionably low. Hence, acquirements, which in older and more enlightened countries would scarcely raise an individual to mediocrity, will here place him in a commanding station. Those who attain to superiority in the community of which they are members are relatively great. Literary excellence in Paris, London, or Edinburgh is incomparable with the same thing in Philadelphia, New York, or Boston: while each of these, in turn, has a standard of merit, which may be contrasted, but cannot be compared, with that of Lexington or Cincinnati.[21]

To a certain extent provincial intellectual life benefited from the same difficulties of transportation and communication that stimulated manufacturing in the small towns of the trans-Appalachian West. There was enough communication with the metropolis to maintain cultural aspirations but not enough to stifle local activity through domination by metropolitan products, whether in manufacturing or in intellectual life.[22] The large-scale social and economic transformations that would ultimately undermine local life were becoming apparent as early as the 1830s, but it was not until after the Civil War that Americans began to realize their implications. The consequences for civic professionalism were noted by Henry W. Bellows in 1872.

> Thousands of American towns, with an independent life of their own, isolated, trusting to themselves, in need of knowing and honoring native ability and skill in local affairs—each with its first-rate man of business, its able lawyer, its skilled physician, its honored representative, its truly *select-men*—have been pierced to the heart by the railroad which they helped to build. . . . It has annihilated their old importance . . . removed the necessity for any first-rate professional men in the village, destroyed local business and taken out of town the enterprising young men, besides exciting the ambition of those once content with a local importance, to seek larger spheres of life.[23]

Bellows, I suspect, expected the establishment and ultimate hegemony of translocal structures of intellectual life and standards of competence to be accomplished through the ascendancy of an urban-based metropolitan system. In such a cultural model, which implies the legitimate concentration of elites, local organizations of intellectual life would be "federated" under metropolitan auspices. Americans, for example, might have followed the contemporary model of the British Association for the Advancement of Science, which united local, provincial societies in a national framework. American scientists were familiar with the BAAS, but when they organized the American Association for the Advancement of Science a different pattern emerged. The AAAS provided an institutional umbrella for individuals and was organized internally by developing disciplines.[24]

As it turned out, neither city nor metropolis shaped intellectual life. The collapse of intellectual vitality in American towns and cities coupled, perhaps, with an antiurban resentment of the metropolis opened the way for the rise of a multicentered and nonlocal system of professionalism stressing individual membership and the fragmentation of elites. That an urban-based metropolitanism failed to develop cannot, however, be blamed entirely upon provincial antipathy to the metropolis. Urban culture itself was in crisis. America's largest cities were no longer able to organize a vital, rigorous, and coherent intellectual life.

The culture of professionalism arose as an alternative to the dis-

organized urban culture characteristic of the third quarter of the nineteenth century, and it pointed in new directions. If urban culture had
been centripetal, encouraging the convergence of specialisms, this new
professionalism was centrifugal. Charles W. Eliot, whose reforms at
Harvard helped to advance the new professionalism, was one of the
earliest to notice this phenomenon. Writing in 1854, when he was
twenty and apprehensive about his future, he observed: "What a tremendous question it is—what shall I be? . . . When a man answers that
question he not only determines his sphere of usefulness in the world,
he also decides in what *direction* his own mind shall be developed. The
different professions are not different roads converging on the same end;
they are different roads, which starting from the same vantage point
diverge forever, for all we know."[25]

Intellectual specialization took on a new character in the process
of becoming a system of disciplines. No longer an emphasis within a
shared public culture, each new disciplinary profession developed its
own conceptual basis. Each became a distinct "epistemic community."[26]
Disciplinary peers, not a diverse urban public, became the only legitimate
evaluators of intellectual work. If the civic institution pattern of intellectual life had woven together the various threads of intellectual life,
the fabric of urban public culture was riven by the end of the nineteenth
century. Knowledge and competence increasingly developed out of the
internal dynamics of esoteric disciplines rather than within the context
of shared perceptions of public needs. This is not to say that professionalized disciplines or the modern service professions that imitated
them became socially irresponsible. But their contributions to society
began to flow from their own self-definitions rather than from a recip-
rocal engagement with general public discourse.

The process of transition from urban-based to disciplinary intellectual life was complex, and its history reveals fleeting glimpses of what
seem to have been alternatives. The American Social Science Association, for example, might be interpreted as a national version of civic
professionalism. Its leaders represented traditional professions, and the
organization's constitution expressed a hope of bringing together men
and women at "both the local and national" level to address broad
social questions. Internal differentiation was based upon the definition
of four areas of public concern rather than on disciplines or subdisci-
plines. By the end of the century, however, it was clear that the future
for the social sciences belonged to professionalized disciplines associated
with university departments.[27]

The community of scientists and intellectuals in Washington during the Gilded Age apparently had yet another model in mind. They tried to advance a disciplinary professionalism that was national in scope within the context of a shared urban culture by federating the disciplines in a local organization that offered public lectures. But the lectures and discussions associated with the urban culture component of this organizational strategy rather quickly lost significance.[28] Professional discourse was treated as a serious activity, while the manifestations of traditional urban culture were relegated to the status of mere entertainment.

The beginning of this schism can be seen as early as 1839, when Horace Mann praised the Lyceum and the public lectures typical of urban culture as "interesting and useful" while at the same time complaining that they tended toward "superficiality." He allowed that the "dim and floating notions" they offered might be acceptable for general topics, but he insisted that in areas that pertain to one's "immediate employment or profession" such knowledge would be "not simply useless, but ruinous."[29] Without precisely following Mann's analysis, a number of historians have also detected serious weaknesses in midcentury urban culture.[30] Such words as *flatness, superficiality, sentimentalism, ineffectual, confused, lax,* and *simplification* recur in historical writing about the period's thought. How can we explain the emergence of these intellectual problems? My argument is that a large part of the explanation can be attributed to changes in the city as a context for intellectual work. It no longer provided an effective audience.

Earlier, in the mideighteenth century, intellectual community had been available in American villages, towns, and cities. While a real distinction must be made between learned and popular traditions, the two could be bridged. Elite culture depended upon and extended popular culture. It was possible for intellectuals to speak to the pace of local thought and still address serious issues in a learned tradition that was at least dimly familiar to their local community of auditors or readers.[31] Yet this intellectual community was fragile. It was vulnerable to the changes in scale, the calculation and ambition, and the cultural diversity that emerged over the course of the nineteenth century. Although a variety of formal institutions maintained this intellectual community into the nineteenth century, it began to unravel after the 1830s, particularly in the larger cities that might have assumed the role of metropolis for the United States.

Intellect's clear association with general urban elites had achieved for it a certain legitimacy and hegemony within society in the eighteenth and early nineteenth centuries. The social fragmentation, isolation, and anonymity that characterized the chaotic mid-nineteenth-century city eroded these customary sources of intellectual authority. Neither personal knowledge nor clear social categories were available to organize and discipline intellectual life. Intellectual distinctions were blurred, and the identity of audiences became rather diffuse.

Urban intellectuals in the midnineteenth century confronted the difficult task of winning acceptance of their special competence in a milieu of strangers. With traditional rituals of accreditation abandoned, producers and consumers of intellectual work found it increasingly difficult to fix on the cues that made coherent intellectual discourse possible. Lacking a solid impersonal basis for establishing a relationship with their audience, urban intellectuals relied on their personalities and the appearance of intimate disclosure to establish the trust and authority essential for intellectual community.[32] But personality was a poor substitute for the shared intellectual framework and clear social categories that had earlier given shape to local intellectual life. In such a situation, the eighteenth-century penchant for argument gave way to the quest for "influence."[33]

Henry Ward Beecher exemplified this pattern of intellectual life and revealed its weakness. The structure of discourse within which he operated as one of New York City's most notable intellectuals did not demand—or allow—hard thinking and vigorous argument. Self-display, sentimentalism, posture, gesture, and preoccupation with external appearance characterized his thought and preaching style. In an important sense he was for theology what Barnum was for art and natural science.[34] And the new professionalism—whether manifested in academic theology or in the Metropolitan Museum of Art—represented an attempt to reform this disorderly pattern of intellectual life.

Those who sought a more penetrating and rigorous intellectual life rejected and withdrew from the general culture of the city in order to embrace a new model of professionalism. Intellectual purposes were thus clarified and made less complicated. Edwards A. Park, in a lecture in Boston to the Massachusetts Congregational Clergy, urged his colleagues to "conduct our scholastic disputes in a scholastic way" for "we do wrong to our own minds when we carry out scientific difficulties down to the arena of popular dissension." Rather conventional formulas were sufficient to fulfill their pastoral duties. Park proposed, in effect, to separate the serious technical role of professionals from their responsibility of supplying usable philosophies for the general public. In time, as Bruce Kuklick has demonstrated in the case of Harvard philosophy, even this compromise was eroded by the complete triumph of the technical over the public role of philosophy.[35]

Intellectual life was tightened as people of ideas were inducted, increasingly through the emerging university system, into the restricted worlds of specialized discourse. The quest of professionals for the authority to define valid knowledge within disciplines is often interpreted as an expression of class interest, and to a degree it was.[36] But the new professionals were seeking intellectual security as much as social privilege and power. The new disciplines offered relatively precise subject matter and procedures at a time when both were greatly confused. The new professionalism also promised social guarantees of competence—certification—in an era when criteria of intellectual authority were vague and professional performance was unreliable.[37]

Urban and professional cultures were also connected with alternative ways of defining and attempting to solve problems. The authority of disciplinary professionalism was linked to new perceptions of the nature of "reality." Representatives of urban culture—from Daniel Drake to P. T. Barnum—had assumed that reality was generally accessible to common observation.[38] However democratic, this naive empiricism was gradually rejected as inadequate. The new professions were associated with a growing sense that understanding must penetrate internal qualities, processes, and structures. Serious intellectual problems and procedures were largely reformulated, most notably in respect to scientific work and in the analysis of society (social science).[39] Valid knowledge, formerly concretized in individual relationships to nature and society, now seemed to be defined in forms and processes one step removed from direct human experience.

Certainly we must welcome the new power and rigor that the disciplinary professions brought to a disorganized nineteenth-century intellectual life. Yet the twentieth-century hegemony of the new professionalism remains problematical. As Edmund Wilson pointed out in *The Wound and the Bow*, powerful new weapons are often inseparable from serious disability. Rigor and intellectual security were gained at the cost of making the parts of American intellectual life more powerful than the whole. Was an intellectual community that comprehended the whole of life compatible with the new professions? When the character of modern professionalism's relation to the social whole was becoming apparent, Alfred North Whitehead pointedly observed: "Each profession makes progress, but it is progress in its own groove. But there is no groove . . . adequate for the comprehension of human life. . . . Of course, no one is merely a mathematician, or merely a lawyer. People have lives outside of their profession or their business. But the point is the restraint of serious thought within a groove. The remainder of life is treated superficially, with the imperfect categories of thought derived from one profession."[40]

The various patterns of intellectual community that have consti- tuted effective audiences for American intellectuals deserve finer analysis than can be offered here. But even this necessarily schematic analysis of the city and the professions as alternative communities of discourse expands our understanding of the historical configurations of American intellectual life. And it suggests a fruitful approach for a history of the life of the mind in America.

When Merle Curti first presented his "social history of American thought" to the profession in 1943, his goal of linking social and in- tellectual history was not assumed to be at all problematical.[41] In recent years, however, social and intellectual history have been increasingly uncomfortable in each other's company. In looking for terms of rap- prochement with social history, intellectual historians have been unduly attentive to the quantitative emphasis of much American and French social history.[42] A more fruitful approach to a social history of ideas is to focus on the way in which the social organization of knowledge affects the style, content, and social significance of intellectual activity.

By directing our attention to the social framework of intellectual life, the activity of the mind can be firmly located in time and place.[43] Writing intellectual history from a local standpoint becomes an exciting possibility. Here the full institutional matrix of intellectual life can be studied in sufficient detail to grasp the way in which specific ideas or ways of thinking develop, gain hegemony or lose significance, and are used in particular settings. We would learn much from studies of the changing social framework of knowledge in a particular locality over two or three centuries. How do various structures of discourse succeed each other over time and interact with each other? How are these changes related to the larger systems of ideas, social structures, and economies that find concrete articulation in a given locality?

These questions point toward a social history of ideas that can analyze the structures within which ideas are formulated, appropriated for use, and achieve hegemony in a given society. These issues are central to understanding the life of the mind because it is within these structures that reality is defined, and changes in the perception of reality are as- sociated with changes in these structures over time. My emphasis here on the social foundations of intellectual life is not intended to deny that the life of the mind is enmeshed in a world of ideas. The structure of ideas must be studied closely by historians, but this work must be matched by study of the structures within which ideas are developed, modified, and transmitted. Such a study will advance our understanding of how the various structures of discourse available to Americans for organizing intellectual life have enhanced (or hampered) their ability to penetrate "the nature of things."[44]

❧[2]❧ Science and the Culture of American Communities

The argument outlined in the previous chapter is here developed in a quite specific field, the history of science. The essay had a considerable effect on discussions of the historiography of early American science, and much of the work it calls for has now been done—though I cannot claim more than simultaneous discovery. By a coincidence this essay was published before the more general one that here precedes it. It was prompted by a request from the editor of the History of Education Quarterly, *Paul Mattingly, that I review the collection of Daniel Drake's writings and the first volume of the Joseph Henry papers. With one condition, it was an opportunity I could not resist. I asked permission to add Neil Harris's* Humbug, *and I proceeded to work out in this one field the ideas I was developing. The essay has the limitations of its origin as a review essay. And it was an early venture. Yet both of those circumstances give it an energy, a speculative quality, and a sense of discovery that I still appreciate. It was published as "Science and the Culture of American Communities: The Nineteenth Century,"* History of Education Quarterly *16 (1976): 63–77.*

HISTORIANS OF EDUCATION HAVE BROADENED THE SCOPE OF THEIR SPECIALTY in the fifteen years since Bernard Bailyn published his influential book, *Education in the Forming of American Society* (1960). The new educational historians have examined a wide range of social institutions involved in education, ranging from the family to the media. Yet curiously little study has been devoted to the transmission of scientific ideas in America.[1] We know much less than we ought to about the countless local scientific and "literary" societies that played an important if as yet unspecified role in the diffusion of scientific ideas.[2] We know little more about the scientific curriculum of educational institutions at all levels. Although we have fine biographies of such academic scientists as Asa Gray and Louis Agassiz, there are no general studies of natural philosophers in antebellum colleges comparable with those we have of moral philosophers.[3] More generally, the meaning of science to various social groups remains largely unknown.[4]

The publication of the selected writings of Daniel Drake (1785–1852), a physician and amateur scientist identified with Cincinnati, and the publication of the first volume (of a projected fifteen) of *The Papers of Joseph Henry*, nineteenth-century America's most important if not necessarily best scientist, suggest how much historians have overlooked. The fascinating pages of these volumes will, I hope, bring an end to this neglect.

Joseph Henry, an experimental physicist, is best remembered as the first head of the Smithsonian Institution. From that post, which he held from 1846 until his death in 1878, Henry played an instrumental role in the development of a national scientific community in the United States. Henry's career can be divided into three segments: the Albany years, from his birth in 1797 until 1832; the Princeton years (1832–46); and the Smithsonian years. This volume covers the first of these periods, including his childhood, student days, and his first years as a teacher and practicing scientist. The absence of documentation relating specifically to Henry for the first twenty-five years of his life might have been a disaster for this initial volume had the editors been less imaginative. But they brilliantly turned this misfortune into an opportunity "to describe the Albany milieu as an influence on Henry's scientific growth." Albany was the eighth largest city in the country in 1830, and Nathan Reingold and his assistant editors portray a "varied and vigorous provincial culture" there.[5] Most important for Henry's scientific development were two institutions whose histories are well documented and interpreted in this volume: the Albany Academy and the Albany Institute. These institutions, the pride of the city's elite, were where Henry received his education and where he later taught and presented his first scientific papers.

What kind of scientific education was available to Henry at the Albany Academy? The documents and editorial commentary in this volume suggest that the quality of scientific instruction was much higher than many generalizations in American educational history would lead one to expect. The Albany Academy was not typical of all academies; its curriculum compared favorably with most colleges. Yet its example (even if it were singular) reveals the academy in its heyday as an enormously effective institution.

The documents taken from the academy archives tell us much that is important about the curriculum and governance of the academy, but the editorial annotations identifying every person mentioned in them make these records even more valuable. This scholarship must have been arduous, but it paid off. It enables the reader to trace the social network of the cultural leadership in a nineteenth-century city. And what one finds is a broad spectrum of the community elite—business-men, medical men, and politicians—actively involved in amateur scientific and general cultural and educational matters.

The selection of Daniel Drake's writings that Henry D. Shapiro and Zane L. Miller have edited is obviously less ambitious than the Henry papers project, but it is valuable for many of the same reasons. Unlike Henry, Drake was a man of ordinary intellect. Yet he is deservedly remembered in this volume that was published as part of the sesqui-centennial celebration of the University of Cincinnati, one of the many educational institutions that can claim Drake as a founding father. It is probably safe to make the generalization that Drake participated in the founding of all the many scientific institutions established in Cincinnati before 1840, including a college and medical school, a museum, a scientific journal, and several scientific and literary societies. This volume includes Drake's statements about his intentions and hopes for several of them.

Unlike the editors of the Henry papers, however, Shapiro and Miller fail to use Drake as a vehicle for systematically exploring the culture of a leading western city. Since Miller is an excellent urban historian who has written on a later period of Cincinnati's history, one might have expected his introductory essay to describe and assess the urban culture within which Drake sought to encourage science. Instead he wrote about Drake's social and political "whiggery," a discussion that is paired with Shapiro's equally conventional explication of Drake's Baconian philosophy of science. Why did Miller write about political ideology rather than about Cincinnati? It was not, I hope, because he felt that his urban specialty was not particularly relevant to the study of a scientist. Antebellum science, like Drake himself, was community oriented, and the urban historian can enrich the study of American science by exploring the urban context of scientific activities.[6] What scientific institutions were developed? In what kinds of communities? Why? What kinds of scientific work were undertaken? What kinds of scientific ideas were communicated? Who participated? For what reasons?

Drake, who symbolized this kind of urban cultural and scientific activity, offers an exciting opportunity to pursue these questions. Baconianism and whiggery, admittedly, were important to Drake, but he seems to have seen himself fundamentally as an urban cultural booster. Near the end of his career he gave advice to his medical students in Cincinnati that might well have summed up his own life.

> You will realize, I trust, that you are not doomed to spend your days among rude and ignorant backwoodsmen; but in the midst of intelligent and refined communities; and that you should, by deep and protracted study, prepare yourself for such associations; for building up a profession worthy of such a state of society, and for performing an honorable part in a thousand works of learning, science, charity, and patriotism.[7]

Urban historians who have examined other western cities demonstrate that this cultural purpose was not unique to Drake or to Cincinnati.[8] I chide Miller for failing to pursue this urban theme because the preoccupation of historians of science with the scientific community needs to be balanced with a study of the place of science in American communities.[9] And this work seems to be in the natural province of urban and educational historians.

These volumes, by raising the question of science and community, suggest new approaches to subjects of interest to historians of science, education, and cities. I propose in what follows to note some of the major issues in the traditional historiography of American science and to suggest briefly some of the ways a focus on science as a cultural activity in American communities relates to these questions and opens new areas for research.

Since 1948, when Richard Shryock published his famous article on "American Indifference to Basic Science during the Nineteenth Century," historians of American science have been preoccupied with the supposed absence of significant contributions to "pure" science by nineteenth-century Americans.[10] Critics blame American practicality while defenders of American science cite Henry, who seemingly stood on a level with his famous British contemporary Michael Faraday. Recently, historians have begun to realize that this approach to national science, alternately self-consciously depreciatory and chauvinistic, leads only to impossible problems of definition and standards of comparison.[11] For the social historian of science, the question is not whether Henry was a better scientist than Faraday but rather what Henry's career indicates about science as a cultural activity in the United States.

There is another related problem in most writing on the history of American science. It is, following Herbert Butterfield's apt terminology,

"Whig history" that views the past in terms of the winners, those ideas and institutional settings that survived to find a place in contemporary science.[12] This approach is a form of presentism that distorts the past. Specifically, it suggests that before the emergence of modern science Americans were not involved with science in any important way. Such a darkness-and-light framework should be familiar to historians of higher education. Until recently, the negative evaluations of the old-time college by those men, like Andrew D. White, who spoke for a new kind of education were accepted uncritically by historians. The ideas of White and his generation of reformers won, and we work in research universities. But this institutional triumph does not mean that they were objective observers of what they set out to destroy.[13] Just as historians of higher education have tended to view the antebellum college from the perspective of proponents of the university, so historians of science may have identified too closely with those scientific promoters like Henry who created the modern pattern of professional science in America.[14] By accepting their assertions about the indifference of Americans to science, historians have ignored the vigor and pervasiveness of a different kind of science, a community-oriented science that is symbolized by Drake and which, incidentally, nourished the young Henry. A more accurate (and truly historical) portrait of nineteenth-century American science will require us to distance ourselves from both the old and new models of science.[15]

Such an approach will have to treat science as a cultural activity and not something independent of time and place. Two ideas developed by Thomas Kuhn seem relevant here. The first is his concept of the "paradigm" within which "normal" science is pursued. This is a relativistic notion that allows the historian to take seriously those ideas that were important in the past but which have since been shown to be "wrong" or naive. The second is his concern for the community or audience to which scientific work is directed and which provides standards of evaluation.[16]

Here is where the question of disciplines becomes important. Charles Rosenberg has recently urged historians to study the social history of American science through its professional disciplines. The "scientist's basic unit of orientation," Rosenberg argues, "is his discipline." "It is his discipline which defines his aspirations, sanctions ambitions, rewards ultimate achievement."[17] This was probably true by the end of the nineteenth century; earlier, however, men's lives were more oriented to their community than Rosenberg allows.[18] In fact, the great story of nineteenth-century science is the shift from community-based amateur science to national and international professional disciplines. The most important scientific development of the nineteenth century, to paraphrase Alfred North Whitehead, was the discovery of the method of discovery. This, Whitehead observes, represents the "change from amateurs to professionals." While there were anticipations in the past and earlier examples of "specialism" in science, "the full self-conscious realisation of the power of professionalism in all its departments, and of the way to produce professionals" was a nineteenth-century achievement.[19]

It distorts the nature and significance of this transformation to see all developments in the early nineteenth century as incipient professionalism. Just as the college was not the university writ small, so science in antebellum America was not simply a prelude to what came after the Civil War. It was at least partly an alternative. When George H. Daniels, in his study of science in Jacksonian America, identifies forty-one of the fifty-six "leading scientists" of the period (selected on the basis of their publication) as "professionals" because they were employed as college teachers, he forgets that the college was not a university or even the germ from which the university later grew.[20] He also fails to recognize the degree to which the antebellum college was a community institution and not the nationally oriented university that became the home of scientific professionals later in the century.[21] Drake, whose 700 (!) publications qualify him for Daniels's list, provides an example. Although he held a professorship during much of his life, this was but one element of his participation in and identification with local cultural life. He identified with communities, not professional career lines.[22]

Nonprofessional interest in science during the Jacksonian period was tremendous. Alexis de Tocqueville declared that science in America attracted a "multitude" while Harriet Martineau remarked upon the scientific literacy of Americans. This interest seems to have been pervasive in small as well as large communities. When Sir Charles Lyell visited the United States, he not only found "crowded audiences" listening to scientific lectures in Boston but also discovered that the residents of a small village in Maine were interested in his geological finds.[23] When the American Antiquarian Society sent out a call in 1812 for "curiosities" to stock its cabinet, a flood of responses was received from throughout the nation. And a half-century later, when the American Museum of Natural History was founded (1869), a circular sent through the towns and villages of New York produced hundreds of rocks, shells, dried insects, and pressed plants.[24]

How was this scientific knowledge communicated to the general American population? The answer seems to lie in a process of cultural decentralization and diffusion. Cultural institutions that had in the eighteenth century been the monopoly of a few seaport cities were replicated in town after town in the nineteenth century.[25] The many cities and towns founded during these years established, or tried to establish, a full complement of urban cultural institutions. Part of the impetus was the urban imperialism and municipal pride stressed by Daniel Boorstin, but it was also an expression of genuine concern to live as civilized people.[26] While Boorstin's point about civic boosting is important for any study of local cultural institutions, it should not obscure the role of changing intellectual aspirations that accompanied this institutional dispersion. Enlightenment ideals of science did not die with Thomas Jefferson and John Adams. In altered form they survived into this period. Indeed, the impact of romantic thought may have given them a new force among a wider population by suggesting to Americans a democracy of intellect and by giving science a romantic attraction through its association with the sublimity of nature.[27]

In 1820, while explaining the need for the Western Museum Society, Drake emphasized that migrants to Cincinnati "were detached from civilized portions of the old world, and brought . . . the tastes, propensities and passions, which belong to a refined society." Yet he also recognized that the culture of these institutions would be local and amateur, not international. These institutions, in town after town, were community wide: all members of the community participated, and they made the best of the available talent. Drake made this point in an anniversary address (1814) to a literary society that he had founded.

> Learning, philosophy and taste, are yet in early infancy, and the standard of excellence in literature and science is proportionally low. Hence, acquirements, which in older and more enlightened countries would scarcely raise an individual to mediocrity, will here place him in a commanding station. Those who attain to superiority in the community of which they are members, are relatively great. Literary excellence in Paris, London or Edinburgh is incomparable with the same thing in Philadelphia, New York or Boston: while each of these, in turn, has a standard of merit, which may be contrasted, but cannot be compared, with that of Lexington or Cincinnati.

The scientific and educational institutions Drake founded in Cincinnati were not intimidated by professional or cosmopolitan standards of excellence. Rather they operated, as Charles Cist wrote in 1841, on "the principle of mutual instruction." The "whole community" participated in the effort to nourish whatever cultural resources existed in the city.[28]

Science was a fundamental part of this cultural activity in Cincinnati and elsewhere. Museums and lyceums were especially important in nourishing this science. The Western Museum that Drake helped found in 1820 had explicit scientific purposes. "The plan of our establishment," Drake declared, "embraces nearly the whole of those parts of the great circle of knowledge, which require material objects, either natural or artificial, for their illustration."[29] During its first years of existence the museum also supported John James Audubon in his work of drawing the birds of America. Yet the museum remained closely tied to the culture of the community, and the dividing line between the pursuit of science and popular amusement was blurred. The people of Cincinnati satisfied their scientific curiosity and found amusement in the same institution.[30] The lyceum was a companion institution. Between 1831 and 1845, sixty lyceums were chartered in Ohio. They began as societies for mutual instruction, but after 1840 they increasingly became stops on a national lecture and entertainment circuit.[31] And the Western Museum eventually crossed the line it had formerly blurred and became merely a commercial amusement palace. In their early phases, however, the museum and the lyceum seem to have been effective community-oriented sources of scientific instruction.

Such community-oriented institutions were not limited to the West. It was the local culture of Albany that supplied Henry's scientific education. Dr. T. Romeyn Beck, a founder and the principal of the Albany Academy and Henry's mentor, was a wide-ranging amateur who played a role in Albany not unlike Drake's in Cincinnati. The Albany Academy and the Albany Institute were clearly community oriented. The publication series of the institute, for instance, was conceived as a local thing, representing Albany. The minutes of the meeting where the project was inaugurated in 1824 read, "There cannot be any doubt but that a well conducted publication would subserve the interests of Science & Literature in this place."[32] A couple of years later Henry's inaugural lecture as Professor of Mathematics and Natural Philosophy in the Albany Academy was obviously addressed to the academy and the city of Albany—and was printed in the local newspaper.

What makes Henry so interesting to the cultural historian is that unlike Drake, Beck, or James Hall, a talented paleontologist who remained his whole life in Albany, Henry rejected this local culture for a professional career. Because of the scarcity of documentation of Henry's personal life during this period, his motives remain shrouded in uncertainty. But the documents in Reingold's first volume clearly describe the process.

In 1831 he published the results of a major experiment in elec-
tromagnetism in Benjamin Silliman's *American Journal of Science and the
Arts*. This placed Henry into what appeared to be an international race
for priority with James Forbes in Edinburgh and Michael Faraday in
England, and Silliman began regularly soliciting Henry for a paper as
each issue went to press.[33] Simultaneously, Henry seems to have become
less and less content with the prospect of being merely an ornament to
the cultural life of Albany, and he began to orient himself toward a new
kind of science. As part of this shift, he became hostile to the amateurs
and popularizers who characterized community-oriented science. When
a relative wrote on behalf of a local mechanic who wanted to know
how to construct the electromagnet that Henry had reported in Silliman's
journal, Henry complained, "There are at the present time many in-
genius but illiterate mechanics engaged in attempts to invent self-moving
machines." This, he concluded, "does not tell much for the diffusion of
Knowledge among the mechanics."[34]

The correspondence relating to Henry's move to Princeton in 1832
reveals him weighing his prospects as a modern professional. The local
community means nothing; his professional opportunities mean everything. Responding to a "feeler" from John Maclean at Princeton, Henry
wrote, "My only views at present are to secure a comfortable support
for my family and next to establish and to deserve for myself the reputation of a man of science." "Any honourable situation," he continued,
"which would afford me superior advantages to those I now possess for
prosecuting them [his researches] will be acceptable."[35]

Henry was not after status in Albany as a leading member of the
community in which he was born; he wanted a new kind of status, that
of a scientist (a word that would come into use in its modern meaning
in the 1840s). He went on to become the driving force in the creation
of a national scientific community in the United States, through his
work at the Smithsonian and by playing key roles in the founding of
the American Association for the Advancement of Science (1848) and
the National Academy of Sciences (1863). Along with the research university, these institutions provided the setting for the fully matured
professionalism that characterized American science at the end of the
century.

This structural shift in the institutional basis of science is related to
important changes in the intellectual style of science. In the midnineteenth century scientific thought was not considered to be different
from any other kind of thought. In the mind of the average American

there was little difference between the lyceum speaker who showed examples of nature's wonders and the stump politician who explained the virtues of his party. They would be evaluated by the same standards. By the end of the century, however, "science" had become something different and was removed from the ordinary experience of Americans.[36]

The style of thinking common to popular and scientific thought in Drake's generation was a rather simple empiricism. It was concerned almost entirely with the direct observation of surface appearances. Its powers of explanation were quite limited, but it did have the advantage of being "democratic." As Drake observed, anyone could see, hear, and feel.[37] This unsophisticated scientific empiricism was most evident in the way Americans responded to museums, and Neil Harris's insightful and illuminating book on P. T. Barnum and his American Museum in New York City brings us close to the cultural meaning of this mentality.

Where others have found only a series of unconnected humbugs in Barnum's career, Harris finds an underlying pattern, a particular "approach to reality and to pleasure." Barnum, Harris points out, drew upon the scientific curiosity of Americans and offered them a chance to "figure out" how things worked or whether something was fake or not. "The objects inside the museum, and Barnum's activities outside," he writes, "focused attention on their own structures and operations, were empirically testable, and enabled—or at least invited—the audiences and participants to learn how they worked." This "operational aesthetic," as Harris calls it, relieved visitors to the museum from "the burden of coping with more abstract problems. Beauty, significance, spiritual values, could be bypassed in favor of seeing what was odd, or what worked, or was genuine."[38]

Like Drake's science, Barnum's museum was democratic. Individualism, Tocqueville remarked, encouraged Americans to rely upon their own perceptions, and Barnum played on this. The famous "Feejee mermaid" hoax provides an example. Barnum did not claim that it was really a mermaid. He said rather that some authorities said it was genuine while others claimed it was a fake. His handbills declared, "Who is to decide when the doctors disagree?" Everyman, of course. He need only rely upon his sense of sight and touch: "If it is artificial the senses of sight and tough are ineffectual—if it is natural then all concur in declaring it *the greatest Curiosity in the World.*"[39] Interestingly, it seems to have been precisely this simple scientific curiosity tapped by Barnum that gave Henry's career its first big push. Much of his fame during the Albany years came from the electromagnet he built that was capable of lifting a thousand pounds. He gave one to Silliman at Yale, and after

Silliman used it in a scientific lecture he wrote to Henry, "*Here* it excites unqualified admiration & an audience of 300 looked at its performance last week with astonishment."[40]

This popular curiosity about scientific matters is impressive, but one must be careful of celebrating the general cultural style it represented. It was a crude empiricism that betrayed a propensity to oversimplify and evade problems and to think in terms of surface and appearance.[41] Professional science challenged this form of empiricism.

The divergence of professional science from amateur science and popular culture begins to become apparent by the 1840s. While amateur geologists concentrated on the feel and appearance of materials, professional geologists were turning toward chemical and fossil analysis. In natural history the Linnaean system of classification, which relied upon external appearance, was replaced by the more theoretical natural system. A correspondent of Asa Gray pointed out the consequences in 1842. "The natural method," he wrote, "takes botany from the multitude, & confines it to the learned."[42] This split between popular and professional natural history (and science in general) deepened as the century proceeded. In the last quarter of the century, it caused great anguish for the professionals associated with the American Museum of Natural History as they discovered that philanthropists who provided funds for its operations consistently supported "naked eye" science more generously.[43]

Two kinds of science had developed by 1870. One, which I will call vernacular science, was community oriented and popular; the other was esoteric and professional.[44] The former was superficial but expressive of the community while the latter was more profound at the cost of severing scientists from the public they needed if their work was to be supported.[45] Much that has been labeled anti-intellectualism by scientists has in fact been a product of their inability to explain the nature of scientific work to those outside of specialized disciplinary communities, to the public living in American communities, to the Daniel Drakes.

After about 1870, professional scientists, especially those trained in Germany where professionalism was most developed, often mistook the incomprehension of their colleagues in the liberal arts colleges as simple anti-intellectualism rather than as a manifestation of the fragmentation of knowledge that accompanied professionalization. By accepting these complaints at face value, historians have misunderstood the changing place of science in higher education. I. B. Cohen, for example, cites an incident related by Ira Remsen, a chemist who had studied in Göttingen and who would later be the first professor of chemistry at the Johns

Hopkins University, to illustrate "the general atmosphere with regard to science" at Williams College, where Remsen had taken a position in 1872. At a faculty meeting held in the college library, one of Remsen's colleagues picked up the latest issue of the *American Journal of Science*, which included an article by Remsen. The colleague noted this, and he tried, without success, to read the title aloud. There followed, in Remsen's words, some "good-natured fun." Remsen added, "I felt that in the eyes of my colleagues I was rather a ridiculous subject." This classic example of what professionalism was doing to the liberal (now interdisciplinary) ideal of knowledge provided Remsen and Cohen with an example of anti-intellectualism. "This story," writes Cohen, "typical of the period, indicates that research and knowledge were clearly not considered to be very important in American higher education."[46] One need not defend the commitment to intellect at Williams to argue that such an interpretation misses the most important point, the changing definition of science itself.

Without further study, little can be said of scientists' efforts (or lack of them) to explain their work to a larger public. Some notable scientists, Louis Agassiz, for example, went on the lecture circuit in an attempt to bridge the gap. Yet the temptation to play to the crowd and to grossly oversimplify scientific concepts in such presentations was difficult to resist. To the degree that scientists succumbed, they unintentionally misled the public about the nature of science in ways embarrassingly similar to the charlatans they sought to expose. Some of the most professionalized scientists faulted Agassiz on this ground. They apparently turned to their classrooms, to textbook writing, and to E. L. Youman's *Popular Science Monthly* as responsible ways of reaching a nonprofessional audience.[47] With the passage of time, however, the "language" of professional and vernacular science increasingly diverged, and even these forms of communication became problematical. It is also possible that, as science found a secure institutional setting in the new universities, in government agencies, and in industry during the early years of the twentieth century, the whole effort of communicating complex scientific ideas to the public seemed less pressing to scientists.[48] Scientists may have concerned themselves only with those who controlled these new centers of power. If so, this still leaves open the question of what definitions of science were proposed and accepted, implicitly or explicitly, as scientists shifted their orientation from local communities to the dominant national institutions of American society.[49]

In the long run, of course, the professional pattern of science triumphed over the vernacular.[50] In the 1850s, 1860s, and 1870s, however, both systems were vigorous. Perhaps this state of institutional and intellectual coexistence (or disorganization) offered the possibility of bringing popular culture and professional science into a harmonious and mutually beneficial relationship. Instead conflict was the order of the day, and an incident in Albany during the 1850s provides a particularly graphic example of what this conflict meant.

Several civic leaders in Albany, particularly James Armsby, a physician, and Thomas Olcott, a banker, proposed to establish an astronomical observatory. The required money was raised, and Ormsby MacKnight Mitchell, the amateur scientist who had established Cincinnati's famous observatory a decade earlier, was hired to head what was named the Dudley Observatory. As the building neared completion in 1855, however, Mitchell found it necessary to return to Cincinnati, and he resigned. Armsby went to the meetings of the American Association for the Advancement of Science in order to consult with the nation's leading scientists about a replacement for Mitchell. Benjamin Peirce, Harvard's noted astronomer, was happy to recommend his former student, Benjamin Gould. He also suggested that the observatory purchase a heliometer, a highly sophisticated instrument used for determining longitude and which was unavailable in any American observatory. Armsby and the trustees took Peirce's advice. Indeed they were so flattered by the interest of the scientists that they appointed Peirce, Henry, and Alexander Dallas Bache to an advisory Scientific Council. As a result, the institutional structure of Dudley Observatory combined the two kinds of science, vernacular and professional, in the trustees and the Scientific Council.

Conflict was immediate; it was also protracted and unseemly. The trustees had envisioned the observatory as a community cultural resource. They were willing to pay for quality, but they also hoped that the community would be able to use the telescope for star gazing. Gould, however, was determined to make Dudley Observatory "a place for careful unostentatious investigation, rather than an exhibition of brilliant-looking instruments and curious contrivances." The Scientific Council supported Gould; indeed they had recommended him precisely because he was capable of using the heliometer to test theories considered important by the national scientific community. But the trustees had no understanding of these esoteric purposes, and after much controversy Gould was fired.[51] This incident is often cited to demonstrate indifference to "pure" science in nineteenth-century America. In fact, neither side showed any interest in "practicality"; both groups sought to satisfy an intellectual curiosity after their own fashion. Rather, two kinds of science and community were in conflict, and they never understood each other.

The battle between these two patterns of science before the triumph of the universities has yet to be fully explored. We, who find a serious social and political problem in the chasm between the scientific "expert" and the "public" and who are worried about the intellectual consequences of the high walls separating the professionalized disciplines, must understand why men like Henry abandoned community for professionalism. What was gained? What was lost? If the community-oriented pattern of scientific education nourished a shared scientific culture, it failed to produce sophistication and depth. Yet we might also ask whether a professionalism completely alienated from community can achieve the wisdom and insight that we seek.

Historians of science have been interested in the growth of a national scientific community; urban historians might well study science in American communities. And a full cultural history must assess the changing roles of these two kinds of community in the creation and transmission of scientific ideas in America.

❧[3]❧ The Erosion of Public Culture: Cities, Discourses, and Professional Disciplines

If the previous essay traced a narrow thread of my theme, this one broadens the canvas. It is the broadest conception of the issues. It is also important for a modification of the essentially two-stage model of the framing offered in chapter 1. Here I identify an intermediate culture of American higher learning. Like Louise Stevenson in her book Scholarly Means to Evangelical Ends: The New Haven Scholars and the Transformation of Higher Learning in America, 1830–1890 *(1986), a book published after this essay originally appeared, my aim was to establish an intermediate organization of intellectual life as distinct, not merely transitional. I make a great deal of a social crisis that I define in urban terms. While holding to that centrality, I would now allow other developments to share more fully in my account: geographical expansion, religious transformation (evangelicalism), market capitalism, and the radical expansion of suffrage (white men).*

Because of the work of Leonore O'Boyle ("Learning for Its Own Sake: The German University as Nineteenth Century Model," Comparative Studies in Society and History *[1983]) and Charles McClelland, especially his essay on Berlin in a book I edited,* The University and the City: From Medieval Origins to the Present *(1988), I now understand that Americans seriously misunderstood the case of Berlin and the German university. Were I to undertake this study today, one of the questions that would loom large is the reason for this misperception or misrepresentation of the University of Berlin by American metropolitan cultural reformers. Since I wrote this essay, Mary Kupiec Cayton has published important work on audience reception of midnineteenth century urban cultural production, and that perspective would very much enrich this essay. (See her "The Making of an American Prophet: Emerson, His Audiences, and the Rise of the*

Culture Industry in Nineteenth-Century America,'' American Historical
Review [*1987*].*)*

This essay was written for presentation at the Davis Center Seminar at
Princeton University in 1979. Thomas Haskell, who read that version,
solicited a revised one for publication in Thomas L. Haskell, ed., The
Authority of Experts *(Bloomington, Ind., 1984), 84–106.*

THE INSTITUTIONAL STRUCTURE OF INTELLECTUAL LIFE WAS RADICALLY TRANS-
formed in the United States between the Civil War and World War I.
The product of these changes was a system of professionalized, academic
scholarship that brought a very high proportion of learned discourse
under the aegis of the university and gave power to a wide range of
professions on the basis of authority conferred by a university connection. A number of fine historical studies of the "revolution in higher
education" and of professionalization of science and scholarship have
made the outlines of this story reasonably familiar.[1] With this essay,
however, I propose to place this innovation in the context of a wider
social and cultural problem. I want to direct attention to the subtle but
vital relationship between a crisis in urban culture and these changes
in the social organization and authority of knowledge, particularly in
reference to serious social inquiry and commentary, what we now call
the social sciences.

The events that precipitated the academic revolution are not to be
found exclusively within the history of higher education or even of the
professions. My argument is that a perceived failure of urban culture
and a sense that the city presented a new kind of intellectual problem
decisively shaped the professionalization of discourse about society in
the United States. Placing developments in this context illuminates the
relationship of knowledge in professional disciplines to the general culture and reveals in a somewhat novel way the intellectual and moral
problems inherent in our contemporary configuration of intellectual life.

My approach to this topic has been guided by assumptions that
should be stated at the outset.[2] I believe that a coherent structure of
discourse is an essential foundation for a satisfactory intellectual culture.
Intellectual work, I think, takes place within an institutional matrix that
confers authority and concentrates attention on selected ways of per-
ceiving and interpreting experience. Communities of discourse supply
collective concepts, mechanisms for exclusion and appropriation, and
give institutional force to the paradigms that guide the creative intellect.

We ordinarily think of universities and the professional disciplines in these terms, but they apply, I am convinced, to earlier periods when the social organization of knowledge took different forms. Before the rise of modern professionalism there were identifiable audiences that judged and affected the work of American thinkers. The city and the cultural institutions it nourished once aspired to and often accomplished this task.

In early modern Europe and even into the early nineteenth century, the learned world—by then no longer sustained by the church—was identified with "Society," either at the court or in cities, rather than with colleges and universities. It was a world created by a leisured aristocracy, an aspiring bourgeoisie, and elite members of the professions.[3] Paris represented the model, and Goethe's praise for its service to artists and writers is both famous and succinct. "Conceive a city like Paris," he told Eckermann in 1827, "where the highest talents of a great kingdom are all assembled in a single spot, and by daily intercourse, strife, and emulation, mutually instruct and advance each other; where the best works, both of nature and art, from all the kinds of the earth, are open to daily inspection."[4] Stated differently, Paris offered mutual criticism, recognition for talent, models and standards, museums and libraries.

In the American republic, of course, there was no court. Nor did America's provincial cities absorb all serious intellectual discourse. But with the partial exception of the denominational community of discourse associated largely with Princeton Presbyterians, aspirations and to a large degree reality placed intellectual life in the nation's cities.[5] A dense network of personal associations and urban cultural institutions made the nourishment of intellectual life a dimension of the urban experience.

The learned world of Philadelphia, New York, and Boston, as well as of such lesser cities as Albany or Cincinnati, was an association of gentlemen.[6] The conjunction of learning with wealth and power was easily recognized within the city, and this gave authority to the city's learned circle. This pattern was sustained by the sociology of the city. As Sam Bass Warner demonstrated in the case of Benjamin Franklin's Philadelphia, the city was characterized by an inclusive diversity.[7] Physical closeness and personal interaction characterized the city, but this did not imply the disorganization of urban roles. Nor did diversity and personal association imply equality. A clear sense of social place and obligation was impressed through personal relations. Precisely because established social categories and cues signifying them were so clear, learned discourse had its own well-understood order.

The advancement of learning in eighteenth- and early nineteenth-century American cities was a civic role, and the substantive meaning of this culture was improvement, personal and social.[8] The educated and powerful worked to establish a cluster of urban institutions that nourished cultural life: libraries and philosophical societies, mechanics and agricultural associations, historical societies, colleges, and small, informal discussion groups devoted to mutual education. Culture and learning had a distinctive and from our perspective notably preindustrial quality. Instead of the language of scholarly productivity and the creation of knowledge, phrases so common in the age of the university, we find in earlier diaries and correspondence such key words as cultivation, pleasure, and improvement.[9]

Intellectual life was rooted in a mix of urban cultural institutions. Only later would one of these institutions, the college converted into the university, achieve hegemony in intellectual life and transform the urban-based world of learning into university scholarship.

Benjamin Franklin best represents the activist, pragmatic, and institution-founding character of early American civic humanism. His autobiography has made everyone familiar with the range of his interests and with his good works as a bourgeois citizen of Philadelphia: the Junto, the Library Company, the American Philosophical Society, the University of Pennsylvania. Only in his genius, however, was Franklin unique. Compare, for example, the less well-known Samuel Bard of New York. Bard was the son of John Bard, a physician who had, in fact, been associated as a young man with Franklin's Junto and who had organized in New York a "Weekly Society of Gentlemen" in 1750. The younger Bard, Samuel, also a prominent physician, assumed a leading role in the creation of a series of civic institutions that advanced learning in New York. He founded the New York Hospital as a teaching hospital in 1771, and he was a leader in the transformation of Kings College into Columbia. He was also importantly involved in the development of the New York Library Society, the New York Historical Society, and the New York Society for Promoting Useful Knowledge. One could mention others in New York, equally obscure today, equally central to the advancement of culture in the early republic: William Dunlap, Samuel L. Mitchill, John W. Francis.

The civic institution model of intellectual life continued into the nineteenth century. But it was neither firmly rooted in provincial America nor productive of the brilliance to be found in European capitals or even such provincial cities as Edinburgh. Its weakness and fragility made it vulnerable in the face of rapid urban expansion and the democratic ideology nourished in the age of Jackson. By midcentury, the social foundations of this traditional pattern of civic culture were being dissolved by social change, and this produced a profound cultural crisis.

Population figures reveal the magnitude of urban change. The population of the nation's largest cities soared between the first census in 1790 and the seventh in 1860. New York represented the most dramatic case. Manhattan, the home of 33,131 in 1790, had a population of 813,669 in 1860. Including Brooklyn, New York's population already exceeded one million. Philadelphia grew from 42,520 to 565,529. For Boston the numbers are smaller, but the growth from 18,038 to 177,840 transformed the culture of that city.[10]

The result was urban chaos. The impress of numbers, coupled with the development of unprecedented cultural diversity and an egalitarian ethos, obliterated the social connections that had woven together the public culture of the colonial city and that had nourished an acknowledged learned society with shared purposes, traditions, and rules of discourse. By 1900 the city was reintegrated on new principles. A new vision of urban order found expression in spatial specialization, social segmentation, and bureaucratization. The eighteenth-century city of inclusive diversity was replaced by the twentieth-century city of "closed social cells." A sense of order was maintained by minimizing contact and keeping it within specialized institutional channels.[11] The reordering of intellectual life—the creation of academic disciplines or intellectual cells—proceeded in a parallel pattern and from the same perception of urban disorder.

The middle years of the century, however, were years of confusion and frustration. Between about 1840 and 1875 the old pattern had collapsed and the new had not yet been perceived. Intellectuals looked about for viable institutional means of achieving social order and for a way of restoring order and authority in intellectual life.[12]

The connection between unprecedented urban growth and the difficulties of midcentury intellectual life has eluded historians but not those intellectuals who lived through it. In an essay titled "The Intellectual Life of America," published in the *New Princeton Review*, Charles Eliot Norton began by contrasting the Boston of Emerson's youth with Boston of the Gilded Age. Earlier, he emphasized, "the community was more homogeneous and its members were acquainted. . . . There were more common and controlling traditions and associations." Emerson's thought and convictions had been nourished in this context. Now, however, men of intellect found little to sustain them in the city. They must "adapt themselves to a comparatively low plane of intellectual life." The urban and democratic transformations of a half century had blurred intellectual distinctions and eroded the authority of the social institutions that had supported them. "The principle of equality," Norton complained, "is extended into regions where it has no proper validity. Our public life, our literature, our journals, our churches, our amusements, our politics, all exhibit a condescension to the crowd. . . . There is a lack of independence and of leading; a lack of superior excellence in nobler fields of effort and expression."[13]

There was in the midcentury city no coherent and demanding institutional structure for intellectual culture. Instead of a clearly signified—and often personally known—community of discourse that established intellectual authority, the urban intellectual, now standing essentially alone, faced a heterogeneous, anonymous, and vastly expanded audience.[14] The city had once ordered relations between writer and reader, speaker and hearer. It no longer did so.

The traditional connection of "society" and intellect was severed. Society retreated into the tight and mannered world of sociability that Edith Wharton would later describe.[15] Where there earlier had been established mechanisms of recruitment into the professions and learned society through family connection and elite sponsorship, the Age of Barnum witnessed an intellectual free-for-all, as all manner of men sought an audience in the city's public culture. "The mind of each," Tocqueville noticed as early as 1830, "is . . . unattached to that of his fellows by tradition or common habits."[16] Traditional signs and institutions of trust and authority in intellectual and other matters were devalued, a fact which provided material for Herman Melville's *Confidence Man* (1857).[17]

Urban institutions, with their conversation and lectures, that had once been the medium of a vital intellectual life came under criticism for their "superficiality." Horace Mann, for example, complained in 1839 that the Lyceum and public lectures characteristic of urban culture offered "dim and floating notions" that might be acceptable for general topics but which in areas pertaining to one's "immediate employment or profession" were "not simply useless, but ruinous."[18]

During the next quarter century the issue became more pressing and the relation between specialized knowledge and an interest in general cultivation of knowledge more problematic. In 1867, two years before he became President Eliot of Harvard, Charles W. Eliot observed that intellectuals faced great difficulty in finding their public in a way "consistent with self-respect, independence, and mental uprightness." The public culture of midcentury cities, because it was so lacking in rigor and was so receptive to "loose and inaccurate statements," posed a threat to the careful investigation and "single-minded" mode of in-quiry characteristic of the scientific method.[19] We all know, of course, that Eliot found a solution to this problem in the elective system and in a graduate school based upon professional disciplines. But this so-lution was not so much a reform of urban culture as a withdrawal from it. Before the creation of the graduate school, there were important attempts to reform the intellectual life of cities.[20]

The problems faced by urban intellectuals were fairly clear. How does one achieve intellectual authority in a society of strangers? How does one locate an intellectual community with shared purposes, stand-ards, and rules of discourse in the heterogeneity of the midcentury city? Could the diverse and anonymous audience presented by great cities constitute a viable community of discourse?

I have identified three distinct responses to this crisis of the city and of intellectual life. None of them, as it turned out, determined the shape of modern intellectual life, but all are interesting and revealing. One of them is exemplified in the career of Henry Ward Beecher, another found its clearest expression in the proposals of Henry P. Tappan and others for the creation of an urban university in the American metropolis, and the third is symbolized by the American Social Science Association.

In retrospect, Henry Ward Beecher may not seem to qualify as an intellectual, but in the New York of the 1870s he stood for the life of the mind.[21] Beecher accepted, even embraced, the new conditions or urban intellectual life. He acknowledged that the diverse urban audience the city had thrown up to the intellectuals might pose difficulties, but it was, he explained, the "atmosphere in which all high scientific truth and research, and all learning, in its amplest extent, are . . . to find their nourishment and stimulation." These new circumstances implied, how-ever, that preachers and other intellectuals would have to "develop new resources" to "maintain [the] authority and influence" once vouchsafed them by tradition and social connection.[22]

In the Yale lectures on preaching, which he delivered between 1872 and 1875, Beecher outlined his strategy for intellectual influence. The central problem he confronted was that of addressing a heterogeneous and anonymous urban audience. He recognized that it was possible to create specialized audiences in the city, but he rejected an intellectual life that was confined in "a single groove." The task of modern intel-lectual life, Beecher believed, was to speak "to the whole people."[23]

He offered the new science of phrenology as an aid in this effort. With knowledge of its principles, a public speaker could by visual inspection immediately learn the character of the anonymous individuals in the audience. "You must know what men are, in order to reach them," and with phrenology, Beecher explained, this can be achieved. "It has been the foundation on which I have worked."[24]

It was Beecher's notion of personalism, however, that was his most important contribution to the quest for intellectual authority and influence in the city. Beecher told his students at Yale that all depended on one's success "in opening the hearts of your hearers." With Beecher, formal discourse dissolved into a personalism that relied upon personality and the appearance of intimate disclosure. His sermons and lectures were "familiar conversations"; sympathy, not shared intellectual purposes or traditions, would provide a common ground for the urban audience. "I aim to make them feel my personality."[25]

Beecher's approach to the problem of modern intellectual life is revealed in his discussion of the proper architecture for churches and lecture halls. Traditional church architecture, a legacy of formalism and ceremony, established a wide gulf between the preacher and the congregation. When the preacher as an individual was less important than traditional ritual, this was appropriate. But in modern times, Beecher explained, the "church is a household, and . . . a preacher has a personal influence on men." The architecture of the church must bring the preacher "face to face with other men" and nourish the informal influence characteristic of street-corner discussions. The minister must be physically near the audience, and the congregation must be able to see the whole body of the preacher—not just the head and chest—so that they might feel his full "magnetic influence." When Plymouth Church in Brooklyn was built for him, Beecher told the architect, "I want them [the congregation] to surround me, so that they will come up on every side, and behind me, so that I shall be in the center of the crowd, and have the people surge all about me." The completed church was, in Beecher's words, "perfect, because it was built on a principle,—the principle of social and personal magnetism, which emanates reciprocally from a speaker and from a close throng of hearers."[26]

Beecher must be credited with confronting the crisis of urban culture; he recognized and adapted himself to the social scale and diversity, isolation, anonymity, and egalitarianism that eroded customary sources of intellectual authority in New York. With traditional rituals of intellectual accreditation and of formal discourse abandoned, producers and consumers of intellectual work found it increasingly difficult to fix on the cues that made a coherent and rigorous intellectual culture possible. Beecher grasped the possibility of relying on personality (not character,

which depends on personal knowledge) to establish the trust and authority essential for the conduct of intellectual life in a milieu of strangers.[27]
A combination of self-display and sentimentalism brought Beecher the
"influence" he sought. But whatever Beecher's personal success, personality was a poor substitute for the shared intellectual framework,
personal knowledge, and accepted social categories that had earlier given
shape to urban intellectual life. Intellectual distinctions in Beecher's New
York were blurred; the structure of intellectual life in the city did not
demand of Henry Ward Beecher participation in formal discourse or
disciplined argument. The unhappy result, in the eyes of a contemporary,
was "the union of moral philosopher and comedian."[28]

The Beecher-Tilton adultery scandal provided E. L. Godkin with
the occasion for a penetrating analysis of the crisis of urban culture and
of the inadequacy of Beecher's response to it. The actions of the prin-
cipals in the scandal and the reaction of the larger public, Godkin reflected, demonstrated a fuzziness of moral categories, the disarray of
contemporary intellectual discourse, and a collapse of professional
standards.

The problem, as Godkin saw it, was that "a large body of persons
has arisen," taught by common schools, newspapers, lyceum lectures,
small colleges, magazines, and the like, "who firmly believe that they
have reached in the matter of social, mental, and moral culture, all that
is attainable or desirable by anybody, and who, therefore, tackle all the
problems of the day." The result, he declared, "is a kind of mental and
moral chaos." Henry Ward Beecher's personalism reflected this problem
instead of overcoming it. Godkin observed

> that Mr. Beecher's preaching, falling on such a mass of disorder, should
> not have had a more purifying effect, is due, we think, to the absence from
> it of anything in the smallest degree disciplinary, either in the shape of
> systematic theology, with its tests and standards, or of a social code, with
> its pains and penalties. What he has most encouraged, if we may judge by
> some of the fruits, is vague aspiration and lachrymose sensibility.[29]

The discipline that Godkin missed in urban culture was precisely
what Henry P. Tappan and others had proposed to supply in the 1850s
through the creation of a great metropolitan university in New York
City. If the college had been one of many urban cultural institutions
that were held together by an interlocking leadership supplied by "society," the midcentury reformers' vision of the urban university placed
it at the center, with a coordinating and directing role in the city's
intellectual life.

When one realizes that this early impetus for the creation of an American university originated in an urban crisis, the later emergence of the university in America fits into a broadened perspective. While it must still be said that university reformers found the colleges wanting, the source of their concern demands reinterpretation. The problem was not so much that colleges were ineffective institutions, but rather that a general and profound perception of disorder in urban culture caused intellectuals to ask something radically new of higher education. Urban culture at midcentury was defined in terms of the university and, perhaps more important, the academy was itself defined in terms of urban culture rather than as the collection of professional disciplines that it became.

There is no little irony in Tappan's ambition. The most compelling spokesman of his generation for New York City as the center for intellectual life and for the central role of a university in creating such a cultural capital, Tappan was dismissed from his professorship of moral and intellectual philosophy at the University of the City of New York (NYU), an institution that might have aspired to the role he envisioned. Even more: he is remembered in the history of higher education for making the beginnings of the modern university in a small midwestern town as president of the University of Michigan.[30]

In *University Education*, published in 1851, Tappan complained of "hosts of mere expert empirics, who without learning succeed in gaining a reputation for learning and . . . invade the most sacred offices of society." A great university, he suggested, would restore the intellectual authority of those who deserve it. It would enable the public to "begin to comprehend what scholarship means" and it would demarcate advanced scholarship as the special province of "a few men of great and cultivated powers."[31]

His proposed university was to be an urban institution. He stressed the historic association of learning with cities, particularly commercial cities, and he declared that New York had reached a stage in its historical development that demanded achievements of a higher order than bricks, banks, and water systems.[32] Cities by their very nature produce a "wonderful influence" that encourages accomplishment in art, science, and literature. "It is," he observed, "the influence of words, of looks, of manners. . . . Men talking daily with men like a common stock of information and ideas, and keep each other's minds at work." He admitted that there is often too much excitement—"too much talking, hearing, and seeing, going about, and not enough still thought; but, nevertheless, here, more than in any other form of life, men are sharpening each other's wits."[33]

If, as he thought, the United States could support only one real university, it ought to be in New York. Although it would be a national institution, he stressed that it was to be in its essential character an institution of the city. He carefully distinguished between a major institution located in the city—as the Royal Society was in London—and a civic institution that was of as well as in the city. His model for New York was Berlin, where the university stood first among a diverse cluster of distinguished cultural institutions. A city of learned societies, he declared, needs a university as its core. "Nothing in a great city can take the place of a great university."[34]

At a time when cultural life seemed confused and diffused, Tappan offered the university as a vehicle of reform. "A great Institution would collect together all that is now scattered and isolated among us, to be the home of scholars, the nurse of scholarlike endeavors, the regulating and harmonizing center of thought and investigation." The university would establish the institutional foundations for a "learned class" in the city, and the "population would feel the plastic power of intellectual development and progress" through "public lectures under the direction of an elite corporation."[35]

The details of his plan reveal the directing and consolidating role of the university in the city's intellectual life. Columbia, New York University, and the Free Academy (City College) would be reduced to gymnasia within an educational system capped by the university. But his vision embraced the reform of urban culture, not just the city's formal education system. Various scientific and literary societies in the city, including the city's theological seminaries, the newly established Astor Library, and the projected Cooper Union, would be coordinated under the aegis of the university. Thus all the city's "Institutions of learning would grow into a harmonious whole."[36]

Professors would participate in civic culture, and the city's finest nonacademic minds would be associated in various ways with the university. Professors would be "required to give popular courses to the public" in addition to their lectures in a prescribed field to "Academical Members of the University." This wider audience of educated adults would share in the consolidated resources of the university. "The result," Tappan wrote, "would be that the libraries, cabinets, laboratories, and lecture rooms of the University would become the resort of students of every grade; it would thus become the great centre of intellectual activity" in the city and, by extension of the city's metropolitan role, the nation.[37]

Tappan's dream of reform was not a solitary one. Indeed, the leaders of the American scientific community, the so-called Lazzaroni, took up a similar plan during the 1850s. Alexander Dallas Bache, echoing a privately circulated plan developed by Benjamin Peirce of Harvard, proposed for New York City "a great University of the arts and sciences in which the practical man may meet on equal terms with the scholar." He suggested that scholars from all over the nation be brought to New York to assume lectureships of a five-year term at the university. Here they would be at the center of a cluster of urban institutions even more diverse than Tappan had imagined: the Chamber of Commerce was as prominent as the Astor Library in Bache's list. With the university providing direction and clear standards of excellence, intellectual life in the city would unite "men of progress, scholars, practical men, mechanics, artists."[38] Civic culture and academic life would meet, even merge into one another.

While these visions of an urban university clearly anticipated in some respects the later research university, it is important to recognize the ways in which they represented an extension of the older civic culture model of intellectual life. Academic culture and civic culture remained one. The proposed university, like the earlier learned associations, had an extensive sense of its constituents. Recall: membership in the earlier learned associations was inclusive rather than exclusive. Some members were devoted entirely to research and the creation of new knowledge; they were recognizably professionals. A larger number were more routine practitioners. Finally, there was a group of members we might call "cultivators." These were men and, rarely, women of broad culture who endeavored to keep involved in the world of learning through direct participation.[39] One difference between Tappan's proposed urban university and the research university that came to prevail in the United States is that this latter group has been largely excluded from academic culture. This exclusion has consequences for the life of the mind for it was cultivators who provided the link between the world of advanced scholarship, of disciplinary discourse, and the public culture of cities.

This great metropolitan university was not established, and during the 1860s cultural reformers looked to other institutional reforms. Perhaps the centralization and the standards they sought could be achieved outside the context of higher education. E. L. Godkin, a major spokesman for cultural reform from the 1860s through the final ascendancy of the university, described such a plan in the pages of the *Nation*. Lamenting the "disintegration of opinion" in modern, urban society, he called for "greater concentration of instructed opinion." He endorsed a proposal to create an Institute in New York that would provide a center for intellectual life in the city and the nation. If, Godkin speculated, the institute, along with local "academies under it all over the country," provided "better means of communication . . . to those interested in or engaged in the cultivation of science, arts, or literature," it might overcome the "spirit of mob" by "infusing . . . discipline and order" into American intellectual life.[40]

Nothing came of this proposal for a New York Institute, but at about the same time a group of reformers and intellectuals, primarily from the Northeast, who were interested in the study and reform of social problems organized themselves into the American Social Science Association (ASSA). It aimed to organize discussion, at local and national levels, on all aspects of social life of interest to concerned citizens. Franklin B. Sanborn, the association's guiding spirit, explained that "the double duty of all social sciences is to learn patiently what *is*—to promote diligently what *should* be."[41] The organization would, it was hoped, consolidate information about society and reform and give the authority of organization to sound opinion.

Members of the ASSA recognized that modern intellectual life required a division of labor, but the division they adopted reflected the concerns reminiscent of civic culture rather than the disciplinary divisions that would be institutionalized in the departmental structure of the modern university. They collected facts within a framework that consisted of the commonsense beliefs of informed and concerned citizens. Hence the ASSA was organized into five "departments," each generously inclusive: Education, Health, Jurisprudence, Finance, and Social Economy. Social concern, not method or "field," differentiated these areas of inquiry. Although academics participated in the proceedings of the association, they constituted a minority.[42] And one looks in vain for the "scholarly" question as a focus of inquiry.[43]

The ASSA represents a bridge between civic culture and university culture. By 1900, the difference between these two models of intellectual life would be clear and unbridgeable. But for a decade after the founding of the Johns Hopkins University in 1876, the tradition of civic culture was still strong. Even Daniel Coit Gilman was concerned about the relation of the university to it. One of his first acts as president of Johns Hopkins was a gesture to civic culture: the establishment of a series of public lectures in Baltimore that would, he said, demonstrate "the methods and principles on which we rely."[44] Even more important was Gilman's response in 1879 as president of the ASSA to Benjamin Peirce's proposal of 1878 that the ASSA be merged with Johns Hopkins. Peirce

envisoned the university giving direction to a metropolitan or nation-
alized intellectual enterprise that would associate the activities of academic and nonacademic social inquirers to the benefit of both.[45] Gilman's initial reaction to Peirce's plan was favorable, though noncommital.
By 1883, however, Gilman had decided against the merger, apparently
finding the civic culture tradition without real promise. (The public
lectures were ended about this time.) He turned instead to a vigorous
encouragement of the disciplinary associations that transformed American intellectual life. A Johns Hopkins professor organized the Modern
Language Association in 1883, another the American Historical Association in 1884, and yet another the American Economic Association
in 1885. Johns Hopkins professors played important roles in the founding of the American Political Science Association and the American
Sociological Association in 1903 and 1905.

Peirce's proposal evidently forced Gilman to think about the limits
of traditional social inquiry and to think of the university as something
that transcended this older organization of intellectual life. In a speech
at Johns Hopkins in 1885, Gilman identified civilization not with the
city—the usual equation—but with the university.[46] A year later, in an
address at Harvard, Gilman argued that "the discovery and development
of unusual talent," the task of the university, could not be accomplished
through civic institutions, such as libraries, museums, and the like, nor
in the "seclusion of private life." It requires, he declared, "favorable
opportunities for intercourse with other minds" available only in the
university. With Gilman we have the solution to the collapse of orderly
discourse in the city. Gilman praised the university for allowing men of
intellect to withdraw from the "turmoil" and "distractions of modern
civilization"; the university alone allowed the "cultivation of a spirit of
repose necessary for scholarship."[47]

When attempts to reform the intellectual culture of the city failed,
Gilman and others carved out bounded space where intellectual discourse
would be safe. Academics were not unique in this respect. Boundary
setting and cultural purification were major themes in the late nineteenth-
century urban experience. Many groups pulled back from indiscriminate
participation in urban life, seeking comfort in sharper and more exclusive cultural self-definitions.[48] Just as the spatial reorganization of urban
life in the 1880s and 1890s produced specialized land-use patterns
and segregated residential areas, so the shared cultural space of early
nineteenth-century urban intellectual life was abandoned for more specialized communities of intellectual discourse.

Emergent professionals wanted to distinguish themselves from the swirl of amateurs, popularizers, and charlatans associated with urban culture—and for valid intellectual as well as selfish personal reasons. In a disciplinary community, genuine intellectual accomplishment would find protection from the competing and often superficial demands of a heterogeneous public. Professional institutions were, as Thomas Haskell points out, "a way to *insure* that each audience would find its proper guide; that moral and intellectual authority would be possessed only by those who deserved it."[49] The disciplines also supplied a common method and shared problems. Hence social prestige and intellectual security were dual—and welcome—benefits conferred by the establishment of professional disciplines following upon an era when both were highly vulnerable. Yet, in this largely successful quest for order, purity, and authority, intellectuals severed intellectual life from place, specifically from its historical association with the city and thus from the public culture the city had nourished. What remained in the city lacked a center, and it lacked institutional authority.

If the social history of the city made the reform of the institutional basis of intellectual discourse essential, it also produced new perceptions of society that demanded intellectual innovation. And this new intellectual style was more easily assimilated into the disciplines than into the older civic culture.

The city's social complexity seemed to require a more penetrating form of social analysis than amateurs displayed. Amateur social observers, even those in the ASSA, assumed that social reality was generally accessible to common observation. For them, practical acquaintance rather than theory conferred authority. For example, in the opening address of the ASSA's New York meeting in 1874, George W. Curtis declared that Sanborn's "practical acquaintance" with the work of social improvement "gives authority to every word that he says upon the subject [of social science]."[50] The social perceptions of Sanborn and those he represented were based on a naive empiricism. Problems were typically defined in terms of particularistic and direct inquiry, using concepts shared by the general public (e.g., the reformation of criminals, divorce, better houses).

By the 1880s, however, the immensity of the material fact of urban and industrial society threatened to overwhelm intellectuals. The world around them seemed not to be known, and the customary modes of social inquiry did not seem to make it any more comprehensible. The interconnectedness of outwardly discrete social facts could not be grasped by common observation, and without such understanding the mass of social particulars was dispiriting. Professional sociology offered esoteric theory that would demonstrate these connections and force understanding out of the confusion of social facts.[51] Valid social knowledge, formerly concretized in individual relationships or institutions, now seemed to call for definition in terms of processes and interconnections one step removed from direct human experience. The perceived need for such esoteric knowledge served, as it always has, as the basis for the creation of privileged intellectual authority.

Albion W. Small, the founder of academic sociology at Chicago, explained that the subject of the discipline was not the immediate, concrete, or commonsense evidence of social pathology that concerned amateur social inquirers, but rather "society." The "near-infinity of group relationships and processes" that defined this sociological entity represented a new "conception of reality." Sociology, Small declared, rejected "all the traditional ways of interpreting human experience" and offered "a new procedure toward all problems and conduct of human life."[52] Franklin H. Giddings of Columbia, the other major spokesman for academic sociology, agreed with Small. In an address to the ASSA in 1894, he contrasted the emerging discipline of sociology with the amateur social inquiry that went under the name of social science. He objected to the eclectic character of social science. It seemed to include everything as its subject matter and anyone as a practitioner. A much sharper definition was possible for sociology. It is not concerned with particular social facts nor with groups of them. Nor is sociology philanthropy. It is a science concerned with the "first principles" of social phenomena. "For some time past," he declared, "it has been apparent to the discerning that this unified, coherent, philosophical 'sociology' was destined to displace or to incorporate and co-ordinate the fragments of 'social science.' " In place of "nebulous and vague" social science, he offered a "clear and precise" sociology.[53]

Although Small and Giddings disagreed in some details about the precise place of sociology among the new academic disciplines, they agreed that it represented a new and esoteric order of conceptualization that distinguished it from all earlier social inquirers. It had a clear object of inquiry, a shared method, and an identifiable special audience, all of which protected academic sociologists from the chaos of thinkers and ideas in what was soon to be stigmatized as the "popular" culture of the city.

There is a wonderful irony in all of this, and we must not miss it. The social complexity and confusion of urban life was embraced by academic social scientists as their special subject. The special capacity of their disciplines made them, so they said, uniquely able to grasp, interpret, and control this new social world. Yet, while making this positive claim, they created the university as an intellectual refuge where they could avoid the city's complexity and disorder in the construction of their discourse. To avoid misunderstanding, let me stress that I am not asserting any kind of social irresponsibility on their part. Indeed, professional service to the city as client was central to their emerging professionalism.[54] My point, however, is that they defined their relationship to the city in terms of the academic division of intellectual labor, rather than any "ordinary" definition of urban concerns inherent in a widely shared public culture.[55]

The failure of midcentury cultural reformers to create a viable urban culture in New York made the United States, in the words of James Bryce, "the only great country in the world which has no capital." The absence of a capital was important, according to Bryce, because "the heaping together of the forces of rank, wealth, knowledge, intellect naturally makes such a city a sort of foundry in which opinion is melted and cast." Neither New York nor any other American city was able to assume this centering role which, in fact, creates a public culture.[56] Without this counterweight of urban culture, intellectual life in the United States took on a heavily academic and relentlessly specialized character. Serious thought in the United States, more than in England or France, is overwhelmingly concentrated within academic, disciplinary communities.[57]

American social scientists achieved intellectual legitimacy and authority by creating specialized and certified communities of discourse— that is, professional disciplines. However successful this strategy proved to be in ordering discourse and securing professional status, it generated a "centrifugal tendency" in American intellectual life, producing island-communities that reduced the common universe of discourse to an exceedingly limited sphere.[58] The academic disciplines in America have been astonishingly successful in producing new knowledge, but their almost complete hegemony in our intellectual life has left Americans with an impoverished public culture and little means for critical discussion of general ideas, as opposed to scientific or scholarly expertise.[59]

PART II.
TWENTIETH-CENTURY PATTERNS

❧❨4❩❧ E.R.A. Seligman and the Vocation of Social Science

If the essays in part I explored the nineteenth-century origins of academic culture, the essays in part II, including this one, explore variant patterns of academic identity and its relations to public life. In this study I place E.R.A. Seligman at the center of an effort to map what I take to be the modal pattern for academic intellect in the social sciences in the twentieth-century United States. My concern is to explore the boundaries recognized by academic intellectuals. It is a story of developing boundedness, of the rise of expertise at the expense of a public conversation.

Had I taken into account gender difference, I strongly suspect that there would be another theme here. Two vectors of development would be revealed. The one here outlined would be predominantly male, but we would notice another represented by the work of women trained as social scientists. They would not appear as frequently in academic careers; they more often were found in the emerging social service field. They were often experts, but of a different sort, often rather nearer the front lines of the provision of social services. While the male social scientists aspired to interact with political and economic elites, their female counterparts had far more significant contact with client groups. Neither, however, addressed the public directly; both in their different ways held back from democracy, each preferring a version of expertise.

The movement to "objective" social science is complex, and it is not (at least in the beginning) identified directly with quantification. Quantification emerged among social workers, predominantly women who were not academics. It was an explicitly reforming strategy. One might call it objective (in that it strove for accuracy), but it was not neutral. Only when academic men adopted such methods in the late 1920s was it associated with the vision of an objective and neutral social science that had no room and no need for political dialogue. This point, along with many other brilliant insights, may be found in an article that came to hand only after this book was in press: Linda Gordon, "Social Insurance and Public Assistance: The Influence of Gender in Welfare Thought in the United States, 1890–1935," American Historical Review, 97 (1992), 19–54.

I dealt with some of the issues raised here in New York Intellect *(1987), but the constraints of length and the focus on the city in that book made the tracing of this academic story impossible. So when Lawrence Stone invited me again to present a paper to the Davis Center at Princeton, this time in the fall of 1987, I took advantage of the occasion to write this paper. I have since revised it (1991), but it has not been previously published.*

THEODORE ROOSEVELT AND WOODROW WILSON WERE MANIFESTLY DIFFERENT political figures, as was suggested by John Milton Cooper's characterizations of them as "the warrior and the priest."[1] This difference should not, however, be allowed to obscure their shared (and important) relationship to the new social sciences that emerged in American universities during the last quarter of the nineteenth century. These two men are our best-educated twentieth-century presidents. When we think of them struggling with their competing programs in 1912 (the "New Nationalism" of Roosevelt and the "New Freedom" of Wilson), we should recall that both of these men pursued advanced study in the social sciences. Both studied political science in the earliest and most highly regarded graduate programs; social science was for them a preparation for public life.

Roosevelt was a student in John W. Burgess's program in Public Law in Columbia's Faculty of Political Science, then closely associated with the School of Law, where Roosevelt was officially registered. Wilson was trained in Herbert Baxter Adam's famous Historical Seminar at the Johns Hopkins University. These educational accomplishments are, of course, well-known facts of the biography of each man. But thinking of them together points us to a generational experience that in turn enables us to sense how deeply entwined were civic purpose and academic innovation in the 1870s and 1880s. The idea that in Gilded Age America, the milieu of Boss Tweed and Mark Twain's not so fictionalized Senator Abner Dilworthy, young men of civic, even directly political, ambition would turn to graduate education in the social sciences is odd. But remembering the electoral contest of 1912 may make it seem less odd.

The creation of the American graduate school in the 1870s and 1880s should be understood in this civic context. It was precisely the Theodore Roosevelts and Woodrow Wilsons whom the founders hoped to equip for public careers. Only later, in the 1890s, when higher education generally began to expand and the classical curriculum declined did the market for academic social scientists emerge. That turned academics at Columbia and elsewhere to reproducing themselves.[2]

When the Graduate School at Columbia was established in 1881, it was intended to train men in "the mental culture" (hardly the language of later social science expertise) that would prepare them for careers in the "civil service" or as "public journalists" or for the "duties of public life" generally.[3] The official language at Johns Hopkins, where Woodrow Wilson enrolled in 1883, was less explicit on this point, but one cannot but notice the large number of journalists, social reformers, and political figures who passed through the Historical Seminar there.[4]

The institutional innovations that produced the modern structures of higher learning were born within the context of a civic culture. Moreover, the first results of that process of academic invention remained within the civic tradition. The culture of that moment of birth anticipated neither "expertise" nor the modern pattern of academic training within disciplines that are also professions and careers. Indeed, at the Johns Hopkins University, the pioneer graduate school, prospective graduate students were informed in 1877 that the institution offered "advanced instruction, *not professional.*"[5]

The academic transformation that created and won legitimacy for professional disciplinary intellect did not play itself out linearly, nor was the geographical space in which innovation occurred neutral. One of my purposes here is to explore the way in which local circumstances can affect the configuration of both the thought and the structure of a translocal intellectual culture. My argument is that the interplay of the political and intellectual issues characteristic of life in a great metropolis played a significant role in shaping—defining the constitution of—the national academic culture, at least in the domain of the social sciences. I hope to show through my narrative that New York's social scientists, E.R.A. Seligman in particular, assumed a definitive role in the constitution of the social sciences in the United States. At the same time, I will propose, much more briefly and, perhaps, paradoxically, that New York, though crucial in this national formation, was never effectively incorporated into it.

A second theme is explored here. I have been struck by the way in which the issue of the class location of intellectuals has been woven

into the discourse of the emerging social sciences and into their institutional elaboration. I make this observation fully aware of the excellent
scholarship on the social and intellectual history of the development of
the American social science, particularly that of Mary Furner, Thomas
L. Haskell, Peter Novick, and Dorothy Ross.[6] My contribution is—in
the face of such existing work—necessarily well bounded, but it does,
I think, further illuminate an important theme in any determination of
the public role of social science and the definition of social science as a
vocation in the United States.

It is, or ought to be, axiomatic that some mix of social motive and
conceptual logic is causally operative in the development of intellectual
institutions. But in certain circumstances the causal significance of one
or the other may be enhanced. The emergence of professional social
science provides such a case; the social motive played an especially
significant role. What enabled this? It was something noticed—in a
somewhat different context—by Roger Geiger in his recent book *To
Advance Knowledge: The Growth of American Research Universities, 1900–
1940*. He pointed out that, in the social sciences, professionalization (the
elaboration of the modern structures that support social inquiry) proceeded in advance of the knowledge base. This sequence, he argues,
reverses the pattern in the natural sciences, and it means that the professionalization of social science was embedded more significantly in
social history.[7]

Let me be clear. My claim here is very limited but not, I hope,
unimportant. A class interpretation is not being offered; rather I am
proposing an interpretation of the way the discourse of class was entangled with the work of defining academic culture. What I want to
stress is not class interest or social control (though both are present);
rather I am attending to the difficulty of establishing the class identity
of academic intellect and the implications of socially grounded per-
spectival constraint. The problem of class affiliation (understood by some
in this story as a voluntary identification) was crucial to the politics and
discursive construction of academic social science, particularly in establishing the terms of its relation to public life.

The intellectual "gentry" of the midcentury civic culture did not
face this problem. They accepted the notion of hierarchy rather easily
and identified themselves with the established classes, the dominant
classes. Their concern was not one of class identity or affiliation but
rather one of achieving the public authority to which they believed
themselves entitled. They represented themselves rather directly as the
"best men," those in whom capacity and authority properly resided,

even if complete social assent to this understanding was somewhat elusive.[8] The younger social scientists, possessed of stronger democratic sympathies, had a harder time of it; they wrestled with the question of their relation to the class system.[9] Could they assume affiliation with the dominant class or accept incorporation into it? Or might they best associate themselves with a rising class (or potentially rising class), meaning the working class? Was it possible to establish for themselves a free-standing space, beyond the class system? After Karl Mannheim's essays of a half century ago on the sociology of knowledge and culture, these are not particularly novel or original issues.[10] Yet the directness of their address impresses one with the significance of the issue throughout the whole period here being considered. This discussion—at times an ac-rimonious one—was integral to the making of academic social science in America.

In the 1880s, when the first professional, disciplinary social science associations were founded (the American Economic Association in 1885, the American Historical Association in 1886), it was difficult for any sentient being to avoid the language of class. The Knights of Labor, Haymarket, the founding of the A.F. of L., Henry George's mayoral campaign, these major and many minor events forced Americans into the sort of class awareness that is so compelling in the first pages of Edward Bellamy's *Looking Backward* (1888) or in Henry George's earlier *Progress and Poverty* (1879).

While this context has not been lost on historians of academic culture, it has been difficult to link the context with the shaping of social discourse without flattening experience and falling into a crude for-mulation of the social control thesis. But by remembering that cities provide a node of connection between society and culture, that place gives sharper focus and form to the interplay of thought and society, one might suppose that an urban perspective may achieve some leverage on this problem. In New York City it is possible to achieve sufficient concreteness of description to illuminate that dynamic.

The Henry George campaign provides a window through which we might begin our examination. The mayoral election of 1886, held at a moment when social tensions in the nation had seemingly reached a flashpoint, was a curious as well as an important election. The election was unusual in the extraordinary quality of the three contestants. In retrospect, the election is curious in that the two losers, Theodore Roosevelt and Henry George, are better remembered than the winner, Abram Hewitt.

George, of course, was the dramatic center of the contest. For many, the meaning of the George compaign lay in its promise (or in its fearful specter) of a working-class reform politics.[11] E. L. Godkin, speaking for the aging metropolitan gentry, had no doubts about the implications of George's campaign—or about his own class allegiance. To give legitimacy even to George's *candidacy* was to invite an "interest" politics that could generate class conflict. Such a politics, he worried—and worried quite explicitly—would deny a political role for those, like himself, qualified to govern by their morality, knowledge, and wisdom.[12] Godkin not only knew where he stood, he was prepared to counsel his fellow gentry and the so-called dominant classes generally that they ought to stand with him. The rising generation of intellectuals was less certain. This generation, the first to embrace the new social sciences, wavered for a long moment before resolving the problem of identity posed by the class division of the 1880s.

The 1886 campaign attracted the interest of two ambitious and talented young members of the newly established Columbia University Faculty of Political Science. Their contrasting experiences during and after the election of 1886 bring us directly to the issues that are the subject of this essay.

Daniel DeLeon and E.R.A. Seligman were both of Jewish descent. DeLeon was a Sephardic Jew born in Curaçao, the son of a doctor, whereas Seligman had been born into a prominent and highly cultivated German-Jewish banking family in the city. The first, whose early life experiences were scattered over several continents, always considered himself as an outsider, a marginal man. Seligman, however, was used to the inner society and security of wealth and power.[13]

DeLeon, who had studied in a German gymnasium and at the University of Amsterdam, entered Columbia Law School in 1876, receiving an LL.B. in 1878. He was deeply interested in diplomacy and international law, especially as it concerned Latin America. When a Prize Lectureship was established to honor graduates of the Faculty of Political Science (or the School of Law, provided that they had taken significant course work in political science), Professor John W. Burgess, founder of the graduate school, turned first to DeLeon, who, as Burgess affectionately recalled many years later in his autobiography, "knew more international law and diplomatic history than any man of his age I had ever met."[14] Appointed Prize Lecturer in 1883, DeLeon began his quite successful lectures on international law.

The Seligmans of New York were wealthy, cosmopolitan, and civic spirited. Their philanthropy was a major source of support for Felix Adler's Society for Ethical Culture and for other good causes. The Seligmans were assimilated and patriotic. Edwin Robert Anderson Seligman, born April 25, 1861, was named for the Union officer commanding that beleaguered fort in Charleston harbor. He graduated from Columbia in 1879. On the advice of Burgess he traveled to Europe for study at the universities of Berlin and Heidelberg as well as the Sorbonne and the École libre des sciences politique in Paris. He returned to Columbia to take a Ph.D. in 1885, receiving in that year, like DeLeon, appointment as a Prize Lecturer. Seligman, too, had been quickly identified by Burgess. "I found his wide relationship and acquaintance with men in the business and financial circles of New York a very great help in the work of the development of the institution." The older man "marked" the younger one "for a colleague."[15]

Both of these favored men were anxious to influence public life, and in their ambitions Burgess must have recognized his own hopes for the Faculty of Political Science. But it was not yet clear just how the university and its faculty would be a civic force. DeLeon, as it turned out, took a path that would be rejected, while Seligman, pursuing another, effectively defined the professional relationship to public life that would become dominant in the United States. Seligman, whose "quasi-public work," as he called it, was extensive and influential, addressed public issues, mostly in the field of public finance and taxation, after the manner of a German professor.[16] He acted as an insider, as a consultant to the government, advising, for example, the Ways and Means Committee in the development of the first income tax legislation. DeLeon, by contrast, was drawn to mass movements, preferring to address the public directly.

In 1886, soon after his three-year lectureship was renewed, DeLeon became involved in the Henry George campaign. President F.A.P. Barnard and many trustees were shocked that someone publicly known as a Columbia professor should be associated with the "monstrous agitation" of the George candidacy. DeLeon was warned of the impropriety of this public visibility, but toward the end of the campaign he nonetheless chaired a George meeting on campus at Madison Avenue and Forty-ninth Street. Barnard immediately asked the trustees to dismiss DeLeon. The grounds were clear enough; he was championing a "movement which is regarded by this body as menacing the destruction of the existing order of civilized society."[17] Burgess, however, resisted the move. His social and political views were profoundly reactionary, yet he was committed to academic freedom. Burgess argued that DeLeon was performing his appointed duties, and the young man was allowed to keep his lectureship.[18]

But the story does not, of course, end there. Seligman, who opposed

George and who in 1890 publicly debated George's theories of taxation under the auspices of the American Social Science Association, was advanced to an adjunct professorship in 1888 and to a full professorship in 1891. DeLeon was not similarly elevated. When his second three-year term expired, Columbia offered him no further affiliation.

It is not clear that DeLeon, who thereafter established himself as the leader of the Socialist Labor Party, greatly regretted his banishment from the academy. With an intoxicating dream of intellect affiliated with a mobilized working class before him, he had come to feel, as he told Seligman, that intellect in the academy was too distant from the "stirring and pregnant" events of the times.[19]

Influence for him meant direct engagement in popular political controversy as a spokesman for the working classes. Such was not the emerging university model of influence. The university at this very moment, with the image of the German professor looming large, was making itself a vehicle for an alternative mode for intellect in public life. While the emerging social scientific professorate sought influence, they did not propose to get mixed up with the swirl of popular debate in the press and lecture platform. Instead of such public and political contention, the aim of the professors, with the support of university administration and, in time, trustees, was the affirmation and institutionalization of the authority of experts.[20] Both George and DeLeon rejected this vision of the social role of trained intellect, but over the next century it was Seligman, not DeLeon and George, who proved the better prophet.

The causes of this academic consolidation of intellect are manifold and complex. Let me suggest, however, that events in New York in the 1880s were more than symbolic; they were part of the cause of what happened. For the alert the message was clear. It was not difficult to grasp the sort of intellectual engagement with society and politics that would be welcome in the university. Surely that recognition affected the ambitions that scholars brought to their years of training and their careers as social scientists.

The ascendancy of the university brought, as its origins and as the context of its development might suggest, a narrowing in the spectrum of legitimate social analysis. Neither George's single-tax theories, nor anarchism, nor socialism could be addressed respectfully and freely in the public arena by academics. Not only did the new social scientists accept these boundaries, they sought to establish their distance from—and effectively delegitimate—the social analysis offered by ignorant politicians and untrained journalists—whether on the right (Godkin) or the left (George).

It is important to recognize the complexity of this contest. The young social scientists probably moved the general discussion of economics to the left of where it was when they came of age. If they shunned radicalism, they did not hesitate to attack the laissez-faire conservatism of Godkin and his ilk. In this instance, then, progressive public policy ideas were advanced under a professional aegis that was self-protecting and that effectively narrowed the terrain of academic discourse.

Even in the rare case of an academic willing to acknowledge and debate George, discourse proceeded from the position of authority. Seligman again provides us with an example. In debating George at a meeting of the American Social Science Association in Saratoga in 1890, Seligman declared—with supreme professional confidence—that no one "with a thorough training in the history of economics" can be an advocate of the single tax. In biology, metaphysics, and astronomy, Seligman insisted, "we bow down before the specialist." With the expertise of the seminar room available, why, he asked, should we take seriously the ideas on economics expressed in popular books, in newspapers, and on public lecture platforms?

Henry George angrily rejected Seligman's assertion of academic authority. "Political economy," he countered, is not at all like astronomy or chemistry. It concerns "phenomena" that "lie about us in our daily lives, and enter into our most important relations, and whose laws lie at the bottom of questions we are called on to settle with our votes." If we cannot properly debate and understand them, "then democratic republican government is doomed to failure; and, the quicker we surrender ourselves to the government of the rich and learned, the better."[21] While the matter is more complicated than either man understood, it is remarkable as well as important that the power of George's retort has been so rarely recognized in the academy.

E.R.A. Seligman's was the first generation of academic social scientists in the United States.[22] As his voluminous correspondence reveals, Seligman was an acknowledged leader of those social scientists.[23] His extraordinarily successful career was exemplary. He served on the Columbia faculty for forty-five years, achieving a singular influence in faculty affairs. In his discipline, too, he was a dominating figure. But his disciplinary influence was, it is important to say, organizational. He provided leadership in the institutionalization of the profession; he was not a man of fruitful theoretical ideas.* At the remarkably young age of twenty-five, for example, Seligman collaborated with Richard T. Ely

---

*In this he is to be contrasted with two Columbia colleagues, John Bates Clark, who was one of the formulators of marginal economics, and Wesley Clair Mitchell, who developed the theory of business cycles.

of the Johns Hopkins University in founding the American Economic Association (1885). Later, Seligman joined with John Dewey, Arthur O. Lovejoy, Ely, and a few others to found the American Association of University Professors, and he was the author of its famous founding statement on academic freedom, "General Declaration of Principles" (1915).[24] By the 1920s, he was recognized and respected as an elder statesman of the now well-established social sciences. For this reason— and because of his wide-ranging erudition—he was chosen to be editor-in-chief of the landmark fifteen-volume *Encyclopedia of the Social Sciences* (1930–35).

Across these busy professional years, Seligman continued his family tradition of civic service. He was active in founding the City Club, University Settlement, and Greenwich House, and he participated actively in the work of the Society for Ethical Culture. A founder and first chairman of the Board of Trustees of the New York Bureau of Municipal Research (1907), he served as well as an expert adviser on many city, state, and federal commissions, including the President's Commission on Statistical Reorganization (1908), the President's Unemployment Conference (1921), the Mayor's Tax Commission (1914–16), the League of Nations Committee on Economics and Finance (1922–23), and the State Tax Commission of New York (1930–32). Many of his books were also addressed directly to current public issues; his study of *The Income Tax* (1911) was, for example, an important contribution to the movement for a progressive income tax.

Seligman was well situated to assume a key role in the institutionalization of the new social sciences. He was in the nation's most important city, a center of highly sophisticated financial and economic thinking to which he had access. He was also a member of what was, between about 1890 and 1915, unquestionably the best social science faculty in the nation. Columbia had as well another advantage. Its work in social science was generally perceived, along with that being done at the new University of Chicago (founded in 1891, as its letterhead indicated, by John D. Rockefeller), as centrist or moderately reformist. Columbia was thus situated strategically in the middle, distinguished from Harvard and Yale, with their relatively weak and quite conservative departments, and from the strong but radically tinged departments at Johns Hopkins and Wisconsin, the successive homes of Richard T. Ely, who was early in his career identified as a radical. Seligman's discipline, economics, was recognized, moreover, as the central social science discipline. It was the most developed as a science, and it was the one that was oriented most immediately and directly to the social issues that made the 1880s and 1890s such stirring times in America. The paradox of progress and poverty, to take George's phrase, was becoming too pressing to ignore. Jacob Riis's "other half" had to be reckoned with, and the freewheeling "robber barons" had to be constrained, if not completely controlled.

The dangers inherent in the social turmoil associated with laissez faire capitalism undermined the moral absolutism of classical economics, whether pronounced by Godkin in the pages of the *Nation* or by Professor William Graham Sumner in his classroom at Yale. Economics as a "science" was, as Seligman put it in his address as president of the American Economic Association, "a product of [the] social unrest" associated with such conditions. The new economics imported from Germany by the young and ambitious social scientists rejected both the abstraction and the moral absolutism of the older generation's classical economics in favor of a historical approach. Insisting upon the importance of the actual historical context of economic life, the new economists were, in Morton White's neat phrase, in revolt against the formalism of the Godkins and Sumners. Arguing the "essential relativity" of economic doctrine, Seligman explained that proper policy was relative to the conditions of "time and place."[25]

Empirical investigations of actual conditions would, the younger academic economists believed, justify intervention not as a general principle, but rather on a case-by-case basis. If Godkin and Sumner addressed the public in the language of moral absolutes, as jeremiahs, the new social scientists offered empirically grounded principles of intervention in particular cases in the interest of the general welfare. Under the cover of what they called the historical method, then, Seligman and others engineered an ideological victory. It was also a professional victory; such an understanding of political economy assumed a permanent and continuous role of expertise for historical economists who would monitor changing conditions and suggest changes in public policy to meet such conditions.

Seligman staked out an intermediate position for himself and for his profession. Situating himself between the old laissez faire economists and the more radical new economists of the Ely stripe, he pressed for ameliorative and realistic rather than radical or utopian social change. To this end he urged economists to concentrate upon methods, facts, and processes rather than upon the making of moral judgments or ideological statements.[26] The shape of expertise as Seligman came to represent it emerged out of a complex social and ideological debate. The debate revolved about the question of the social location, or class affiliation, of academic intellect. Seligman's role in resolving the disputed issues was significant, probably even decisive.

In helping to found the American Economic Association (AEA) in 1885, Seligman had sought, with considerable success, to restrain Richard Ely's radicalism. He was less anxious to achieve ideological purity than was Ely, recognizing that the wider spectrum of economic opinion incorporated, the more authoritative the AEA would be as a *professional* body. This strategy conferred the standing it would need in the next decade when, as Seligman and others had anticipated, the organization was called upon to defend the new academic professionals.

The decade of the 1890s, a troubled decade of Populist insurgence and labor conflict, saw several economists and other social scientists fired or threatened with dismissal for their "radical" beliefs. Seligman may have been financially independent, but he understood that any profession unable to protect the livelihood of its members in good standing was not much of a profession. The AEA and its notables had to do something, and they did. What is most interesting about this episode is not the story of the individual cases that arose, but rather the pattern of response to them by Seligman and the AEA. That pattern defined the bonafide economist as well as the limits of professional respectability and protection. Little was said directly on this point, but, as with DeLeon's dismissal at Columbia, the message of organized social science was unmistakable.

Seligman and the AEA went to the defense of academics who, in their view, addressed economic issues reasonably within the purview of their supposed technical competence, even if their views on these matters were unorthodox. They were also anxious to speak out against excessive and especially arbitrary trustee power over academics, arguing always that academic performance could be judged only by peers. Both of these concerns were present when, for example, Seligman encouraged his fellow economists to defend Edward A. Ross, who was fired on orders from Stanford University's single and dominating trustee, the widow of Leland Stanford. Ross's professional standing was publicly defended, and networks of influence were used to secure another academic position for him.

But those academics who spoke directly to the public, as opposed to addressing peers or established political or economic elites, and who spoke in favor of a broader range of radical proposals were not defended. Even someone so prominent as Richard T. Ely found himself all alone when a small group of Wisconsin trustees charged him with teaching "socialism." He survived the ensuing "trial," and Wisconsin still prides itself on the ringing defense of academic freedom that was announced as its conclusion. But anyone who examines Ely's career after the ordeal, which included the experience of being abandoned by the profession, will notice that his social views were substantially and consistently moderated. He turned to scientific investigations of an increasingly statistical sort, and he stopped speaking to popular audiences on political issues.[27] In a less public way, others got the message. Henry Carter Adams left Cornell quietly, fearful that making an issue of his firing would mark him. He went to the University of Michigan, learning in the process that it was best to make his influence felt as an adviser to legislators or to government regulatory agencies.[28]

By 1900, the result of the academic freedom cases was a stronger profession and one that favored the center. Academic economists were both less conservative and less radical. And they were less likely to make direct public appeals or frankly ideological statements. Investigation and objective data became more important than ideas. The academic ideal of the unremitting research for knowledge, whether trivial or not, was born. In the words of Mary Furner, the closest student of the relation of these cases to the formation of the social science disciplines, the right of "direct appeal to the public on controversial social questions was retained as a theoretical right, but economists were expected to channel most of their reform efforts through government agencies or private organizations where scholars could serve inconspicuously as technical experts, after the political decisions had been made, rather than as reformers with a new vision of society."[29] The academic freedom cases of the 1890s did not, in other words, produce free men of ideas addressing a civic body; their resolution revealed a professorate seeking incorporation into the major institutions of society.

Neither the AEA in the 1890s nor, for that matter, the American Association of University Professors (AAUP) in 1915 stood forthrightly for the freedom to express radical or controversial views. The real issue for them both was professional, not civic or intellectual. They defended expertise in its proper arena, and they strenuously asserted that academic peers, not trustees of universities, were the only legitimate judges of academic performance. This definition of academic freedom was a remarkable and enduringly important accomplishment within the context of the history of universities, but we must recognize its limits in the public realm. It did little to enhance the vitality of public discourse; it almost certainly worked in the opposite direction. It is useful in this connection to note that the positions of the AEA and the AAUP— specifically Seligman's statement of the AAUP's founding principles in

1915—contrast with the far broader First Amendment emphasis of the National Civil Liberties Bureau (later the American Civil Liberties Union) founded in New York by Roger Baldwin during World War I.

The position taken by Seligman and his colleagues on the academic freedom cases was in part strategic: they adopted a policy that seemed most likely—under current conditions—to win significant gains in the status and autonomy of professional social science. But this strategy was embedded in a larger and more fundamental intramural discussion among economists. Like literary intellectuals during the same period, the academic social scientists had to face the question of their relation to the class system.[30]

For some conservative economists, of course, the issue was easily disposed of. Since they denied the existence of "classes" and, thereby, class conflict, there was no problem of class location. But that particular form of blindness to experience and faith in ungrounded logic failed of wide acceptance. The annual meetings of the AEA in 1898 and 1899 became wide-ranging discussions of the relation of class standing and professional ambition. In both years it was the presidential address of Arthur T. Hadley, president of both the AEA and Yale, that sparked the highly charged debate. Hadley, something of a moderate, tried to avoid the whole issue, calling upon the economist to look after the whole, as the "spokesman of all." John R. Commons, later famous as a labor economist and historian at Wisconsin but in the late 1890s working for the Bureau of Economic Research and lecturing at Cooper Union in New York after having been dismissed from Syracuse University for his radical views, immediately objected. Historical circumstances, Commons declared, required that economists become the experts of one class or the other. They must, as he put it, gain the "ear either of those who control legislation or of those who are striving to get control." Commons felt that, just as Adam Smith has associated himself and his theories with a rising class, so the new economists, if they were to have real historical influence, must do the same.

It was Commons's intervention, not Hadley's address, that became the focus of the discussion, and it was Seligman who offered the most sophisticated response. Unlike many of his fellow center/liberal economists, Seligman was not afraid of Marx. A few years later, he would publish an important book, *The Economic Interpretation of History* (1902), a book sympathetic to Marx's historical analysis, if not his revolutionary politics, and a book that influenced Charles A. Beard, then a graduate student at Columbia. If Seligman accepted the existence of classes and even the conflict of classes and interests, however, his concern, as always, was in reconciliation. "I should certainly take issue with Professor Commons that the economists can serve the public only through the class." While "the statesman may have to appeal to class interests in order to secure his practical ends," the economist must reject any class affiliation. "The economist," he explained, "tries to represent the common interest of society." Accepting the historical fact of "class struggles," Seligman asked economists to assume a role of reconcilers, molding conflicting interests into a "harmony of interest."[31]

Seligman admitted that in the past political economists may have been associated with the dominant classes, but now, he insisted, economists will exert influence only if "economic theory becomes broad enough to represent all interests, instead of the interests of only a single class." Commons, however, was not persuaded. The economist, he responded, "cannot represent society as a whole. If he claims to do this, he really means that he wishes to have things as they are." Karl Marx and Henry George, he told his colleagues, had more influence than the academic economists. The reason for this was clear to Commons. It is "because they represent the radical classes that are acquiring political power." The discussion concluded with the almost forgotten Hadley declaring himself in "total disagreement" with Commons.[32]

Neither Commons's nor Hadley's views prevailed, but Seligman's did. His vision of the expert, working within dominant institutions, somewhat isolated from public opinion and free of politics, became the foundation of a putatively neutral professional social science in America.[33] Within a very few years, surprisingly enough, Commons shifted his own views, coming to a position quite close to Seligman. Having changed employment, moving from the radically tinged Bureau of Economic Research to the National Civic Federation, an organization representing mostly reform-minded corporate capitalism and organized labor, Commons reconsidered. His experience at the federation, where he was closely associated with Samuel Gompers, President of the A.F. of L., led him to adopt the trade unionists' vision of organized labor improving itself through collective bargaining. Making reference—almost certainly—to Gompers' bête noir Daniel DeLeon, Commons expressed his distrust of those "intellectuals" who identify themselves as spokesmen for labor but whose grand reforms look too far beyond the simple interest of workers in advancing their wages. He learned during these Civic Federation years in New York, as he later wrote in his autobiography, "that the place of the economist was that of adviser to the leaders," whether of labor, capital, or government, and "not of propagandist to the masses."[34]

Seligman's vision of academic intellect fit nicely with the ideal of university service articulated by early-twentieth-century university builders. In a modern and increasingly organized society, the university could offer invaluable expertise to economic and political elites, upon whom they were dependent for funds. Three great universities were built upon this vision of service; by World War I all were centers of social science research. Two were great urban universities, and the other was a state university. The University of Chicago achieved eminence by using its home city as a laboratory of social science; the University of Wisconsin won distinction with its state-oriented and reformist "Wisconsin Idea"; and Columbia took advantage of New York's metropolitan standing to associate itself particularly with national service.[35]

Everyone understood, however, that public service and advocacy would help neither the university nor the individual professor were it to become identified with dissent. The service ideal established a link between the university and a significant sector of the public, but not the public in general. "The modern university and the academic professions arose," Steven Diner wrote, "because advocates of a new kind of higher learning sold their ideas to persons of wealth, social prestige, or political influence."[36] To say this much is not to say that the university was captured by rich reactionaries. If Charles Beard—when he resigned from Columbia in 1917—characterized the trustees of Columbia as being "reactionary and visionless in politics, narrow and medieval in religion," such was not always the case, even at Columbia.[37] During Seth Low's presidency of Columbia in the 1890s and at many other distinguished universities, the trustees and the larger elite constituency of universities were drawn for the most part from the newer and more aggressive modernizers of the governmental, corporate financial, and professional elite.[38] It was possible, as Seligman well understood, to propose to these leaders rather advanced ideas, even the income tax, if they were presented as neutral and scientific policy options. Technique, not rhetoric, offered the promise of influence. The reformist ambition of the professional social scientists could be realized through technical innovations within an accepted order of things. Such efforts, cast in the interest of enhancing the general welfare, were often welcomed; they were at least tolerated. But questioning fundamentals, "radicalism," was beyond the legitimate range of the service ideal.

If Presidents Nicholas Murray Butler at Columbia, William Rainey Harper at Chicago, and Charles R. VanHise at Wisconsin embraced the service ideal from the outset in the interest of winning the financial support of the established classes, one errs in equating these presidential motives and policies with the ambitions of the new social scientists.[39] The presidential embrace of the powerful did not mean that academic intellectuals aimed to do the same. Yet the new social scientists certainly stood to gain both intellectually and socially from the service ideal pressed by the presidents. It advanced their scholarly ambitions by opening the path to public work and legitimating the professor as adviser to power.

Some form of social engagement with established power was inherent in the German historical method.[40] Formalist theories of society and economics did not invite such engagement, but the historical method implied, even demanded, involvement in business and government. Such an approach to social inquiry, to social knowledge itself, was given a formal philosophical basis in the pragmatic philosophies formulated by William James and, especially, John Dewey. Under the influence of pragmatism, social truth and active experience in the world would be assimilated. By the canons of pragmatism, social scientific ideas could be validated, tested for their truth value, only by judging the effects of particular social interventions.

Participation in public affairs had, as well, psychological appeal. The younger academics were haunted by the "fear of being remote," fearful of being trapped in genteel culture.[41] They wanted contact with society and its problems, and they oriented their scholarship toward action. Even history, not a policy science, was cast by James Harvey Robinson, particularly in his famous course on "The History of the Intellectual Class of Europe," in terms of "social betterment and intellectual reform."[42]

There were, then, real attractions to the service ideal propounded by the university presidents. Yet there was a problem, too, not so much a political problem as a definitional one. What was the core responsibility of academic intellect? This question was raised most directly and in the most extreme form by Thorstein Veblen in *The Higher Learning in America*.[43] Veblen's book was, among other things, a caustic attack on the alliance represented by the service ideal. Speaking in the name of an uncompromising, independent, and critical intellect, he insisted that the object of higher learning was thinking, not service to businessmen or anyone else, including undergraduates, who by all reports were indeed exceedingly ill served by Veblen's teaching style.

Although *The Higher Learning in America* was based on his experience at the University of Chicago (1893–1906), Veblen did not publish the book until he came to wartime New York to write for the *Dial*. The timing and the place were particularly fitting. Not only New York's literary intellectuals but the city's academics as well were driven to ponder what the war experience revealed about intellectual life in New York and America.[44] For some, the collaboration of professors and universities in the war effort validated the service ideal and the role of the expert. For others, however, the war exposed something desperately wrong with these visions, something that seriously undercut the dream of the professor as an intellectual.

If the First World War was a decisive moment in the transformation of intellectual life, it is perhaps useful to seek a slightly longer view of the change before examining the war and its immediate effect. Intellect at Columbia, one cannot help feeling, was at its most open, adventurous, and vital (a favorite word of the time) in the decade after the university's sesquicentennial in 1904, the year, incidentally, of John Dewey's arrival at Columbia. Dewey and several of his new colleagues, particularly Franz Boas, Charles A. Beard, and James Harvey Robinson, were vastly extending the range and methods of social research, rejecting categorical analysis for contextualism; refusing formalism, abstraction, and logic for actual experience; and, above all, casting aside absolutes as they came to understand society, in Dewey's phrase, as "something still in the making."[45]

Perhaps the archetypal work of this new and exciting spirit was Beard's famous study of the Constitution. It is both well known and true that Beard's motivation, at least in part, for writing *An Economic Interpretation of the Constitution* (1913) was to undermine the absolute and sacred authority of that eighteenth-century document at a time when the Supreme Court was invoking it to strike down progressive social legislation. But we err if we see only politics and miss the important intellectual agenda behind its writing, one Beard boldly announced in the first chapter. Referring unmistakably, though not by name, to the work of Burgess, Beard proposed a new approach to the study of public law. Heretofore, Beard argued, analysis of the Constitution and law generally had been juridical, that is formal, categorical, and absolute, not historical. The book was conceived as an experiment in the method of placing law into the context of the real historical forces and interests involved in its making.

Columbia put all of this intellectual excitement on display in a series of lectures in the 1907–8 academic year. Organized in part to counter the developing specialization of the graduate school, the lectures were intended to let the various parts of Columbia, as well as the public, know something of the range and quality of work being done at the university. The lectures were "well attended," not only by students and professors but also by the "outside public."[46] They ranged over the whole spectrum of disciplines, the natural sciences, the social sciences and humanities, and the arts, but here I want to direct attention to only four, the lectures by Beard on politics, Robinson on history, Boas on anthropology, and Dewey on philosophy.

Beard, already thinking along the lines that shaped his famous book on the Constitution, insisted that analysis be rooted in "social realities," not "abstractions." One must, he explained, incorporate the social, historical, and economic elements if one is to find the "whole man" in political life. Robinson, rejecting the tight political focus of earlier historians, presented his vision of what—a few years later—he called the "new history," a history concerned with the social "process as a whole." He urged that political, economic, social, intellectual, and scientific threads be brought together in history with the aim of "explaining the immediate present." Boas elaborated the method and concerns of his new discipline, but he refused to enclose himself within it, and he insisted that the study of primitive societies was vital to modern life. The discovery of "the relativity of the values of civilization," he explained, is important for our "common everyday life" because it makes us open to other cultures and more critical of our own.[47] These professors were not contained by the service ideal of expertise; they strove for direct contact, open communication, with the educated public.

The most exciting lecture was Dewey's. Anticipating the argument he would make two years later in "The Influence of Darwin on Philosophy," his famous essay commemorating the fiftieth anniversary of *The Origin of Species* (1859), Dewey began by criticizing Plato's quest for utopian absolutes and Aristotle's tendency toward "the idealization of the existent." Rejecting absolutes and embracing change, Dewey asked philosophy to engage life as it is now and to accept responsibility for current conditions. There is, he insisted, no "ethical science" independent of actual social life, and the task of intelligence is to create and maintain "more and better values here and now." Invoking the lessons of "evolution," he urged the study of "the conditions out of which come the obstacles and the resources of adequate life." The pragmatic or democratic intellectual must develop and test "ideas which, as working hypotheses, may be used to diminish the causes of evil and buttress and expand the sources of good." Without such active, critical intelligence in the world, he warned, we are necessarily victims of "class-codes, class-standards, class-approvals" and the captives of "practices and habits already current in a given circle, set, calling, profession, trade, industry, club or gang." He concluded by calling upon intellectuals to constitute a social intelligence both organized and free.[48]

For these men, the new social science promised to free knowledge and, by implication, social power from class power. The crisis of war, however, would show the liberation to have been confused at best, chimerical at worst. If Dewey's words seemed clear in 1907 or 1908, only a few years later they would be full of ambiguity. If Randolph Bourne and Max Eastman thought that what they learned from Dewey sustained resistance to war, others would find support for their pragmatic, contemporary war service. There are hints of the problem in the lectures themselves. They exude a sense of intellectual excitement and good will, but they lack anything approaching a realistic understanding of the relation of intellect to power.

The war, however, forcibly intruded the elemental fact of power into the world of academic intellect. Most academics could not resist the lure of power; they succumbed, and so did Dewey. But Dewey (and Beard and Robinson) were shaken by the failed promise of war as an arena of expertise. And they understood the issue in terms of the class position (or class possession) of social scientific knowledge.

To understand these issues, we must consider in some detail academic affairs at Columbia during the war. President Butler outlined the "mobilization of Columbia University" for war in a remarkable document, *The Organization of Columbia University for National Service*.[49] Within the Economics and Social Service Corps, Charles A. Beard was designated to head the Civics Division. It was a supremely ironic designation. Beard would, as it turned out, give Columbia a civics lesson, but not the one Butler intended.

If in some respects the service role of the university was enhanced and consolidated, the war also brought to a head long-simmering opposition to Butler's definition of the university and his manner of administration. Before the war it had seemed difficult, for some at least, to specify the distinction between the professor as intellectual and the professor as expert, but the crucible of war clarified the difference. The intrusion of war into affairs at Columbia tended to impress upon academics the necessity of a choice; either they must assert themselves as free intellectuals or they must become servants of power. Neither a middle ground nor ambiguity fared well in the crisis of war. The postwar resolution of these issues was not absolutely clear. Certainly, the general thrust of events at Columbia was to favor institutional loyalty and service to established power over independent and critical intellect. Yet in the interstices of the university's organized life the critical intellect survived, even if not regularly nourished, to flourish again in the era of World War II.

By 1917, there had been a certain uneasiness and restiveness among the faculty at Columbia for more than a decade. In the immediate prewar years, however, Columbia's troubles found focus in one man, James McKeen Cattell. One of Columbia's most distinguished social scientists, Cattell was also a difficult and fiercely independent man. He joined the Columbia faculty in 1891, as Professor of Experimental Psychology. A year later he helped to found the American Psychological Association, whose president he became in 1895. He edited and published the important journal *Science*, and he was the founding editor of the *Psychological Review*. At Columbia he was an effective teacher, directing more than fifty doctoral dissertations. The first psychologist elected to the National Academy of Sciences, he was, historian Dorothy Ross noted, "second only to William James in the esteem of his colleagues."[50]

With the publication of *University Control* in 1913, he made public his opposition to the "autocratic system" of university administration. Neither as acerbic nor as brilliant as Veblen's "memorandum on the conduct of universities by businessmen," Cattell's book was, nonetheless, intelligent and telling in its criticism. His favored image of the university was that of a free association of intellect, "unhierarchical, democratic, anarchic, in its organization." Linking the rise of universities in America with the rise of trusts, he identified both the "trust promoter" and the university president as "utterly subversive of a true democracy." The modern university president was "not a leader, but a boss."

He proposed that university governance be radically revised. The governing body ought to be made up in equal parts of the faculty, alumni, and members of the community, while deans and the president should be elected by the faculty. Only then, he thought, would the university itself be democratic and thus able to serve "the larger democracy of which it is a part."[51]

Butler did not take to the suggestions. In fact, he proposed that the trustees "retire" Cattell, who was then fifty-three years old and the father of seven children. A number of faculty leaders came to Cattell's defense, including John Dewey and Franz Boas, and Butler abandoned the attempt. But another major episode came in January 1917. When Butler announced that the Faculty Club would be closed to accommodate other activities, Cattell circulated a "confidential memorandum" to the 426 members of the faculty suggesting, among other alternatives, that the Faculty Club be relocated to Butler's official residence on Morningside Drive, which, he surmised, would be vacant "if our many-talented and much climbing President should be swept into the national Vice-Presidency by a reactionary wave."[52] The letter did not remain confidential, and the trustees, Butler, and the faculty were shocked to read it in the city's newspapers. Butler again proposed to retire Cattell.

E.R.A. Seligman, who had been concerned for some time about

the erosion of faculty power in university administration and about several war-stimulated inquiries into faculty opinion, was determined to involve the faculty in the case.[53] Butler and the trustees accommodated him, appointing a faculty Committee of Nine, with Seligman as chairman. After persuading Cattell to apologize for his breach in manners, Seligman and his fellow committee members were able, by June, to stop the move to retire their colleague.[54]

At about the same time, however, the committee gave its approval to a statement on academic freedom in wartime that Butler announced to the faculty and to the public on June 6, 1917. While national policies were "in debate," Butler explained, "we gave complete freedom" to members of the university community.[55] Once the nation had spoken, however, "conditions sharply changed." What had been tolerated before became intolerable now. What had been wrongheadedness was now sedition. What had been folly was now treason. His conclusion was a direct and unmistakable warning to the faculty: "the separation of any such person from Columbia University will be as speedy as the discovery of his offense."[56]

It is important to understand that, however much this statement reflected Butler's own predilections, the statement was approved by a Trustee Committee and the Faculty Committee of Nine, which included Seligman and John Dewey, both founders of the AAUP. But even the AAUP, one must further realize, acknowledged in 1918 that war brought "special obligations." To fail to support the administration and its objectives, the AAUP counseled, would be "to desire the triumph of moral evil in the world."[57]

Such was the context for Cattell's next—and last—act at Columbia. In late August, he wrote to several Congressmen—on stationery that identified him as a Columbia professor—asking them to "support a measure against sending conscripts to Europe against their will."[58] When Butler learned of this, he invoked his June warning and proposed to fire Cattell summarily, without a pension. Seligman immediately intervened, again in the interest of establishing the principle of faculty control. Butler and the trustees saw a different value in the Seligman Committee. It could be used, they rightly supposed, to legitimate their own actions. Becoming by now tired of the exasperating Cattell, the Committee of Nine agreed to his retirement.[59] But the trustees, saying they were acting with faculty approval, fired Cattell, rather than retiring him. They also fired Henry Wadsworth Longfellow Dana, a young professor of English, likewise for his alleged antiwar activities.

At this point, Charles A. Beard offered his civics lesson, and it was a dramatic one. He announced to his classes that the day's lecture would be his last. His resignation, effective immediately, had been submitted to President Butler. Beard's announcement surprised and shocked students and faculty, but it was not a sudden decision. He had been disturbed by affairs at Columbia for some time. A year before he had been called before a trustee committee that inquired into his own views and those of his colleagues, and he had been forced by Butler to fire a perfectly able lecturer in the Politics Department whose pacifist views, once admired by Butler, were now an embarrassment to the president. The firing of Cattell and Dana moved Beard, who in fact strongly supported the war, to a public act. If Butler defended the firing in terms of the obligation of professors to consider the "reputation" of the university in their "public conduct," Beard refused the claim of such institutional values. He stood absolutely for the principle of free speech and the free intellectual.[60]

The *New York Times*, in an editorial on Beard's resignation, declared that "Columbia University was better" for it, but it was, as John Dewey immediately realized, an enormous, irreplaceable loss for Columbia and for academic life.[61] Dewey had already dissociated himself from the recommendations of the Committee of Nine, and he had resigned from it.[62] Two days after Beard's resignation, he wrote Seligman to say that he now was convinced that the committee had erred in its efforts to "smooth over" the real problem at Columbia. They had worried too much about saving the "university from a disagreeable scene." It would have been far better had they acted sooner and much more strongly to defend the integrity of intellect. If they had, "Beard would be our colleague today." By not being courageous enough, we left Beard "in a position where he felt isolated, and without the support of his colleagues."[63] Dewey did not follow Beard's example. He did not resign his professorship, nor does he seem to have been tempted to do so. But he did withdraw substantially from the affairs of the university and increasingly made the city rather than the university the habitat of his mind and work.[64]

As a simple fact, Beard's resignation rocked the literary and academic worlds. But the words that surrounded the act demand attention. Beard's letter of resignation was a reasoned and stinging criticism of the academic intellect of his time. He pointed out that his own early and consistent support of the war was a matter of the public record. But, and this was the nub of it all, the opinion of an intellectual can be trusted by the public only if its "disinterestedness is about all suspicion," if its "independence is beyond all doubt." The public must have reason to believe in the intellectual's "devotion to the whole country, as distinguished from any single class or group." At present, with the university apparently under the control of trustees who deny intellectual independence to the faculty, the public cannot have that faith in a Columbia professor. "I am convinced that while I remain in the pay of the Trustees of Columbia University I cannot do effectively my humble part in sustaining public opinion" in regard to the war or the task of postwar reconstruction.[65]

Responding to Beard—though not naming him—in his Annual Report, Butler made explicit Beard's distinction between the obligations of a Columbia professor and those of an intellectual. Butler also, and not surprisingly, inverted Beard's evaluation of their respective duties. Since professors benefit from the prestige of the university, Butler argued, they had "a distinct, constant, and compelling obligation" to protect that prestige. One cannot, he insisted, be loyal to "humanity" rather than to the institution. Such expressions reveal "muddled thinking," what one has come to expect from "those who, for lack of a more accurate term, call themselves intellectuals." These intellectuals, he informed Columbia's trustees, "know so many things which are not so that they make ignorance appear to be not only interesting but positively important." Yet it was true, he ruefully acknowledged, that they "abound just now" in the city's lesser literary circles and that even in the academy they "are not without representation." But he pledged himself and the university to stand firmly against the "rule of the literary and academic Bolsheviki."[66]

Farther from the actual events at Columbia, from the distance of Newport, Rhode Island, John W. Burgess, now in retirement, observed it all. He knew that something had gone wrong. He would not say so publicly, but privately he worried that his grand hope for Columbia's Faculty of Political Science was being destroyed. With Columbia fallen to such a "sad state," how could it serve as the foundation of "reason" in public life? "Freedom of thought and speech," he urgently wrote Seligman in the midst of the crisis, "is the life of a university." A year later, when Robinson, too, resigned to join Beard in founding the New School for Social Research, Burgess was "grieved." It saddened him that Beard, Robinson, and "the younger men" would abandon the Faculty of Political Science "in order to construct a rival to it." Yet Burgess, whose political and intellectual outlook was so different from those now fleeing Columbia, could understand that their effort was in fact a rekindling of his own original dream. And he did not begrudge them their attempt. "I can understand their point of view," he confided to Seligman.[67]

The effort to establish the New School for Social Research, originally to be called the Free School of Political Science, after École Libre in Paris, arose directly from the perceived constraints on intellect inherent in the service ideal's alliance of the university with the dominant classes.[68] By calling it a free school, they meant free of affiliation with the dominant classes, and by locating it in New York City, they hoped to differentiate it from the national system of academic scholarship.

Although this particular effort was sparked by problems at Columbia, it is important to understand that it was only the most important of several contemporary efforts to free the social sciences from this alliance or to forge a new alliance with the subordinated classes. The Rand School of Social Sciences, founded in 1906, for example, was inspired by Beard's earlier work as co-organizer of Ruskin College for workers, which he had done while a student at Oxford in 1899–1901. Funded initially by Carrie Rand Herron, the Rand School later received increased support from socialist trade unions until, by 1918, in its new quarters at 7 East Fifteenth Street, it provided a social science curriculum for fifteen hundred students, nearly all of whom were socialist workers. Beard, who was already a member of the three-person advisory board, began lecturing there in 1918. A few years later, in 1921, Brookwood Labor College opened in Katonah, New York, forty-two miles north of Grand Central Terminal. Under the inspiring leadership of A. J. Muste, this two-year residential college devoted itself to teaching and research on behalf of peace and social justice for labor. Workers selected by labor unions received training in the social sciences as preparation for working class leadership. Brookwood, the Rand School, and the New School for Social Research were all involved in different ways, moreover, with the Workers' Education Bureau of America, which Charles and Mary Beard helped to found in 1921. It was, indeed, a moment of unusual ferment.[69]

The prime mover behind the New School experiment was James Harvey Robinson, characterized by economist Wesley Clair Mitchell "as a man of ideas, which is not orthodox in a historian."[70] Robinson, an enormously popular teacher of both graduate and undergraduate students, was absolutely committed to independence of thought.[71] He quit Columbia both in protest and in sympathy for his friend and sometime co-author Beard. Beard and Robinson were soon joined by two other Columbia colleagues, both distinguished: Dewey, who did not resign, and Mitchell, who did. Herbert Croly of the *New Republic,* who brought with him economist Alvin Johnson, one of his editors, joined the Columbians. That the early meetings were mostly held at offices of the *New Republic* and that the school was organized in a group of three townhouses near the magazine's own yellow house in Chelsea make an important point about this moment of crisis and ferment: academic and literary cultures were interacting with and sustaining each other. Indeed, after 1919, it would be that intersection of academic and literary New York that would provide the terrain for the development of generations of New York intellectuals.

There was considerable agreement on what the founders did not want and less on what they did want. Probably, however, they all agreed with Robinson that it was to be an "independent school of social science," with neither trustees and presidents nor degrees. The students would be adults who did not need to be persuaded to learn and who would attend for the sole purpose of learning, not to earn academic degrees. The overall design, as Croly put it, was to free social knowledge from the constraints of "individual, national, and class particularism," and the school would avoid the limitations of "excessive specialization."[72]

Within this broad area of consensus, there was room for considerable disagreement. Robinson envisioned an intellectual center, a sort of club where social ideas were discussed by men and women of intellectual distinction. Beard tended more toward a research institution, but he was also attracted to the notion of a place for free and conversational intellect to find itself in the city. Mitchell, too, looked toward a research institution committed to the free pursuit of objective fact, while Croly advocated what we would today call applied social research, with a particular emphasis on the training of experts in labor relations.[73] Even with these unresolved ambiguities, the opening of the school in 1919 was an intellectual event in the city. The faculty was brilliant: Robinson, Beard, Dewey, and Mitchell were joined in the first year by Elsie Clews Parsons, Thorstein Veblen, Emily James Putnam, Graham Wallas, and Harold Laski. The new university was competitive enough from the start to prompt President Butler to condemn the New School as "a little bunch of disgruntled liberals setting up a tiny fly-by-night radical counterfeit of education."[74]

Butler's blast—and others from established leaders—made fund raising commensurate with the school's intellectual standing impossible.[75] But the experiment suffered internal problems as well. A school without an administration could not, as it turned out, avoid internal chaos, and the founders soon parted ways. Croly left first, in the spring of 1921, while Beard and Robinson resigned soon after, at the first signs of incipient bureaucratization. Alvin Johnson suddenly found himself in charge. He saved the New School by converting it into a valuable but harmless center of adult education.[76] The attempt to create an independent school of social science in New York had failed.

Beard, who had gone into the experiment with such enthusiasm, was chastened by the failure. After trying to devise a way for adults freely to associate under academic auspices "in the pursuit of wisdom and knowledge," he concluded that it was a noble but impossible dream. Writing in the *Freeman* in 1921, he asked whether the "modern university" is really a place "where men with an intellectual mission" can "best deliver their message." Has not the printing press, he asked, "made the university obsolete for all except those engaged in cramming candidates for degrees?" For the "true teacher, the restless searcher—out of all things," there is, he decided, "a greater forum than the narrow school room," the printed word.[77]

Mitchell, who had resigned his Columbia professorship, rejoined Dewey at Morningside Heights. Dewey in the course of the war had transformed himself into a public intellectual, receiving a retainer from the *New Republic* with an agreement that they would print whatever he gave them whenever he gave anything to them. He almost ceased being an academic, though he did some of his most important technical philosophy as well as writing and speaking for the public. Mitchell became the model social scientist of the decade. After founding the National Bureau of Economic Research, committed to objective economic research, Mitchell joined with Charles Merriam of the University of Chicago to found the Social Science Research Council. No one who looked at the organization of the social sciences at Columbia or Chicago, the two major centers, could fail to grasp that the institution of social science in the United States after the war was hardly the freestanding realm of intellect sought by either the early Ely or the founders of the New School. Never before had intellect been more thoroughly incorporated into the dominant structures of American society. Men like Mitchell and Merriam brought together, as did the Social Science Research Council itself, government, universities, and the new foundations.[78] And all of this was done under the aegis of objectivity, the very value that Beard, who had become a free intellectual, had come to suspect.[79]

This reorientation of social science can be tracked by comparing the 1907–8 lectures with another series that in 1929 celebrated the 175th anniversary of Columbia's founding. In reading this second set of lectures, one is impressed, unavoidably, with the fact that the intellectual excitement that marked the earlier lectures had been subordinated to the pride of incorporation into society. If the earlier lectures had opened out to the general culture, engaging the intellectual concerns of an educated public, the later lectures explained the inner workings of professionalized disciplines to outsiders. They trumpeted disciplinary progress, particularly the various institutional mechanisms devised to publish scholarship, secure funding, coordinate research, and extend influence.

A Quarter Century of Learning, 1904–1929 is a remarkably complacent set of lectures. The introduction to the volume, written by historian Dixon Ryan Fox, celebrated the enhanced role of the scholar in American life, making specific reference to psychologist J. B. Watson's recent appointment to the vice-presidency of New York's largest advertising firm.[80]

These lectures do not share ideas. Nor do they even announce ideas. Rather they report professional progress. For example, Carleton J. H. Hayes, a distinguished historian working in the tradition of Robinson's New History, began by informing his auditors that the "new history" had won the day. Instead of illustrating this new historiography by exploring the possible links between history and contemporary intellectual and political life, something Hayes was fully capable of doing, he declined to exploit the opportunity. The occasion, he apparently thought, called instead for an account of those institutional developments that marked the maturation of the profession. His lecture thus reads less like the work of a scholar and more like that of President Butler or the head of a large corporation. His comments about the founding of the American Council of Learned Societies in 1919 and the Social Science Research Council in 1923 and his description of lavishly funded collaborative projects (the *Dictionary of American Biography* and the *Encyclopedia of the Social Sciences*) must have impressed the audience. But if any of his auditors had heard the lectures of 1908, he or she surely must have felt some disappointment about the intellectual hole in Hayes'.

Wesley Clair Mitchell, who spoke on economics, took much the same approach, noting the founding of the Brookings Institution in Washington (1916) and the National Bureau of Economic Research in New York (1920). He also endorsed the recent foundation-sponsored trend toward interdisciplinary collaboration in the study of social issues, citing in particular the Social Science Research Council, founded for that purpose and of which he was president.[81] The other lectures were celebratory in the same way. All of it is very impressive, but the lectures mark at once the new status of intellect in society and its retreat from public discourse.

Academic intellect constituted itself more or less along the lines envisioned by Seligman in the 1890s. Yet the terms of this instauration involved a class affiliation that he had been loath to acknowledge. The institutional quest for a social science free of class affiliation died with the failure of the 1919 vision for the New School for Social Research. Efforts to associate the social sciences with the working classes found greater success, but not much, and they did not materially affect the development of academic social science in America.[82]

New York and New York academics played a key role in this institutionalization of social science as expertise. What they devised was embraced by a national system of universities and disciplines. In New York, however, the subject matter of social inquiry was never completely captured by the academy. There was always a venue for the scholar to straddle the academic and literary cultures, as did Dewey, or to flee the one for the other, as did Beard.[83]

Elsewhere in the American academic system, however, there was very little to ventilate disciplinary procedures and boundaries. Even in Chicago, where the social sciences were deeply engaged in the life of the city, where they used the city as a laboratory and were a factor in local administration, there was, as Edward Shils recently wrote, remarkably little contact between the city's literary culture and its academic culture.[84] This division meant that the rich borderland between literary and academic culture was less often trod in Chicago than in New York. However much the University of Chicago's social sciences associated themselves with the city, it was on strictly academic terms. This strategy made the social sciences at Chicago professionally preeminent. New York's social scientific community, clearly inferior to Chicago's after the war, never effectively enclosed itself. It was always open, at least at the top, to the more general political and literary intellectuals of the city. The result was weaker disciplines in New York City, but that may also have made possible the fuller engagement of public life by *academics as intellectuals*, something achieved by Robert Lynd, Richard Hofstadter, Daniel Bell, C. Wright Mills, and Robert Merton a generation later.[85]

❧[5]❧ The Emergence of the New York Intellectuals: Modernism, Cosmopolitanism, and Nationalism

Although this essay draws rather heavily upon the research that became
New York Intellect, *it does something largely precluded by the structure of
that book: here the relations between academic and literary intellectuals are
explored, even emphasized, while in the other study they were discussed
separately. The focus of concern here are themes of modernity,
cosmopolitanism, and nationalism in the interest of showing the phasing of
their emergence as central themes in the intellectual culture of the 1930s,
1940s, and 1950s. The argument, implied as much as it is explicit, is that
the formation of the New York intellectuals—the sociology, the style, and
the substantive concerns with which they have been identified—has a long
foreground. Indeed, the New York intellectuals had been formed and had
established the values, politics, and concerns of the movement before the
generational subset that came to be called "The New York Intellectuals"
arrived on the scene.*

*This paper was prepared for a conference, "The Metropolis
Transformed: Budapest and New York, 1880–1930," which was held in
Budapest in August 1988. It was cosponsored by the American Council of
Learned Societies, through the International Research and Exchange Board,
and the Hungarian Academy of Sciences. This context will explain the
otherwise odd references to Budapest and certain Hungarian intellectuals. It
has not been previously published.*

BY THE 1880S, NEW YORK CITY, LIKE BUDAPEST, HAD DRAMATICALLY TRANS-
formed itself. The population had grown tremendously during the past
half century. If the Chain Bridge marked the expansion of Budapest, so
the East River Bridge (quickly designated the Brooklyn Bridge) gave
New York City a metropolitan scale while it reinforced the city's met-

ropolitan claims.[1] Both cities absorbed massive and polyglot streams of immigration. The cultural aspiration of both cities was increasingly cosmopolitan and sophisticated; both for the first time realistically could claim association with the great cities of western Europe.[2]

In both cities bourgeois culture had established itself, and in New York it became easier and more acceptable to identify the city's culture with that of the nation. Since the Civil War, the *Nation* magazine had been published in New York, and that magazine, along with *Harpers* and, in the 1880s, the *Century*, successfully claimed to be national media of bourgeois culture and politics. In literary history, this consolidation of New York's metropolitan ascendancy is often marked by, if not necessarily identified by, the movement of the novelist William Dean Howells from Boston to New York. By the 1890s, only Paris had more artists than New York, and in New York, largely because of its commercial economy, which drew many business travelers, the theater had long flourished. In urban history, the city's standing was marked by the founding of museums that assumed they were metropolitan *and* national. No other American city during the era would have dared to establish either a *Metropolitan* Museum of Art or an *American* Museum of Natural History. New York had, indeed, become the home (and the voice) of a national, liberal, and genteel bourgeois culture that emerged out of the Civil War, the United States's war of national unification.[3] It would soon become, as well, the staging ground for a generational and modernist revolt against that culture.

Genteel culture found its literal home in the brownstone houses that lined the city's streets. The brownstone is an exclusively bourgeois housing type; the earlier Greek revival town houses that remain today in Greenwich Village were the homes of artisans as well as merchants. But the brownstone, a housing type that developed north of Washington Square after the middle of the century, was the home only of bourgeois families. The working class, different in so many ways from earlier artisans, was also different in its urban housing arrangements: by mid-century the tenement had been developed as housing for workers and the poor.

Life in New York's brownstones, geographically separated from the poverty and despair of the Lower East Side tenement district, was organized around ideals. At the core of brownstone New York's culture was a faith in the universality of moral values and the inevitability of progress. It demanded absolute commitment to the importance and value of Anglo-American literary culture.[4]

This genteel culture reached its peak of influence in the 1880s and early 1890s, surviving past its time into the twentieth century, thus setting the stage for an exceptionally intense drama of generational conflict. At its best and in its own time, however, it was centered in the New York publishing house of Charles Scribner's Sons, where William Crary Brownell, in the role of literary adviser, represented the keenest New York literary intelligence, and in the finely printed and beautifully illustrated pages of the *Century* magazine, edited by Richard Watson Gilder. Brownell and Gilder, the nation's premier book and magazine editors, were the gatekeepers for the brownstone culture of New York; by their decisions, they defined its public existence. They saw themselves as part of and representative of brownstone New York, and they sought to shape the literary expression of that class's ideals.

The modern literary intellectuals who emerged in New York early in the twentieth century defined themselves in opposition to this culture. They rejected not only the philosophy and aesthetics of it, but also the Victorian definition of the relation of intellect to the class system. If brownstone culture assumed that the man of letters was a member of the bourgeoisie, its best representative, the new literary intellectuals of the early twentieth century, the first American writers to call themselves intellectuals, rejected such class affiliation. They articulated, with somewhat less sociological precision, a self-identity much like that of the "free-floating, unattached intellectual" whom Karl Mannheim was at the same time characterizing both as an ideal and as a description of his Hungarian colleagues in Budapest's Sunday Circle.[5]

Partly for reasons internal to the history of the bourgeois class generally and their own families in particular, partly because they were unable to establish any other class affiliation, specifically a working class alliance, these new intellectuals defined themselves in generational terms, as the "Young Intellectuals." This pattern was not unique to America; one finds it in London, Madrid, Rome, Berlin, Vienna, and Budapest, and it later emerged as another of Mannheim's key sociological concepts.[6] The Young Intellectuals, whether in the United States or in Europe, were the first generation to come of age within a bourgeois culture that had consolidated itself politically, financially, and culturally.

For those who sat in brownstone parlors, traditional culture appeared to be quite secure in New York—more so than it in fact was. New York must have seemed an invulnerable bastion of genteel culture and a compelling symbol of capitalist progress. In ways not visible from brownstone windows, however, the city offered considerable resources to those who would subvert that culture.

In fact, one could hardly imagine a better place than New York

City from which to launch an attack upon traditional culture. Not only was the city moving into closer touch with continental intellectual currents, but its rapidly increasing immigrant districts were giving lie to any Anglo-Saxon definition of the city and its culture. To the considerable extent that New York deviated from the Anglo-Saxon norm, the young embraced it. As the young gradually became aware of the socialism and Russian fiction discussed by Jewish intellectuals in the cafe society of the Lower East Side, they discovered a moral intensity that implied a richer, deeper sense of culture than traditional culture seemed to offer. The increasing visibility of poverty and of labor militancy on the Lower East Side—to say nothing of the tragic Triangle Shirtwaist factory fire of 1911, when 146 Jewish working girls died only a block east of Washington Square—suggested an economy of exploitation as much as one of progress. And Tammany Hall was, of course, a continual affront to genteel notions of politics.

The Greenwich Village section of the city, moreover, provided a special kind of sanctuary within the city itself from which to fly the banners of revolt. Surrounded by immigrants, avoided by traffic, situated halfway between the city's two skyscraper districts, Greenwich Village offered a place where it seemed possible to escape bourgeois values and art. Here, in the freer atmosphere of the village, the Young Intellectuals could in word and deed attack conventional notions of family and sex roles, the foundation of traditional culture. What the village seemed to offer was the opportunity to fuse life and art, the personal and the political. "There was," Max Eastman, editor of the *Masses*, recalled, "a sense of universal revolt and regeneration, of the just-before-the-dawn of a new day in American art and literature and living-of-life as well as in politics."[7]

Within the bourgeois city there was, then, a special milieu that nourished the rebellion. It is important to understand the degree to which the cultural revolt in America was headquartered in New York and the extent to which the revolution in New York has defined the basic terms of intellectual culture in twentieth-century America. One cannot but be struck, for example, by the absence of revolt in Boston and by the difference between the rebels in Chicago (native American and aesthetic, with the poet as the characteristic type) and in New York (the more cosmopolitan essayist, linking culture and politics).

There was, however, more than urban social history involved in this cultural transformation, and developments were not contained within Greenwich Village. Morningside Heights, where, as Max Eastman recalled, ideas sprouted out of the walks on the Columbia University campus, provided crucial intellectual sustenance to the revolt. From 1904, when philosopher John Dewey moved from the University of Chicago, until the First World War, when historian Charles Beard resigned from the university and left academic life, Columbia University provided a home and an urban context for a vital and remarkably coherent and self-consciously modern (and antiformalist) circle of philosophers and social scientists. Here America's most advanced philosophical and social scientific thinkers reconceived truth, understanding it not in Kantian categories but as the product of historical experience. They undermined the epistemological project of Kant in favor of history. Steering between idealism and positivism, these philosophers of the *via media*, as historian James Kloppenberg described them, undid the philosophical underpinnings of genteel culture, embracing a positive, even constructive, modernism that pointed toward social democracy.[8]

Admittedly, the New Yorkers were participating in an international critique of idealism and associationism, and in this they joined Wilhelm Dilthey, T. H. Green, Henry Sidgwick, and Alfred Fouillée. It is also true that the groundwork for American pragmatism had been prepared elsewhere: by Chauncey Wright, Charles Peirce, and William James at Harvard and in Cambridge and by Dewey himself at Chicago. But it was in New York that it found its home and entered the discourse of literary and political culture, with Max Eastman, Dewey's graduate student and editor of the *Masses*, providing a vital link between Morningside Heights and Greenwich Village.[9]

Most centrally at stake in the revolt of the younger generation was the definition of culture itself. The Young Intellectuals were self-consciously modern, but they were modern in a rather specific sense. So many definitions of artistic and literary modernism identify it with a rage against civilization, the breaking of form, and even nihilistic futility that we might miss other equally legitimate versions of modernism that are more moderate, positive, affirming, and even reformist.[10] Such modernists were the Young Intellectuals. It was characteristic that in hiring a staff writer for the newly established *New Republic* in 1914, the editor, Herbert Croly, urged him to be "thoroughly critical" of the "actual practice of the arts in this country," but "there must also be a positive impulse behind our criticism."[11]

We also think of modernism as an internationalist movement, either universalizing or interiorizing culture—or both. We do so properly, but often such an assumption misrepresents versions of modernism that are more nationalist in their concerns. While the Young Intellectuals eagerly attended to and celebrated international cultural movements, they remained cultural nationalists. They could be at once, as Lewis Mumford, the closest heir of this generation, had described himself, "unashamedly declarative of our national identity yet equally cosmopolitan."[12]

No individual better expressed the cultural ideal and literary style of the Greenwich Village intellectuals than Randolph Bourne; no magazine more so than the *Seven Arts*, characterized by Henry May as the "pure, distilled essence" of the movement and group.[13] Both Bourne and the magazine were attentive to international developments; indeed, they conceived of themselves as part of an international youth movement. Yet they were fascinated by America. Rejecting the Anglo-Saxon culture of the brownstone elite, they looked to Whitman in order to locate the possibilities of a distinctive, modern, and vital American culture.[14]

Bourne, who was born in Bloomfield, New Jersey, in 1886, of a family with long and deep Anglo-Saxon roots, entered Columbia University in 1909. Few of the Young Intellectuals went to Columbia; most had attended Harvard and Yale. But at Columbia Bourne encountered a wider world than he had ever imagined. He came into contact with a cosmopolitan outlook and the bright children of the Lower East Side. He also studied with a number of Columbia professors who were pioneering the development of the exciting new social sciences, especially Charles Beard and John Dewey. Stirred by the intellectual excitement of the social science faculty, he rejected the "deadening" literature professors, looking instead to "philosophy and history and sociology as the true nourishment of the soul."[15] Under this impulse, Bourne opened the literary mind out to the social sciences and, through them, to society. He became an essayist, establishing the essay as the favored genre of the New York intellectuals.

Bourne also understood the implications of Dewey's revolution in philosophy. Dewey's undercutting of the idealistic and formalistic premises of Anglo-Saxon gentility fed into Bourne's own personal experience; he discovered in the immigrant-filled city the parochialism of the Anglo-Saxon culture of his family. This discovery clarified his desire for a vital rather than emblematic culture in America. Most important of all, Bourne and his fellow intellectuals associated with the *Seven Arts* were certain that cultural and political advance would proceed hand in hand. Like the members of the Sunday Circle in Budapest at the same time, they were convinced that society could be, in the words of the founding editor of *Seven Arts*, "regenerated by art."[16]

Seven Arts magazine is often identified with Bourne; it was there that he published his powerful essays against the war, essays that caused the magazine's financial angel to withdraw support, ending its brilliant career after little more than a year. Yet Bourne came late to the magazine's short history, not appearing in its pages until the second of its two volumes in April 1917. Nor was he ever actually an editor of the magazine.

The founding editors were James Oppenheim and Waldo Frank, both of New York German-Jewish backgrounds. Oppenheim, a poet who secured financial support for the magazine, had attended Columbia for two years before working at a settlement and becoming head of the Hebrew Technical School for Girls. Frank had been raised in wealth, and he came to Greenwich Village after Yale. After reading Van Wyck Brooks's *America's Coming of Age* (1915), they persuaded Brooks to become an associate editor, "thus relieving us," Oppenheim remembered, "of the onus of being non-Anglo-Saxon."[17]

Of the five major editors and contributors identified with the magazine—Oppenheim, Frank, Brooks, Bourne, and the Yale-educated music critic Paul Rosenfeld—all were raised in New York or its suburbs, and three were Jewish. It was, then, a New York magazine, and it was the first example of an ethnic collaboration, Gentile and Jew, that sought to speak for an American national culture embracing "different national strains."[18]

Seven Arts was not to be a "little magazine"; it proposed to speak broadly for an American cultural renaissance. "In all such epochs," the editors wrote, "the arts cease to be private matters; they become not only the expression of the national life but a means to its enhancement." *Seven Arts*, they declared, "is not a magazine for artists, but an expression of artists for the community."[19] Located around the corner from the "291" gallery of Rosenfeld's friend Alfred Stieglitz, *Seven Arts* was an intensely national magazine, promoting a new American culture, while at the same time self-consciously cosmopolitan in outlook and attentive to modern developments on the Continent (not England).

America's entry into the war at once shattered and clarified the cultural movement represented by the *Seven Arts*. When Bourne published "Twilight of Idols," his stinging attack on Dewey for supporting the war, the magazine collapsed. More important, as Bourne observed in the course of the article, it was no longer clear that cultural and political advance went hand in hand.[20]

Bourne feared, as he wrote to Van Wyck Brooks in 1918, that the war "has brought an immense and terrifying inflation to the political sphere, so that for most people nongovernmentalized activity has ceased almost to have significance."[21] The cultural program of the *New Republic*, whose prowar editorials Bourne, one of the magazine's original staff writers when it was founded in 1914, now attacked, was abandoned in favor of political influence.

Bourne noted a peculiar, and disturbing, "congeniality" between the war and the pragmatic intellectuals at the *New Republic*, so anxious to influence the Wilson administration. "The war," he observed in the essay that brought the *Seven Arts* adventure to an end, "has revealed a younger intelligentsia trained up in the pragmatic dispensation, immensely ready for the executive ordering of events, pitifully unprepared for the intellectual interpretation or the idealistic focussing of ends." Reasserting the importance of art, he concluded that, "unless you start with the vividest kind of poetic vision," you may find yourself "happily and busily engaged in the national enterprise of war."[22]

Two other legacies of the war bear discussion here. First there was the Russian Revolution. The success of Lenin and his fellow Bolsheviks in 1917 and the subsequent reality of the Soviet Union became a momentous fact of modern life. And it immediately became a fact of a peculiar sort, capable of extension through space, becoming an almost tangible part of intellectual life in New York. Second, nationalism, inflamed as usual by war, not only brought intolerance, repression, and Americanization programs; it also stimulated in response the formulation of a cosmopolitan ideal, sustaining an urban, ethnically diverse, and antiprovincial notion of intellect that became, as a number of historians have recently shown, a beacon for the *Partisan Review* generation of New York intellectuals in the 1930s and 1940s.

After the Russian Revolution, the sort of innocent, nondoctrinaire, eclectic "revolution" represented by the *Masses* (1911–17) was no longer possible, as its reincarnation as the *Liberator* (1918–24) and the later *New Masses* (1926–48) clearly reveals. Once the Soviet Union existed, a great deal of free speculation became difficult. Concrete positions on its policies seemed to be demanded, and for the first time in America art began to be judged overtly and directly by political criteria, with the idealization of proletarian literature and rejection of modernism. It is fitting, perhaps, that the United States government closed down the *Masses* in New York almost on the day Lenin's triumph made the radicalism of that magazine impossible.

The xenophobia and intolerance stimulated by the war also provided the context for Bourne's powerful and oppositional essay, "Trans-National America," which envisioned a cosmopolitan American national culture. Brownstone culture had failed most obviously in its incapacity to imagine a national culture that included the immigrants who were transforming New York. Bourne, by contrast, saw in the city's newcomers a grand opportunity for youth to liberate itself from Anglo-Saxon parochialism. Not only was he prepared to accept immigrants, he developed a theory of American culture that required the patterns of difference that they constituted.

Beginning with Horace Kallen's criticism of the homogenizing and Americanizing idea of the "melting pot," Bourne elaborated a pluralistic vision of intellectual culture. It was a conception of culture that combined an acceptance of persistent particularism with a sense of common and public discourse. And although it was written after Bourne's break with Dewey, it depended upon Dewey's philosophy, particularly his rejection of absolutes and his emphasis upon the continual making and remaking of truth and culture.

Bourne urged intellectuals to accept the distinctive character of American life; they should stop longing for European models of politics and culture. He rejoiced in America as a "unique sociological fabric," and he asserted that "it bespeaks a poverty of imagination not to be thrilled at the incalculable potentialities of so novel a union of men." He envisioned America in the image of New York—a federation of cultures. Rejecting the legitimacy of Anglo-Saxon dominance, he declared that American culture "lies in the future," and it shall be "what the immigrant will have a hand in making it."[23]

Like Kallen, Bourne welcomed the preservation of ethnic difference, but he was particularly concerned with a unity that could embrace such permanent diversity. He was moved, as David Hollinger wrote, "by the idea of a community of intellectuals, a complex, yet unified, single discourse to which a variety of contingent particularisms would make their distinctive contributions."[24] It was a vision of urbanity and cosmopolitanism that proved itself congenial both to Anglo-Saxon radicals and to the emerging Jewish intellectuals.

One best grasps the radicalism and New Yorkishness of Bourne's essay by following the correspondence between Bourne and his editor. When Bourne submitted the essay to Ellery Sedgwick, editor of Boston's *Atlantic*, the editor had been publishing the New York writer's work since Bourne's undergraduate essay defending youth, "The Two Generations," published in 1912. This established relationship accounted for the publication of "Trans-National America" in the *Atlantic*. Sedgwick did not sympathize with Bourne's argument; he was in fact deeply distressed by it. Speaking in the tones of Boston to New York as well as those of an older gentility, he informed Bourne, "I profoundly disagree with your paper." The United States, at least as Sedgwick understood the matter, was "created by English instinct and dedicated to the Anglo-Saxon ideal." He complained that Bourne spoke "as though the last immigrant should have as great an effect upon the determination of our history as the first band of Englishmen." Insisting that the United States had neither political nor literary lessons to learn from Eastern Europe, he bridled at Bourne's equation of an old New Englander and a recent Czech as "equally characteristic of America."[25]

Bourne's ideal was new and profound in its implications. Yet it was also deeply rooted in the city's social and literary history. Whitman, of course, would recognize it, but so, too, might Henry James. As early as the 1860s, James, more committed to the Anglo-Saxon ideal than Bourne, nonetheless saw certain advantages in America for literature. "I think that to be an American is an excellent preparation for culture. . . . We can," he observed, "deal freely with forms of civilization not our own." If the absence of a "national stamp" has in the past been a "defect," it is "not unlikely that American writers may yet indicate that a vast intellectual fusion and synthesis of the various National tendencies of the world is the condition of more important achievements than any we have seen."[26] And when James returned to New York in 1904 his reaction to the immigrants was more complex than is usually recognized. While it is true that he felt alien in the city of his birth, physically transformed as it was, and worried over the fate of the English language, he also found on the Lower East Side a social and intellectual life containing a "promise of its own consciousness." He even contemplated an "ethnic" synthesis in America that might become "the very music of humanity."[27] Few at the time could grasp it, but the possibilities Bourne and, more hesitantly, James saw in the city of immigrants, not the dominant and narrow Anglo-Saxonism of the time, were to become the basis for the internationalist and cosmopolitan center of art, music, dance, and literature that New York became in the 1940s and 1950s.

The metropolitan and cosmopolitan ideal articulated by Randolph Bourne implied a proliferation of vital subcultures—ethnic, but also aesthetic, geographical, and political. Although he celebrated difference and diversity, he felt that the geographical contiguousness of the metropolis would deny each group the privilege of provinciality. All must be tolerant of others, and they must engage in conversation with each other. What one most notices after the war, however, is a striking shrinkage of the literary imagination and diffusion of literary life into particular locales and coteries.

To make this point, we might notice that the rich interweaving of

politics and culture represented by the Young Intellectuals did not survive the war, nor did their confident assumption that radical or progressive politics and advanced "modern" art were natural partners. For
example, the *Dial*, which had been moved from Chicago to New York
in 1918 with the intention of publishing both Dewey and Bourne, was
nearly torn apart by politics, and in 1920, under the editorship of Scho-
field Thayer, it turned severely, if impressively, to aestheticism and modernism. The *Freeman*, established in 1920 with aims that seemed to
welcome the Young Intellectuals (now getting older), turned out to be
a fundamentally political magazine. To the extent that any discussion
of modernism in the arts appeared in the *Liberator* and the *New Masses*,
it was to condemn it, usually from the perspective of proletarian art.

The shift from the prewar years to the 1920s was anticipated in a
revealing exchange between Randolph Bourne (just before his prema-
ture death in the influenza epidemic of December 1918) and Harriet
Monroe, editor of the influential modernist magazine *Poetry*. Writing in
the *Dial*, Bourne had observed that the real danger for the young artists
was not the philistines, nor was it the Anglo-Saxon traditionalists, but
rather the "undiscriminating" public that wants "the new without the
unsettling." Writers, he insisted, need protection from a "public too easy
to please." He called for a "new criticism" that would address not only
the art, but also the "uncritical hospitality of current taste," that is to
say, the culture.

Monroe responded with a claim that all the artist needed was the
means to get his or her art before the public. Art had no relations beyond
itself for the critic to elaborate. Bourne's rejoinder distinguished his
broader cultural concerns from the aestheticism that would characterize
the twenties. "You can discuss poetry and a poetry movement solely as
poetry—as a fine art, shut up in its own world, subject to its own rules
and values; or you can examine it in relation to the larger movement
of ideas and social movements." He was fearful, however, that to "treat
poetry entirely in terms of itself is the surest way to drive it into futility
and empty verbalism."[28]

It was in the context of the ideals of the Young Intellectuals and
against the background of the shrinkage of the territory of the imagination in the 1920s that Edmund Wilson, the city's most notable twentieth-century critic, fashioned his own career. Fascinated by European
modernism and its American manifestations in the *Dial*, the *Little Review*,
and *Poetry*, as well as in the Provincetown Players theater group in
Greenwich Village, he insisted at the same time that literature must be
in the world. As he picked his way through the shards of the city's

intellectual culture of the 1920s, Wilson was intensely aware that art had become increasingly private and interiorized at the expense of its engagement with the public world.

It was to this problem that Wilson addressed himself in his first book. Realizing that the battle against the genteel tradition had already been won by Bourne's generation, he was free, as he put it, to address the "most recent literary events in the larger international world." The classic works of modernism needed to be understood, and in *Axel's Castle* (1931) he addressed this need. *Axel's Castle*, the title he chose for this study of the symbolist poets, represented the imagination, which Axel did not "want to get out of to participate in reality." What made sense for postwar Europe did not, he thought, make sense for postwar America. Wilson was concerned that the greatest European writers, including Yeats, Proust, and Joyce, so emphasized interior "contemplation" that their work "led to a kind of resignationism in regard to the world at large." They seemed to discourage the will. Writing to his editor, Maxwell Perkins, Brownell's successor at Scribner's, outlining his plan for his book, he explained his own position.

> I believe that any literary movement which tends so to paralyze the will, to discourage literature from entering into action, has a very serious weakness; and I think the time has now about come for a reaction against it. The disillusion and resignation of contemporary European literature is principally the result of the exhaustion which has followed the war; and we in America, in taking from Europe, as we have almost always hitherto taken, our literary standards and technique, have taken also, with the most recent consignments of artistic goods from Europe, a sea of attitudes and ideas . . . which have absolutely nothing to do with the present realities of American life and which are largely inappropriate for us. I believe—or rather, I hope—that the reaction of which I speak may come first in the United States. I seem to see certain signs of it; in another generation or two, we may be leading the world intellectually.

Hence *Axel's Castle* was his attempt to appreciate the technical accomplishments of recent European literature and, at the same time, to insist upon a distinctive American literature, more fully in the world and less "atmospheric."[29]

What Wilson did, and it became clearer in the 1930s, was to try to bring together modernism in the arts and radicalism in politics. In the 1930s, when he turned to the left, he took up his second great theme, "the most recent developments of Marxism in connection with the Russian Revolution," and this supplied the subject for his book *To the Finland Station* (1940).[30] These two books, with their themes of modernism and

Marxism—how to be a radical *and* admire the poetry of T. S. Eliot—
crystalized the intellectual agenda for the "New York Intellectuals"
from the founding of the "new" *Partisan Review* in 1935 into the
1950s.

⚜️[6]⚜️ The Historian and Public Life: Charles A. Beard and the City

In 1982, David Rothman and I organized a small conference under the auspices of the New York Institute for the Humanities on "The Historian and Public Life: Charles A. Beard." Others prepared papers on Beard and the Constitution and on Beard and foreign policy, and I wrote on Beard and the city. It is worth recalling that before 1927, when he and Mary R. Beard published The Rise of American Civilization, *Beard was known primarily as a political scientist and as a "municipal expert." By approaching Beard from this angle I relocated him in relation to professional history and reform intellectuals. Many of my concerns about academic intellect were refracted in revealing ways by approaching him from this perspective. Placing Beard in the context of his municipal reform work enables one to see quite clearly the two modes and phases of his engagement with public life, one based upon empirical data and the other on rhetorical skill. The papers from our small conference were subsequently presented as a session at the 1982 meeting of the American Historical Association. This paper has not been previously published.*

AT A TIME WHEN THERE IS MUCH DISCUSSION ABOUT THE RELATION OF THE historian to life outside the academy, to life in the larger public world, it is worth examining earlier professional self-definitions of historians. Upon close examination, it turns out that our predecessors did not make certain distinctions that we do—and that we have assumed they did as well. They saw, for example, less sharp divisions between disciplines, and they found it easier to move back and forth between the academy and the city. In a recent essay, for example, John Higham showed how closely associated with local civic life was Herbert Baxter Adams's professionalizing project for historians.[1] With this essay, I aim to look into the professional and civic activities of one of the leaders of the generation following Adams's.

Charles A. Beard, it is well known, was an activist who eventually left the academy. My intention here, however, is to explore in some detail a part of his activism less widely known, his experience as a "municipal expert" and his activities as an urban reformer during the Progressive Era. While such an inquiry sheds some new light on Beard's biography and upon urban progressivism, my intentions point in another direction. I hope to elaborate and illuminate the way in which his civic identification and reform interests in New York shaped and were shaped by his sense of the place of the historian in the public world.

The activist life that Charles A. Beard pursued grew, in large part, out of his early confrontation with the industrial city in America and England. While still a student at DePauw University in 1896, he spent a summer in Chicago—he visited Hull House, walked the streets, talked to labor leaders in the aftermath of the Pullman Strike, and was in the city when William Jennings Bryan electrified the Democratic Convention. Mary Ritter Beard, who knew him during these early student years, later wrote that this Chicago experience "made a deep and lasting imprint on his mind and influenced his future activities."[2]

Upon graduating from DePauw, Beard went to Oxford. While he devoted enough attention to his studies to impress F. York Powell, his teacher, his greatest energy and enthusiasm were captured by the English labor movement and the movement for workers' education. While he was in England (we are speaking of the years 1899–1901), Beard played a key role in the founding of Ruskin Hall, now Ruskin College, at Oxford, and he wrote his first book, *The Industrial Revolution*. These activities helped him define a role for himself as a public teacher. This role, which he later played both within and outside the classroom, was acted in England mostly outside the classroom. As director of the Ruskin Hall extension service, he traveled through the industrial cities of England delivering five lectures or more each week to workingmen's and reform groups. In these lectures and in the book he used history to show that society was on the eve of a new age and that technology and knowledge could be used in the service of humanity.[3]

His book *The Industrial Revolution* is in many respects paradigmatic of his life's work. It was written for a nonscholarly audience; indeed, it was written primarily for workingmen, to make them aware of their own history. But it was a serious synthesis. His pragmatic intention is clear in his preface. He presented the book as a "guide for students seeking for the first time the historical basis of modern social and economic problems."[4] Not only is Beard here assuming the role of the public teacher, he also is announcing the problem of society that would preoccupy him through his career as a historian and political scientist: how humans can use their knowledge to come to terms with the conditions of modern urban and industrial life. And here, as throughout his career, the solution is rational planning and administration grounded in a larger sense of purpose than individual greed, though recognizing that interest could not be ignored.

This short book illustrates a quality that distinguished Beard's writing for half a century. For Beard, scholarly discourse and public discourse were not differentiated. This made him a remarkably good textbook writer, and it accounts for the eleven million copies his books sold. For him there was a sort of serious writing that was not, at least not in the worst sense, academic. As both a writer and a doer, he could not be contained by the bounds of discourse of any university or professional discipline. He assumed the existence of a larger public culture, and he took that to be his proper habitat.

He was, by personality as much as by intellectual commitment, contemptuous of universities and professors who, by being silent on social problems, justified the status quo. In *The Industrial Revolution* he savaged the bulk of the professoriate.

> The condition of social health is undoubtedly a subject to which our highest intelligence and our clearest judgment should be devoted. For the most part, however, the learned who are not spending their energies in useful, scientific and critical investigation are busy waging war against ancient devils, fog giants, metaphysical dragons, and especially in drawing salaries from fat livings.[5]

Underlying the critical perspective of *The Industrial Revolution* is a faith that human beings are not a means but an end in themselves. This faith, bolstered by Beard's reading of Ruskin (Mary Beard once noted that for much of his life he carried a copy of *Unto This Last* in his pocket), underlay Beard's fundamental principle of political science. As he stated in 1910 in his first textbook, "Man is not made for the state, if we eschew German political science, but the state for man."[6] Unlike many recent social historians, whose interest in the condition of people's lives leads them largely to ignore the state, Beard felt that the state was vitally important to people's happiness. For him the state was the central object of analysis. This does not mean, as we all know, that he confined himself

narrowly to juridical analysis. Political inquiry, he explained in his remarkable lecture of 1908 on politics, begins with "acts as may be ju-
ristically tested, passes to the acts most nearly related, and then works
out into the general field of human conduct."[7]

My point for now, however, is that Beard had defined himself as
an activist concerned with the social problems of urban and industrial
society before he decided to become a political scientist and historian.
Like Woodrow Wilson and Charles Merriam before him, Beard saw in
the new social sciences a place for political commitment.

To understand Beard's experience as a scholar in urban politics,
one must place him in the context of the professionalizing social science
disciplines. When he entered graduate school at Columbia in 1902, the
several social science disciplines there and at Chicago and Wisconsin in
particular were in the process of defining themselves and their place in
American society. The various studies of Barry Karl, Steven Diner, Thomas
Haskell, Mary Furner, and Laurence Veysey have shown that an explicit
commitment to expert public service, particularly to groups needed by
the university, was a central theme in their quest for prestige and material support.[8] As Steven Diner wrote in his book on Chicago's social
scientists, "significant numbers of professors engaged directly in civic
affairs, knowing that these efforts could enhance their national professional stature and their standing within their own universities."[9] These
new professors, as Merle Curti long ago remarked, dressed, talked, and
acted very much as men of the world.[10] By approaching the city as an
extension of ambitious professional disciplines, these intellectuals effectively redefined the city in functional terms, with the functions defined
by professional organization and research fields, a matter of more than
incidental importance to their careers as well as to our contemporary
efforts to make sense of urban life.

Beard's civic activism should not, therefore, be seen as in any way
detracting from the development of his career. In fact, the period of
Beard's most intense civic activism coincided with the writing of major
works of historical scholarship and with his rapid professional advancement within the academy.[11] The activism was integral to his career.
During the years when he wrote *An Economic Interpretation of the Constitution*, he was deeply involved with the newly established Bureau of
Municipal Research—from 1909 onward he spent three afternoons a
week downtown at 261 Broadway. In 1912, a year before he published
the book on the constitution, he undertook substantial responsibilities
at the bureau's newly established Training School for Public Service; in

1915, the year he published *The Economic Origins of Jeffersonian Democracy*, he assumed the directorship of the school. In fact, the energy and productivity displayed by Beard during these years of scholarship, teaching, and civic activism are awesome. During a period of thirteen years, he authored, co-authored, or edited eleven books, published ten articles in the *Political Science Quarterly* and several others elsewhere, and reviewed at least sixty-five books for various journals.

Beard's civic activities were so compatible with his scholarship in part because they nourished his commitment to the antiformalist movement within the discipline. In his review of Arthur F. Bentley's work and in his preface to the book on the constitution, for example, one can see his concern to get beyond John Burgess's abstractions to the "real" stuff of politics, to the process of political change.[12] This approach not only facilitated activism, but it seemed as well to require it as a source of facts and experience and was thus an avenue of understanding.

Urban politics was a new field in the discipline when Beard arrived at Columbia. Earlier political scientists had not been able to develop the study of urban politics because, under traditional American legal theory, the city was a mere administrative unit of the state, not a political jurisdiction. One of Beard's teachers at Columbia, Frank Goodnow, had recently broken through this block, arguing for political home rule in cities. Goodnow not only gave theoretical justification to a Progressive reform strategy, he created a field of study, municipal politics.[13] While this innovation in American political theory might have led someone like Frederick C. Howe to celebrate the city as the hope of democracy, more penetrating thinkers like Herbert Croly and Charles Beard insisted on the limits of home rule and municipal politics. Although always appreciative of Goodnow's work, Beard observed in, of all places, the preface of his text on *American City Government* (1912) that "there can be no such thing as 'municipal science,' because the most fundamental concerns of cities, the underlying economic foundations, are primarily matters of state and national, not local, control."[14]

Beard swerved from Progressive orthodoxy in another respect. For progressive urban reformers nonpartisanship in municipal affairs was usually linked to municipal home rule. For the professionalizing academics, this linkage was attractive. It gave them the opportunity to be involved in politics without any taint of partisanship that might compromise their claims to professional and disinterested expertise. Beard, writing in the *National Municipal Review*, challenged this progressive shibboleth. First, he insisted, it is fruitless to wish away partisanship. Second, he asked whether it is really true, under modern social and

economic conditions, that national political issues are irrelevant to municipal affairs. His answer was that no municipal problem, whether it
be poverty, housing, unemployment, or whatever—refuse collection
possibly excepted—"can be solved, can be even approached by mu-
nicipalities without the co-operation of that state and national government, and the solution of these problems calls for state and national
parties." Only the Socialists, he remarked, seem to have recognized the
importance of having a unified party position on all three levels of
American government.[15]

No doubt his consistent understanding of the place of the city in
national political and economic development made it easy for him to
move back and forth between the study of municipal affairs and that
of national history. And it prevented him from becoming a narrowly
focused urbanist. As we shall see, he constantly urged his fellow urban
experts to place their work in a wider context.

In discussing the professionalizing context of Beard's urban activism, it is pertinent, I believe, to compare briefly his career to that of
Charles Merriam. These two early leaders of the profession of political
science were both committed to activism, yet they adopted very different
strategies. Merriam was a supremely able academic entrepreneur and
organizer. His influence in the profession and in American society was
based on the nexus of major institutions he brought together: the university, government, social science professional organizations, and philanthropy.[16] This gave Merriam great power, but it also limited him. His
ideas were institutionalized, sponsors had commitments and expectations that he could not ignore, and generations of students, though a
source of power and influence, were surely a constraining responsibility,
dependent as they were on both Merriam's ideas and institutional commitments. He could not move too far from what was acceptable to the
major institutions that gave him his kind of influence. For example,
Barry Karl pointed out that Merriam feared that even getting involved
with Hoover's Social Trends project in 1929 might be too political.[17]

Beard, on the other hand, by leaving Columbia and a few years
later leaving the Bureau of Municipal Research, denied himself institutional support for his ideas. He had to establish his ideas without
students and without funds. But Beard had a freedom denied Merriam
by his sponsors. Beard, as is well known, rebelled against his sponsor
when he resigned from Columbia in 1917. Perhaps less well known but
equally important, he resigned the directorship of the Bureau of Municipal Research in 1921 at least partly because of the interference, again,
of Nicholas Murray Butler. Beard and some of his colleagues were con-

vinced that Butler had persuaded Andrew Carnegie to withdraw his financial support from the bureau because of Beard's supposed "radicalism."[18]

It is ironic that Beard, who so tellingly criticized Frederick Jackson Turner's mythic rugged individualism, was the quintessential individualist, someone who could be contained by no institution. Even when he resigned from Columbia in 1917, he refused invitations from John Dewey and Arthur Lovejoy to join them in the newly founded AAUP. His friend Matthew Josephson said of him, "I have never met anywhere a man who so thoroughly enjoyed his own sense of freedom or who was so jealous of his intellectual and moral independence as Charles Beard."[19] By contrast, Turner, the celebrant of American individualism, was, if we are to believe Ray Allen Billington's portrait of him, the perfect academic organization man, a department builder at Wisconsin—and a man whose greatest influence was through his seminar students.[20]

In view of his separation from the nexus of power and the networks of reform that included Merriam and Butler, Beard adopted a different strategy for influence. To put it most simply he became more and more of a historian and less and less of a political scientist, until by the 1930s and 1940s he was seeking to assimilate all social sciences to history. As a political scientist, both at Columbia and at the Bureau of Municipal Research, Beard conceived of activism as technical expertise, particularly in administration. Beard increasingly recognized—and this was another part of his decision to resign from the bureau—that as one is drawn into such technical matters one's intellectual freedom and one's freedom to act are narrowed by context.[21] After his resignation, Beard assumed increasingly the role of the historian speaking to technicians, urging them to think about larger contexts, particularly the larger economic and political contexts. He assumed the role of publicist for a larger, more inclusive interpretive frame in municipal research.

As early as the first course in politics that he taught to Columbia College undergraduates, Beard had insisted, as he wrote in the syllabus for that course, that anyone specializing in politics ought "to read broadly in the great works on American history, for it is in the record of things done, rather than in theoretical treatises, that the actual operation and spirit of our institutions are to be sought, and practical guidance for the present and the future to be found."[22] In an address to the National Municipal League in 1928, Beard justified his decision to discuss the historical and philosophical aspects of the city's place in the civilizing process instead of "budgets, accounts, city manager plans, and statistical measurements" because of his belief that it is important for "practical persons" to raise their eyes from such matters and listen to "high brow" intellectuals a bit removed from actual doing in the interest of gaining insight into the "more distant outcome of their actions."[23] By 1946, when he wrote a report on historiography for the Social Science Research Council, Beard had made such historical contexts central to all policy discussion. Historical assumptions, he explained, whether explicit or implicit, underlay all discussions of public affairs, including such elementary matters as assumptions about conditions of normality and crisis. History, he insisted, is not just one of many disciplines to be drawn upon. It "includes all the humanistic sciences . . . and it is against knowledge of this comprehensive history that the abstractions of the humanistic sciences are to be checked for validity."[24]

When it was established in 1908, the Bureau of Municipal Research in New York represented an important new chapter in the history of urban reform. It symbolized, perhaps better than any other urban reform movement in the Progressive Era, the ambition of professional, academically based urban policy formulation. The New York Bureau of Municipal Research was, in the phrase of Barry Karl, "the center of an essentially new preoccupation of reform." Its early history, he noted, "provided those first exciting links between philanthropically oriented reform and academically inspired research," marking significantly "new attitudes toward and methods of coping with problems of American urban society."[25] It is in precisely this context that Beard the urban activist is properly placed, although, as we shall see and as was often the case with Beard, he came to see some of the limitations to the approach to urban reform that so captured his enthusiasm between 1908 and 1921.[26]

At the bureau, besides serving four years as director and administering for three additional years the training school (which, incidentally, trained Robert Moses), Beard wrote a number of important reports. These included one on traction in New York; another, *The Constitution and Government of the State of New York*, was a landmark in the development of American administrative theory.[27] He also collaborated with Robert Moses and drafted part of the report on the retrenchment and reorganization of the state government that was commissioned and implemented by Al Smith. And during this period, he advised the mayor of Tokyo and helped to organize there an Institute of Municipal Research. For this work he is still remembered in Japan as one of the fathers of city planning.

Let me briefly characterize the sort of reform movement Beard was involved with at 261 Broadway. More than anything else, the bureau was a fact-finding agency. Its initial statement to the public described its purpose as that of securing "constructive publicity" and scientific methods of accounting in New York. The labyrinth of charter provisions and budgetary practices in New York served to mystify the process and ways of power, to veil it from the public gaze. The bureau sought to demystify and bring policy into public discourse, and they thought the budget was the best vehicle for this.[28]

It was assumed at the bureau that possession of the facts in public would lead to intelligent control. Speaking in 1926, on the twentieth anniversary of the movement for municipal research, Beard expressed his view that "the most significant contribution of our movement . . . is the application of the idea of continuous and experimental research" to municipal administration. It is an example, Beard thought, of humanity freeing itself from "the tyranny of rules of thumb and the blind regimen of nature, becoming conscious of its destiny."[29]

The budget, presented according to proper principles of accounting, represented for these reformers a new and exceptionally powerful tool—of both analysis and management. The budget, Beard wrote in 1912, is "the central problem of the city's administration."[30] Here was reality at its core. (This mystique of the budget, by the way, is not entirely misplaced. It was—and is—an unsurpassed source of both information and administrative power.)

Although the bureau was preoccupied with the economic basis of urban policy, we find at the bureau not the mind of the economist but that of the accountant.[31] Perhaps this mentality, more than the sordid sense of reality that Lionel Trilling and Richard Hofstadter attributed to Beard and some other progressives, led Beard to the Treasury records. The spirit of the bureau was not muckraking—as I think Beard was not a muckraker in his book on the constitution. Budgetary facts were sought as a positive and very powerful tool for understanding process and method—and for making government comprehensible to a public. Describing the work of the Bureau of Municipal Research, William H. Allen, one of the founders, insisted that the organization represented an advance on earlier muckraking and on the "throw the rascals out" approach to urban reform. "There is one thing," he noted, "about our major premise which is new in New York and that is the assumption that the great problem in municipal government is not to stop graft, is not to head off the politician, and not to get good men into office, but rather to keep the public informed of what public officials are doing."[32]

They were not simple budget cutters. One of the proudest achievements of the early bureau was its success in getting the Department of Health's budget substantially *increased* by publicizing it.

Like John Dewey, particularly in *The Public and Its Problems*, Beard and his colleagues at the bureau were seeking to create a public politics, something on the agenda of New York civic reform since the campaigns and mayorality of Seth Low. Citizens can become a public, the reformers believed, only if they have facts. To this end, the Bureau of Municipal Research published 780 pamphlets, bulletins, and reports between 1908 and 1916. One of the bureau's most celebrated projects was the creation of a public budget exhibit, with a variety of striking visual aids. Between 1908 and 1911 more than two million people visited the bureau's exhibit. Beard's faith in the public during these years was extravagant, and like many others he tempered his optimism in the 1920s. But unlike Walter Lippmann and some others, he never dismissed the public.

More than most Progressives and more than most of his colleagues at the bureau, Beard worried about the relation of the expert (academic or not) to American democracy. In his first textbook on American government and politics, he affirmed his faith in the democratic control of experts.[33] As Director of the Training School for Public Service, he confronted the question more directly. The "supreme public question of the hour," he observed, "is whether democracy and efficiency are inherently irreconcilable." He recognized that "democracy distrusts the expert," and he insisted, moreover, that "there is no doubt . . . that much of this mistrust is well grounded and thoroughly justified." He presented two strategies for accommodating expertise to democracy. One was rather conventional for his time. Following the lead of Woodrow Wilson and Frank Goodnow, Beard insisted that administration and politics are two different things. Politics decides what is to be done, and then expert administration simply carries out that mandate as efficiently as possible as a technical matter. I think we can no longer accept such a pure description of administration. And neither did Beard, apparently. His second point subtly undermined his distinction between administration and politics. "The only kind of an expert that democracy will and ought to tolerate," Beard concluded, "is the expert who admits his fallibility, retains an open mind and is prepared to serve."[34] Although Beard did not elaborate, this notion seems to incorporate a dialogic notion of expert knowledge of the sort Robert Westbrook found in the writings of John Dewey during the same period.[35]

In 1921 the Bureau of Municipal Research became another of the several institutions from which Beard resigned between 1917 and 1921 (the other major one besides Columbia being the New School for Social Research, which he had helped found two years before he resigned). Partly, as I noted before, this was a matter of an intensely individualistic personality. But there seems also to have been a recognition that the institutionalization of municipal research and reform had sucked the movement into a rather confined world of technical concerns.[36] And for the next quarter century Beard again and again used his repeated invitations to address his old colleagues at their conventions to urge them to take care not to let technical concerns suffocate the movement. As early as 1926, he objected that most municipal research was too narrow, too exclusively oriented to questions of finance and adminis-tration without considering wider contexts and purposes. He called upon his former colleagues to rise above the "efficient routineer" by mingling "vision with . . . thought, imagination with . . . analysis, courage with . . . research."[37] By 1947, he was challenging every single assumption of the movement in an effort to shake an institutionalized and self-referring reform movement into much needed self-criticism.[38]

Beard was a very early supporter of the emerging city planning profession. One of the distinguishing features of his textbook of 1912 on urban government was the large place he gave to the profession of city planning. For Beard city planning offered a way of addressing the larger economic problems of urban development. Writing in 1911, he defined city planning as "the substitution of scientific organization and prudent forethought for the largely fortuitous results of real estate spec-ulation."[39] Here as elsewhere Beard sought to reunite those two in-quiries and policy orientations that had been torn asunder in the nine-teenth century: economics and politics. City planning, he said again and again, was properly understood as political economy.[40]

In 1926, the year he assumed the presidency of the American Po-litical Science Association, Beard explained to city planners that their accomplishments fell far short of their technical capacities precisely be-cause they did not probe deeply enough into the "economic forces which may be enlisted for or against the dreams and blue prints of artists and engineers." He explained that by attention to economic matters he did not "refer to such matters as the industrial activities surveyed by the New York Plan Committee." He had in mind interest groups. The task of the city planner was to understand the political economy of the city and to use that understanding to advance plans. The planner, Beard wrote, has the responsibility "of analyzing and exposing to public gaze, on the one hand, the various economic interests that are likely to gain more money by keeping things as they are or by forcing an anti-social development, and, on the other hand, the economic groups that may be enlisted in virtue of their practical interests on the side of a comprehensive community scheme." Short of such work, he warned, city planning will find itself where Harvey found medicine.[41]

It is of some importance to understand the way he defined the interests to be found in the city. While he quoted Madison, he tended to define a distinctly modern type of functional interests that are distinct from class interests or more culturally defined interests, such as religious interests. There grow up in cities, Beard observed, "of necessity a real estate interest, public utility interests, various manufacturing interests, commercial interests, shipping and carrying interests, banking interests, an organized labor interest, and office-holding interests, with many lesser interests, dividing the citizens into different groups actuated by different sentiments and views with respect to any concrete readjustment of tangible values by a city plan."[42] By implicitly accepting them all as equal, Beard embraced consensus and pluralism.[43] More important, by defining his groups largely in terms of city functions, Beard advanced a kind of thinking about urban politics that leads to the sort of liberal crisis illuminated in the work of Theodore Lowi. Liberal reform, Lowi has argued, legitimated functional groups, each with a professional ethos, with the result being a series of semiautonomous, self-referring, and largely *ungovernable* power centers within the city.[44]

Speaking more broadly of the city planning movement in the United States, one cannot but be struck by how far from Beard's program it turned out to be. Beard did not jolt the profession out of its technical preoccupations with traffic surveys and zoning. It was, after all, a profession that recognized as one of the crises of the 1930s the dilemma of whether miniature golf represented a commercial or recreational use of land.

But even within the realm of academic urban research the orthodox approach was a radical rejection of Beard. The center of urban research in the United States for most of the twentieth century has been the University of Chicago. And both its sociological and its economic studies emphasized market-determined lines of analysis—leaving public policy, which inhibits such patterns, beyond its ken. The Chicago School, often with financial support from interested parties, *mapped* the workings of the urban market in shaping the housing, transportation, marketing, and demographic character of the city, whereas Beard asked urban researchers and planners to *direct* these developments through some sort of democratic politics.

A comment on a way that Beard's well-known shift on the matter of objectivity and subjectivity in the writing of history bears upon his urban and social concerns will serve as a conclusion. Throughout his career, scholarship and public activity were inseparable, but over time the nature of the linkage changed profoundly. Objective facts, as we have seen from our discussion of the Bureau of Municipal Research, were originally thought to have immediate political consequences. In time, however, he came to believe that facts would have meaning, political and moral significance, only if interpreted through a *prior* and necessarily *subjective* frame of reference. Objective description was no longer adequate as either history or activism.

For Beard, commitment to values was essential to scholarship. It is probably important to note here that, if he reacted against the objective empiricists of the 1920s, he equally rejected the absolutists such as Robert M. Hutchins in the 1930s. He believed that the historian must choose values, even while knowing there was no knowable justification for them.[45] The values the historian must take on faith and the commitment to the direction of history that he must make, according to Beard, made the historian *ipso facto* a man of affairs. Or as Beard put it in *The Open Door at Home*, the historian becomes a "statesman, without portfolio, to be sure, but with a kindred sense of public responsibility."[46] All of this made scholarship a moral and public act.

When Beard rejected his colleagues' claims to objectivity, he denied himself (and them as well) something quite valuable to activist professors. The cloak of objectivity had allowed them to accept consultantships and advisory roles without facing the question of value. Edward Purcell wrote of them, "If their findings were morally neutral, objective descriptions of institutional and human functions, then they were obviously neither being used nor being partisan." What this belief in objectivity did was open "the way for a practical role in society and possible ultimate realization of methods of control, while at the same time suppressing any moral or social doubts about the actual consequences of their actions."[47] Beard was aware that courage and willingness to take risks were at issue. He recognized that his position was that of a lonely publicist, not that of a man seeking influence through the orchestration of major academic, governmental, or philanthropic institutions.[48] His instruments of influence would be the book and the article, not the grant, the research institute, and the consultantship.

Beard's philosophical shift in the late 1920s and early 1930s was important in the movement I have already described from political scientist to historian. Less interested in influencing history through administrative intervention, he increasingly sought to gain influence by providing interpretive contexts, by providing compelling myths about how the society works. In this respect *The Rise of American Civilization* in 1927 leads directly to his famous presidential address to the American Historical Association in 1933, "Written History as an Act of Faith."[49]

During these same years his writing on urban topics revealed his shifting orientation as effectively as did his more well-known historical work. In 1933 he published two essays on a major landmark in American social science and social policy, the study of *Recent Social Trends*, commissioned in 1929 by Herbert Hoover and directed by Charles Merriam and Wesley Clair Mitchell. According to Beard, *Recent Social Trends* reflected "the coming crisis in the empirical method to which American social science has long been in bondage." It had been commissioned by Hoover on the apparent assumption that all important social facts would be collected. Hoover, like most American social scientists, assumed that "once the 'data' have been assembled important conclusions will flow from observing them." Beard challenged this assumption in two ways. First, he asked, What was an important fact, a fact worth collecting? And important to whom, for what purpose? He also asked: "Where do hopes, aspirations, and values come from? From exhaustive surveys of facts? Soon that issue will have to be faced in the intellectual life of the United States."[50]

If Beard saw evidence of the limitations of American social science in the genesis of the report, he found cause for hope in the report itself. "The excellence of the study, apart from the accumulation of significant social materials, lies in the very fact that its sponsors and investigators generally depart from the terms of their Presidential commission and proclaim or assume values that do not flow . . . from their 'data' of 'trends.' "[51] When the report discusses social problems, Beard insisted, it is proceeding in a way that empiricists do not acknowledge. "Problems," he explained, "do not come out of the facts. They are tensions that arise in the human mind when facts are observed. They come from the realm of the human spirit, . . . ever evolving in relation to facts. The Committee has found problems because it has brought to the consideration of the findings minds charged with ideas, ideals, values, and aspirations." In spite of itself, the report suggested to Beard that American social thought was on the eve of an intellectual revolution, "the subjection of science to ethical and esthetic purpose."[52]

For Beard, then, the social scientist and historian must assume the burden of providing large interpretive statements about the direction of social change, and this is their most valuable public act. While specialized research and the collection of empirical data are indispensable tasks, the noblest calling for the scholar is the creation of large historical visions out of a subjective commitment to values and a professional commitment to the rules of evidence. The alternative, which Beard saw at every turn—and which stimulated him to write his essay "That Noble Dream"[53]—had in Beard's view an enormous cost.

It is at this level of concern—at the heart of historical practice itself—and not merely as a "solution" to the employment problems of the profession that we ought to be discussing the historian's relation to public life. Beard lived in a simpler world; his scholarly activism was based upon a belief in progress that did not survive the Depression and war—even for Beard himself.[54] The intellectual complexity of historical scholarship is today greater, as is the social and political context of our work. But we would err not to see the pertinence of Beard's sense of the historian's public role to our own efforts to understand what we are doing and what we ought to be doing.

🎜7🎜 Lionel Trilling and American Culture

Few intellectuals in America have been "figures" in the way Lionel Trilling was in his lifetime and, for that matter, since his death in 1975. He was an academic, but his audience was always general. If many contemporary literary critics see no reason any longer to attend to his mode of critical inquiry, those concerned more generally with the condition of intellect in American culture continue to use him as a reference point, as a lodestone. Many, mostly conservatives but some romantic radicals as well, have canonized him. Under the circumstances, it is often difficult to locate the historical Trilling, but that is what I have tried to do here. Trilling spoke directly to a historical moment, and only if we grasp this is there a possibility that he will speak indirectly but usefully to our own concerns.

I wrote this essay at the invitation of Michael Lacey of the Woodrow Wilson Center, who asked if I would contribute an essay on Trilling to a conference titled "Cultural Criticism in America." The conference, which was cosponsored by the American Quarterly *in celebration of its fortieth anniversary, was held in June 1989. This essay was published in the* American Quarterly *42 (1990): 324–47.*

I thank Quentin Anderson, Denis Donoghue, David A. Hollinger, Carl E. Schorske, and Gwendolyn Wright for their acute readings of earlier versions of this essay, regretting at the same time my inability to respond adequately to the full richness of the commentary they provided. I also acknowledge several fine books on Lionel Trilling that were useful to me: Marc Krupnick, Lionel Trilling and the Fate of Cultural Criticism *(Evanston, Ill., 1986); Robert Boyers,* Lionel Trilling: Negative Capability and the Wisdom of Avoidance *(Columbia, Mo., 1977); Daniel T. O'Hara,* Lionel Trilling: The Work of Liberation *(Madison, Wis., 1988).*

BEGINNING IN THE 1930S, BUT ESPECIALLY WITH THE PUBLICATION OF *THE Liberal Imagination* in 1950, Lionel Trilling advanced a remarkably compelling alternative to the way of talking about politics, literature, and society that had been orthodox among intellectuals and critics on the American left. The essays included in *The Liberal Imagination* all had been published previously, many in the *Partisan Review*, and they reflected that magazine's programmatic ambition to displace Stalinist modes of literary and political judgment.[1] Yet with *The Liberal Imagination*, Trilling reached for a wider and more mainstream audience than the literary and political coterie associated with the *Partisan Review*. He succeeded; the book sold 100,000 copies as one of the first serious paperbacks. Trilling became a public figure, one of the most influential intellectuals of his generation.[2]

If Trilling's project was in part to dissociate himself and American liberalism from the radicalism of the 1930s that seemed to mandate a reading of literature with the aid of political categories that were too crude and mechanical, he was seeking also to establish closer and more sympathetic relations between intellectuals and the cultivated middle classes in the United States. Trilling expected this class, which included a rapidly expanding professoriate as well as educated businessmen, to grow in numbers, significance, and cultural sophistication. His postwar success was inextricably—and quite consciously—linked to its progress. As early as 1939, Trilling had begun to orient his work to this class. In a *Partisan Review* symposium on "The Situation in American Writing," he indicated that his "literary interest" was "in the tradition of humanistic thought and in the intellectual middle class which believes it continues this tradition. . . . It is for this intellectual class that I suppose I write."[3] Among such readers, he found an audience aware of new American political responsibilities and new cultural opportunities. They appreciated the complexity of literature and politics, and they enjoyed as well as respected intellect.

With *The Liberal Imagination*, Trilling endeavored to deepen liberalism (though some then and later would accuse him of subverting it). His use of the word liberalism was sufficiently various to cause confusion. In so careful and subtle a writer, each usage had its own special nuance, but there were in Trilling's *oeuvre* two broad patterns of usage. One designated a liberalism he sought to challenge, the other a liberalism he proposed. The first was in the ordinary sense political, though his interest in liberalism was more precisely in the cultural stances associated with, even determined by, political ideology. Liberal in this sense referred to a wide spectrum of American political opinion, from conventional progressive attitudes to those of fellow travelers and Stalinists. The second meaning, also expansive, was tied more closely to a tradition of humanistic learning than to modern American political allegiances. It was a historically grounded critical spirit, a commitment similar to that recently proposed by the philosopher Richard Rorty in defining the humanistic intellectual: people who "read books in order to enlarge their sense of what is possible and important—either for themselves as individuals or for their society." As teachers, they "instill doubts in the students" about their own self-images and about their own society— all to the end of ensuring "that the moral consciousness of each new generation is slightly different from that of the previous generation."[4]

The version of liberalism Trilling favored and promoted proposed a richer awareness of power and a fuller appreciation of tragedy. Suspicious of Enlightenment rationalism, with its much too easy expectation of liberal progress, Trilling found fortification in Romanticism. The literary company he kept in this enterprise was impressive, and mostly British. Besides Matthew Arnold, the subject of his doctoral dissertation at Columbia in the 1930s, it included Wordsworth and Keats, the writers he most often taught over the years. He also admired John Stuart Mill for his reconsideration of the place of feelings in liberalism.[5]

Trilling sought to impress upon the educated classes of the United States the importance of "moral realism." Reinhold Niebuhr, Trilling's friend and Morningside Heights neighbor, offered similar advice.[6] But there were important differences. Trilling's counsel, wary as he was of activism and commitment, encouraged a worldly and sophisticated hesitation, while Niebuhr's influence urged action. Religion marked another important difference between the two. While Niebuhr turned to neo-orthodox theology, Trilling's thought was secular. He turned to literature rather than to philosophy or theology—and he turned to Sigmund Freud, especially *Civilization and Its Discontents* (1930).

The phrase "moral realism" was first used by Trilling in 1938, but it was in *The Liberal Imagination*, particularly in the much-cited essay on "Manners, Morals, and the Novel," originally published in 1948, that he gave definition to the term. "At no other time," he wrote, "have so many people committed themselves to moral righteousness." Writers and intellectuals praise each other for "taking progressive attitudes" toward society's failures. But, he lamented, "we have no books that raise questions in our minds not only about conditions but about ourselves, that lead us to define our motives and ask what lie behind our good impulses." There was, Trilling feared, a kind of moral passion that could become as dangerous as self-interest, that could become disturbingly imperious. Never before had the "enterprise of moral realism" been "so much needed." He warned liberals that they must be aware of danger even in their "most generous wishes," that there was a possibility that liberals would end up coercing the objects of their genuine social concern. "It is to prevent this corruption, the most ironic and tragic that man knows, that we stand in need of the moral realism which is the project of the free play of the moral imagination."[7]

For Trilling, liberalism, which he considered as a culture rather than an ideology or a political movement, was in peril; its moral authority was threatened and so was its capacity for enhancing the richness of possibility. As liberalism approached Stalinism as a limit, which he feared it was doing, it was in danger of corrupting itself.[8] Such was the great moral crisis that provided the focus for Trilling's early writing, including his novel, *The Middle of the Journey* (1947). As a critic, he took it upon himself to negotiate the liberal intellegentsia through that crisis. The culture of modern liberalism needed more sustenance from literature than writers and critics were providing. The politicization of art in the 1930s, paradoxically, had made literature and criticism less able to supply the nourishment liberalism required.[9]

This political point framed a set of understandings about the task of criticism in America. Trilling found serious fault with the critical practices of both professors of English and the political/literary intellectuals of the city.[10] The problem with academic literary scholarship, he believed, was that its "scientific" or "historical" approach to literature rarely got to the text itself as the locale of meaning. The "sociological" criticism of the literary left, while more vital in important respects, had the effect of crudely reducing literature to political categories. Trilling worried that both the academics and the literary left devalued or, at least, undervalued literature. Trilling's great achievement was to approach literature historically without losing the importance of the literary work itself *and* to read literature in a way that insisted upon literary values while making commentary on that literature in ways that illuminated fundamental questions of society and politics.

What Trilling achieved may be made clearer by establishing his relation to the New Critics, who were more or less contemporary. Usually, they have been seen as quite separate from Trilling. Yet he shared with them an ambition to develop nonpolitical categories of literary analysis. Today we have had some difficulty with the notion of nonpolitical literary categories, and a fair reading of the New Criticism has revealed that it served a conservative perspective. Trilling's politics were, as we shall see, more complicated, as he sought to rescue what he considered an authentic liberalism from the corrupted liberalism of his time. One can say, however, that Trilling and the New Critics joined forces in an effort to displace what had passed for "liberal" literary interpretation in the 1930s and 1940s.[11]

The New Critics gave up more than Trilling. While their approach marginalized biography, history, and culture, Trilling moved to enhance the critical attention given to both history and literature. He established an approach to literature that embraced both the work and its cultural surroundings as the joint objects of critical interpretation.

The most significant point of difference separating Trilling and the New Critics was less a matter of method than of intention. Trilling's central critical concern was less to illuminate literary texts than to use them to explore moral values in modern culture. Trilling was not interested in developing new ways of reading texts, and the critics of his generation who did—such as Cleanth Brooks, Northrop Frye, and William Empson—were engaged in a wholly different kind of work. Only rarely in his studies of writers did Trilling attend to language itself or ask, in Denis Donoghue's phrase, "literary questions."[12] His famous essay reevaluating William Dean Howells does not once quote from a literary text of Howells. One is often struck, as Cornell West remarked, by the "looseness" of Trilling's readings.[13] Not surprisingly, he rarely wrote about poetry, favoring instead the novel, where matters of form and aesthetics were less important, he thought, than social and moral relations.[14] It is surely telling that his principal graduate course, jointly taught with Jacques Barzun, was interdepartmental, "Studies in the Background of Contemporary Thought and Culture."

In an article written to serve as the final chapter of *The Liberal Imagination*, Trilling declared his interest to be "literature in relation to ideas."[15] He lamented the seeming absence of ideas in American literature. He felt that European literature, not American, was "in competition with philosophy, theology, and science." He rejected the Anglo-American notion (identified in his time with T. S. Eliot's observations on the mind of Henry James) that ideas and art did not mix. Indeed, Trilling argued that the artistic power of European literature derived "from its commerce, according to its own rules, with systematic ideas."[16] If contemporary American writing lacked "emotional power," the reason, in Trilling's view, was "the *intellectual* weakness of American prose literature."[17]

Trilling consistently stressed that ideas mattered, and he complained about their absence in classic and contemporary American literature. He was not really a close student of ideas, however, and his command of intellectual history was limited.[18] His focal concern was with values. More precisely, he worried in essay after essay about the moral meaning of one's personal relation to the values of a time and place, always seeking to isolate a paradigmatic circumstance upon which to focus his concern.

Although he came to personify the role of critic in the United States, Trilling often presented himself as an accidental critic. He always insisted that his principal literary ambition had been to become a novelist. He even argued in an autobiographical note that his "work in criticism took its direction from the novel"; thus, it tended to "occupy itself not with aesthetic questions, except secondarily, but rather with moral questions, with questions raised by the experience of quotidian life and by the experience of culture and history."[19] In *Beyond Culture* (1965), he had earlier described his "cultural and nonliterary method."

> My own interests lead me to see literary situations as cultural situations, and cultural situations as great elaborate fights about moral issues, and moral issues as having something to do with gratuitously chosen images of personal being, and images of personal being as having something to do with literary style.[20]

In Trilling's mind, these were the concerns of a novelist, of a European novelist typified for him by Gustave Flaubert.

He claimed yet another affinity with the great tradition of the European novel. Writing in 1940, Trilling observed that it was in those European literatures deeply affected by the French Revolution that the novel took on "its intense life." Why? He maintained that what "animated the novel in the nineteenth century was the passionate—the 'revolutionary'—interest in what man should be."[21] For him, too, the French Revolution so radically had undermined the historical culture of the *ancien régime* that it enabled (or compelled) men and women to consider the creation of their own selves. It also unleashed a utopian politics. Both of these "results" of the French Revolution preoccupied Trilling, politics to a greater degree early in his career, the self increasingly as his career proceeded from *The Opposing Self* (1955) to *Beyond Culture* (1965) and to *Sincerity and Authenticity* (1972).

The tradition of the European novel was only one of the formative influences on Trilling. He was influenced deeply by the ideas and example of Matthew Arnold. Marx and Freud, especially the latter with every passing year, were crucial to Trilling's outlook. These influences on Trilling have been much discussed, however. Not much more can be said about them until the Trilling papers are made generally available to scholars.[22] Here I wish to focus for a moment on Trilling the New Yorker, on the ways in which he was the product of the cultural milieu of that city.

Although Trilling was one of the central figures in the group of writers and critics who came to be known as the "New York Intellectuals," the specific metropolitan experiences of that time and place seldom entered his writings as they did, for example, Alfred Kazin's.[23] None of Trilling's fiction developed an urban theme or even an urban milieu, and his critical writings rarely made an urban reference. Yet Trilling was manifestly the product of the city.

Born in 1905, Trilling described his Jewish immigrant family as "fairly well established" in a "comfortable New York suburb."[24] Few details are in the public record.[25] His father was a tailor, and his mother had grown up in England. She was the apparent source of the name Lionel and of the child's early and appreciative acquaintance with English literature. The family was ambitious for the talented child, and Trilling accommodated, ultimately embracing this ambition. Although it would be hard to prove the point, it may have been that for Trilling, as for other upwardly mobile children of immigrants, the acquisition of culture seemed an emblem of success and legitimation. Again speculatively, Trilling's background and career invite one to look for evidence of a tension between ambition and moral principle. Precisely this issue emerges with great power in Trilling's most famous short story, "Of This Time, of That Place," where a teacher fails to respond to a talented but obviously disturbed student out of a desire to protect his own career.[26]

Trilling and others of the New York Intellectuals are usually thought to have been formed by the 1930s and, thus, by radicalism and Marxism. In Trilling's case, Marxism was more a passing episode without particularly formative consequences.[27] He came of age intellectually in the 1920s, not the 1930s. The formative influences on the young Trilling were the Greenwich Village intellectuals of the World War I era (especially Randolph Bourne, Van Wyck Brooks, and Edmund Wilson); Columbia College, with its commitment to liberal humanism; and the group of Jewish writers associated with the *Menorah Journal*. These cultural resources, available to Trilling in the 1920s (and his twenties), supplemented later by Arnold and Freud, provided him with the critical tools and the critical orientation that he developed so effectively a generation later, in the era of World War II. If anything, Trilling was a foe of the 1930s and the legacy of that decade.

Trilling was an undergraduate at Columbia College from 1921 until 1925, and it was during these years that he began associating with the literary community downtown in Greenwich Village and writing for the *Menorah Journal*. Columbia in those years was probably less exciting than it had been a decade before, when Randolph Bourne had attended and Charles Beard was still on the faculty. For Trilling, however, it represented access to a larger and more cosmopolitan world. Even the Anglophilic curriculum that defined liberal humanism and sought to refine Americans, particularly the ambitious Jewish students who made the college officials so uneasy, seemed to have been liberating in an important sense. The very "canon of the grand style" at Columbia that invites our suspicion today as a display of cultural power may have worked differently for Trilling and other children of middle-class immigrant homes.[28] At any event, Trilling devoted himself to that tradition of liberal learning all his life. Most of his undergraduate teaching from the 1930s to the 1950s was in the Literature and Humanities Program or the Honors Colloquium that had been established by John Erskine, one of Trilling's teachers. Whenever in later years he talked about the condition or future of the humanities, his thinking was explicitly grounded in the commitment to liberal humanism he had acquired at Columbia College.[29]

He was always, however, more than an academic. It was not until 1942 that he publicly identified himself in the *Partisan Review* as an academic; and as late as the mid 1950s, he sometimes identified himself as a critic, novelist, and teacher—in that order. After graduation, Trilling took an apartment across the street from Edmund Wilson's in Greenwich Village, to declare his "solidarity with the intellectual life." In an autobiographical fragment, Trilling recalled his entry into the vocation of literature as being framed by a "sense of national culture" and a "sense of resistance to traditional culture and business culture" that had been developed by Bourne, Brooks, and Wilson.[30]

Heretofore, commentators on Trilling have not noticed how much he worked in a tradition developed by these Village critics. David A. Hollinger, it is true, has pointed out the importance of the "cosmopolitan ideal" of Bourne in the formation of the "liberal intelligentsia" in America, including Trilling.[31] However, there are more detailed similarities between the program of the earlier Young Intellectuals and the critical stance assumed by Trilling. He can be seen as a continuation of this earlier formation of intellectuals.

Like Trilling and his *Partisan Review* circle, the *Seven Arts* magazine group (also a collaboration of Jews and Gentiles) was interested intensely in the prospects for intellectuals in American society. While they sometimes spoke of "social justice," the more pressing question for them—as for Trilling—was that of the "quality of intellectual life and the quality of emotional life."[32] They, too, distinguished between ideas and ideologies, favoring the former. Independence was the keystone for their definitions of themselves as intellectuals. In the wake of World War I, when pragmatism and liberalism had seemingly been transformed into war administration, Bourne and Brooks stressed the inadequacy of a liberalism that lacked "poetic imagination," a phrase very much in the spirit of Trilling's *The Liberal Imagination.*[33] In the essays of Bourne, moreover, one finds the first expression of that special literary style later associated with the New York Intellectuals, what Irving Howe has called the style of "brilliance," a style wonderfully exemplified by Trilling.

Trilling was aware of the priority of the earlier generation of Village intellectuals. He recognized Brooks's *America's Coming of Age* (1914) as a "work of critical genius," and he acknowledged that Van Wyck Brooks set out the critical program both for the Young Intellectuals of the World War I era and for Trilling's World War II generation. In 1954, when Brooks had abandoned his earlier cultural radicalism and had become an object of contempt in the *Partisan Review* circle, Trilling publicly remembered the older man's service to American criticism. Reviewing Brooks's autobiography in the *New York Times Book Review*, Trilling characterized the vital message and influence of Brooks.

> That ideas should be related to the actual life of a people, that the national existence should be of a kind that permitted ideas to affect it—this was the burden of the early work of Mr. Brooks that won the enthusiasm of the young men between 1914 and 1924.[34]

The *Menorah Journal* was crucial to Trilling's development. Trilling's association with it derived from his always qualified Jewish identity, though there was an important connection between the journal and the Young Intellectuals.[35] Neither the *Nation*, the *New Republic*, nor the *Freeman* gave him any ground "upon which to rear an imagination of society." But the "Jewish situation," as he understood it through the *Menorah Journal* and its editor Elliot Cohen, "had the effect of making society at last available to [his] imagination" in a way neither Herbert Croly, nor H. L. Mencken, nor, for that matter, Henry Adams could. At the *Menorah Journal*, where he published his early fiction and wrote reviews of Jewish novels, he came to understand and use ethnicity and class as social categories.[36]

Much has been written by Trilling and by his commentators about the role of Jewishness in his development. In general, Trilling refused to identify himself as a Jewish writer. As he put it in 1944, "I cannot discover anything in my professional intellectual life which I can specifically trace back to my Jewish birth and rearing."[37] We probably could take him at his word, at least in this narrow construction of the issue. Yet there was a way in which his relationship to his own Jewish identity seemed to have prefigured the complex pattern of exploration and evasion that marked his work.

The first fiction he published in the *Menorah Journal* illustrates my point. "Impediments," published in 1925, was written while Trilling was still a Columbia undergraduate. It was set at Columbia with a student serving as the first-person narrator. The prefiguring to which I referred occurred early in the story, when the narrator spoke of another Jewish student named Hettner. Trilling described Hettner as "a scrubby little Jew with shrewd eyes" who was "writhing beneath a depression." The narrator feared that Hettner would invade his own vulnerable self. Hettner "forced" the narrator to engage him in "perfunctory courtesies," including joining him in walks between the different campus buildings. The narrator was pleased that these walks were short enough to confine the conversation to the "fewest of subjects, and these [he] was careful to make the most impersonal." The narrator's reflections at this point seemed to anticipate what would be a more general characteristic of Trilling's intellectual and emotional style as a critic.

> I always felt defensive against some attempt Hettner might make to break down the convenient barrier I was erecting against men who were too much of my own race and against men who were not of my own race and hated it. I feared he would attempt to win [himself] into the not-too-strong tower that I had built myself, a tower of contemptible ivory perhaps, but very useful.[38]

The final formative influence of the 1920s was the philosopher John Dewey. In Trilling's posthumously published autobiographical notes of 1971, the only name written in capital letters was that of JOHN DEWEY. Not only did Trilling call himself a pragmatist and naturalist, but he recalled the influence of Dewey at Columbia. "Intelligence" infused the atmosphere. The centrality of mind was assumed, particularly mind brought to bear on experience with the intention of giving it direction.[39] As he did for many others in the 1920s and even the 1930s, Dewey represented for Trilling the possibilities of humanism. In his book *Matthew Arnold* (1939), Trilling placed Arnold in the context of what he described as a Deweyan project, "bridging the gap of poetry and science." Speaking to this point, Trilling used the phrase "imaginative reason," a phrase that might have come from Bourne's criticism of Dewey, criticism that Dewey incorporated into his work in the 1920s.[40]

Like Dewey, Trilling did not believe in "disinterested contemplation."[41] Literature and language were rhetoric, always seeking to persuade—hence some of the limitations of *The Middle of the Journey*. Trilling's understanding of mind was always, as Denis Donoghue pointed out, essentially "pragmatic," concerned with consequences more than with possibilities.[42] As late as 1974, a year before his death, one could detect traces of his Deweyan or pragmatic concern for the consequences of ideas as a measure of truth.[43]

Trilling took Dewey as his guide on the social definition of the self. Even though Trilling was a close student of Freud (and Dewey was not), it was a Deweyan sense of the ethical self that enabled Trilling to move so easily between self and society, and in an essay on John Dos Passos in 1938 he cited Dewey's *Ethics* (1908) as an authority on selfhood, moral choice, and agency.[44]

One recognizes the source of Trilling's forceful defense of Dewey's work—called it "monumental"—against the criticism of Alfred Kazin in *On Native Grounds* (1942).[45] Yet there is an important difference between Dewey's understanding of truth or knowledge and that of Trilling. For Dewey, truth and the determination of truth are inherently democratic and participatory, while Trilling is much more likely to associate truth with order and even hierarchy. This tendency is most apparent late in his career, especially in his Jefferson Lecture, *Mind in the Modern World* (1972), but one can detect it in earlier works as well, even, as Denis Donoghue suggested, in some of the phrasing of his novel, *The Middle of the Journey*.[46]

Trilling, then, worked within a fairly dense and well-articulated critical tradition. Many of the strengths and weaknesses of his own critical enterprise were forecast either in his sense of himself as a child of immigrant Jews or in these formative influences: the faith in art over politics; the awareness of the plurality of American experience; the Deweyan sense of self, society, and ethics. Trilling never bothered to place these influences—as well as those of Arnold and Freud—into any kind of theoretical coherence; rather, he understood himself to be a practical critic, responding to his sense of the contemporary cultural circumstance with available tools.

The liberal humanism that in large part had formed Trilling seemed flaccid and vulnerable by the 1940s. It had been corrupted, Trilling felt, directly by Stalinism and more obscurely but more importantly by fellow traveling, one of the points of his novel *The Middle of the Journey*. In the preface to *The Liberal Imagination*, Trilling worried that liberalism was not being toughened—in the realm of ideas—by a conservative challenge. He feared that the decline of vital ideas invited action, action wrapped in ideology and, thus, hostile to the rich pluralism of American life. Hence, he announced his intention to place liberal ideas "under some degree of pressure," sorting out "weak" or "wrong" expressions of a larger liberal heritage with which he obviously identified. Sensing that the tendencies of American liberalism in the 1930s and 1940s had been to "simplify" and to deny the "emotions and imagination," he set before himself the job of recalling "liberalism to its first essential imagination of variousness and possibility, which implies the awareness of complexity and difficulty."[47]

While Trilling's target was "ideology with its special form of unconsciousness," there was also an implication in what he was saying that favored hesitation over commitment, appreciation of complexity over action. Trilling urged naive American liberals, blinded by optimism and ideology, to attend to a phrase from John Keats, one of his favorite writers. "Negative capability," as he explained it, meant a "willingness to remain in uncertainties, mysteries, and doubts" and to recognize that such is not "an abdication of intellectual activity. Quite to the contrary, it is precisely an aspect of their [writers'] intelligence, of their seeing the full force and complexity of their subject matter."[48] This notion summarized Trilling's way of resisting liberalism's moral weaknesses—from the absolutes of the Stalinists, to naive fellow travelers, to formulaic liberals.

The opening essay in *The Liberal Imagination*, "Reality in America," was a devastating attack on Vernon L. Parrington's *Main Currents in American Thought* (1927–30). The essay also challenged the judgment of liberal intellectuals who praised the fiction of Theodore Dreiser. In both cases, he objected that political or ideological criteria were replacing literary and intellectual ones. Parrington offered an ideological reading of American literary history, while only ideological sympathy could excuse Dreiser's failings as a writer.

Trilling began by attacking the title of Parrington's trilogy. Thoughts or ideas, Trilling charged, are not found in a "current." Rather ideas are found in a dialectical contest within culture, even within individual writers. Trilling's particular interest was in those artists "in any culture" who contain a "large part of the dialectic within themselves." In them, he proposed, one gets to "the very essence of the culture," and the sign of their significance is that "they do not submit to serve ends of any one ideological group or tendency."[49] To see ideas, literature, or truth in any other way, according to Trilling, was to simplify and to narrow imaginative possibilities—and thus political possibilities.

Parrington used a liberal formula that relied too much on the manifest political content of literature. This formula left him unable to accommodate in any adequate way the achievements of Poe, Hawthorne, or James. (In a later chapter of *The Liberal Imagination* Trilling would defend James's *The Princess Casamassima* [1886] as a work of powerful political import.) The problem was a much too restricted understanding of reality, democracy, and politics. More important, however, he insisted that there was a chronic failure among liberal intellectuals to understand the way literature, both fiction and criticism, entered into the political and cultural life of a society. From Bourne and his circle and from Arnold (and his own study of Arnold), Trilling understood literature to be useful to the political life of a nation only in a most general and indirect way. To ask for more direct political lessons would be destructive to serious literature.

The logic behind Trilling's criticism of liberalism pressed him to expand the domain of the political. Anxious to displace overtly political definitions of art and, one suspects, the claims of commitment inherited from the 1930s, Trilling proposed that "our definition of politics" incorporate "every human activity and every subtlety of every human activity." He realized "manifest dangers" in such a strategy, but he anticipated "greater dangers in not doing it." Unless we insist that politics is imagination and mind," he wrote ominously, with the Stalinist reference clear, "we will learn that imagination and mind are politics of a kind we do not like."[50]

It has been argued by Grant Webster, among others, that Trilling's great contribution as a critic was to bring the standards of literary complexity to the politics of the 1940s.[51] But the achievement is more ambiguous than Webster realizes. Texts are neither coterminous with nor the same as society, and literature is not the same as politics. To look for the richness and complexity of literature in political discourse or action is to insist upon a standard that invites disappointment. It is a categorical error to treat literature as politics, a point well made by Trilling. It is equally an error to treat politics as literature. By Trilling's standard it is hard not to be disillusioned by practical politics, as he apparently was. Ironically, the notion of politics advanced by Trilling may have served to undermine a needed political realism. (Machiavelli was never cited by Trilling.)[52] Trilling may thus have weakened rather than strengthened the moral foundations of American politics.[53]

There were peculiarities in Trilling's understanding of society. Though he spoke of variety and pluralism, it was variety without real difference.

Society was, for him, universally middle class. Questions of morality were not usually social questions; they were almost always personal choices, the moral dilemmas or burdens of the modern self.[54] This emphasis was no doubt in reaction to the "sociological criticism" of the 1930s; but the farther Trilling got from the 1930s, the farther society, in any way that involves social conflict, receded from his criticism. Late in life, recalling the influence of Marx and Freud on his intellectual formation, he stressed that they taught intellectuals that "nothing was as it seemed, that the great work of intellect was to strike through the mask." Both of them, but particularly Freud, also offered a structure of ideas that at once deeply invaded the private life and brought into the open its connection to public life. Both Marx and Freud, Trilling recalled, asked "unremitting questions about motive and intention," and so did Trilling.[55] It is striking that these lessons should have been learned. Trilling brought together Marx and Freud in a way that emphasized the individual, not the social. Motive and intention loomed larger than conflict and oppression.

With the publication of *The Opposing Self* in 1955, Trilling's criticism found a sharper focus in the exploration of psychocultural patterns, moving from the public realm of politics to family life and what he called the "conditioned self." Two essays were particularly important in this respect. One, the essay on John Keats that developed the notion of "negative capability," celebrated the virtue of contentedly being suspended in uncertainty so that it invited at least a political quietism. For Americanists, the key essay in *The Opposing Self* is "William Dean Howells and the Roots of Modern Taste." First delivered as a lecture at Harvard in 1951, after the success of *The Liberal Imagination*, the essay on Howells not only sought to rehabilitate the reputation of that writer, but did so in ways that affirmed limits and conventionality.

He appreciated Howells's concern with the middle classes and the quality of middle-class family life. Modern diffidence about Howells, he observed, may have said more about our own extreme commitments— to form and to evil that may have diminished too much the self and pleasure. Contemporary readers may be too much drawn to the excitement of the modernist historical necessity of disintegration and, thus, be offended by Howells's "moderate sentiments."[56] Trilling, however, was ready to defend middle-class domesticity. Later, in a preface to a reprinting of Tess Slesinger's novel of the 1930s, *The Unpossessed*, Trilling would criticize yet more strongly the intellectuals for their refusal to recognize family and domesticity as positive values, even as sources of wisdom about the "conditioned nature of life."[57]

But this was a special case of Trilling's increasing concern with the

conditioned as opposed to the willed self. If earlier he had been concerned with individual moral choices and obligations, in *The Opposing
Self* and even more in *Beyond Culture* (1965) his concern was increasingly
the vulnerability and coherence of the self. The "old connection between
literature and politics," he conceded in *Beyond Culture*, "has been dissolved."[58] With *The Opposing Self* and *Beyond Culture*, Trilling let go of
his Arnoldian (and Deweyan) reform program, becoming more and
more interested in the moral fate of the self. Assisted by his reading of
Freud, he shifted from meliorism to pessimism, from the public to the
private, from politics to psychology.

The appearance of *The Opposing Self* produced worries among many
intellectuals; the critic they had embraced as the guide to the liberal
imagination, in the phrase of Joseph Frank, might be serving up a
"conservative imagination." Frank feared that the emphasis on conditioned life struck at the heart of liberalism. How, he asked, could de-
terminism be freedom? There were areas, Frank insisted, where the will
fruitfully might intervene. Trilling did not seem to appreciate this. In
puncturing short-sighted optimism and utilitarianism, Trilling had served
liberalism well, Frank acknowledged. "But in defending the conditioned
on the level of middle-class values, and in endowing the torpid acceptance of these values with the dignity of aesthetic transcendence,
Mr. Trilling is merely augmenting the already frightening momentum
making for conformism and the debilitation of moral tension."[59]

Frank surely captured a tendency, but he did not attend sufficiently
to the complexity of the notion of "will" in Trilling's work. It was a
key concept, and one about which Trilling had ambivalent and changing
feelings. In general, he feared will, especially the easy triumph of will.
He also insisted that only a commitment to will and its exercise against
resistance would make for anything worthwhile, whether in art or politics.[60] The point at issue, however, was not simply that of will, which
seemed to have tortured Trilling, but that of his easy acceptance of a
middle-class and business civilization in the 1950s. If he once shared
his generation's contempt for the business class and the injustice of the
capitalist system, postwar prosperity seemed to have pushed that concern aside for Trilling, as it did for others.

Trilling served the intellectual life of the United States very well,
invaluably so in the 1940s and early 1950s, less importantly after that.
He had a special and vital message that needed saying. Yet he needed
to say it, one suspects, at least in part to account for his own inability
to commit himself. It could be said that his celebration of complexity
over commitment represented a private evasion with public benefits.

The critical vocabulary he developed in public theorized his personal dilemma; his private uncertainty was transformed into a public ideal of moral responsibility that nourished a critical spirit.

In favoring the classic writers of Europe over those of the United States, Trilling seemed to devalue American literature. Yet he effectively brought European and American literatures into a single conversation. For Trilling—as for the Columbia English and Comparative Literature Department where he studied and taught—English and American literatures were isolated less from other national literatures than is usually the case in the academy. Today, students of American culture and literature tend too often to be parochial, and it is rare for students of comparative literature to attend to their own literature. At Columbia in the 1930s and 1940s, the introductory comparative literature course embraced at once British, American, and Continental writers.

During the 1940s, Trilling focused upon American literary history more than at any other time in his career. Between 1944 and 1951, he taught his only specifically American literature course, a graduate course on American literature since 1870. Most of his critical essays were on nineteenth-century British writers, but in *The Liberal Imagination* one-half of the essays dealt with American writers. (In *The Opposing Self*, the number dropped to two of nine, and in *Beyond Culture*, only one American author is the subject of an essay.)

Only in nineteenth-century realism did Trilling find the sort of materials that suited his critical enterprise. He found this literary form mostly in European writers. Although he expressed "great admiration and affection for the American classics," he insisted in 1939 (and at other times) that "they have been far less important to me than the traditional body of European writers."[61] He found intellectual nourishment in the thickness of the issues embedded in the characters of the nineteenth-century European novel ("brilliant sociology") that he did not find in "mythic" characters like Captain Ahab, free, as Trilling understood him to be, of class and society. He lamented that "American writers of genius have not turned their minds to society."[62] This insight, which would be developed into a notable book by Quentin Anderson, is limited nonetheless.[63] Trilling could gain access to society only through social realism, not through the symbols often so brilliantly deployed by American writers. It would fall to different critics—Henry Nash Smith, Leo Marx, R.W.B. Lewis, and others—who in the 1950s would explore the relation between this fiction and society.[64]

Trilling was able to become the representative intellectual, the voice of liberalism in the postwar years, because of changes in the sociology of the intellectuals (their *embourgeoisement*) and because the middle class itself was changing. In an era of perceived (and real) economic prosperity that expanded the middle class and increased the level of its education, Trilling's issues—"quality of human life" rather than redistribution— were middle-class issues.[65]

He was always aware that the context of his work and influence was a rapidly intellectualizing middle class that needed and welcomed guidance on cultural matters. It was perfectly fitting that so much of his writing in the 1950s should have been in the monthly reports to the subscribers of book clubs, *Griffin* of the Reader's Subscription from 1952 to 1959 and *Mid-Century* of the Mid-Century Book Society from 1959 to 1962. Delmore Schwartz, the poet among the New York Intellectuals, remarked upon this role assumed by Trilling in an arch but penetrating appraisal of Trilling's work published in the *Partisan Review* in 1953, "Mr. Trilling is interested in the ideas and attitudes and interests of the educated class, such as it is and such as it may become: it is of this class that he is, at heart, the guardian and critic."[66]

Such a role had not seemed always possible. Writing as late as 1945, he had observed that "there exists a great gulf between our educated class and the best of our literature."[67] Yet Trilling expressed the hope in *The Liberal Imagination* that the situation was about to change, and in 1952, in his contribution to a famous *Partisan Review* symposium on "Our Country and Our Culture," Trilling announced a monumental shift. "There is," he observed, "an unmistakeable improvement in the American cultural situation of today over that of, say, thirty years ago." The point he had predicted in 1939 as inevitable had been reached; wealth in America, finally, was showing "a tendency to submit itself, in some degree, to the rule of mind and imagination, to apologize for its existence by a show of taste and sensitivity."[68]

Such were the terms proposed by Trilling for intellectuals to accommodate themselves to American life. He proposed a moderation of the sense of alienation among intellectuals, the leaving behind of European ideologies (Marxism), and an energetic exploration of the distinctive and organic pluralism of American life. Intellectuals might do quite well, he supposed, in this postwar middle-class society. There comes a moment, Trilling reflected, "when the tone, the manner and manners of one's own people become just what one needs, and the whole look and style of one's culture seems appropriate, seems perhaps not good but intensely *possible*."[69]

If such accommodation worried Irving Howe and prompted his powerful essay, "The Age of Conformity," it is clear that Trilling's embrace was contingent. The nature of his fascination with middle-class

America emerged in his comments on the work of David Riesman, whom he much admired. A "pragmatic acceptance of society," which was what Riesman proposed, was "morally possible," Trilling thought, only under a particular set of conditions. "It needs an economic situation of at least relative prosperity, and it needs a society which actually is tending toward democracy, a society with a high degree of mobility making for an increasing equality."[70] It was a happy moment: the New York Intellectuals were making it, and so was a huge swath of American society.

To leave it this way would make the matter seem all too crass and self-interested. There is another perspective that suggests the pathos of Trilling's relation to the established classes and culture. Trilling, as R. P. Blackmur pointed out in a review of *The Liberal Imagination*, needed a pattern to work *within*, not *against*. He moved comfortably only within the house of liberalism, making his way through the ideas that are the "furniture of the liberal imagination." In Trilling's work we see, according to Blackmur, "that he cultivates a mind never entirely his own, a mind always deliberately to some extent what he understands to be the mind of society."[71]

Trilling's animated suspension within the middle-class culture of the postwar years makes him seem distant today, more so than his colleague and friend Richard Hofstadter, whose ironic, even bemused, detachment at the time makes him more easily approached today. Although Trilling was fascinated by the pluralistic possibilities of American life, exploring it as far as was possible through the printed word, he attached himself so tightly to his middle-class audience that he constantly, confidently, and effectively used the first-person plural in his essays. As long as that audience was known, as long as he and they shared enough to maintain their conversation, Trilling was secure. By the early 1960s, however, he became less sure of the culture of the middle classes. The collapse of this middle-class consensus was the underlying and worrisome theme, the subtext of his famous essay "On the Teaching of Modern Literature" (1961).[72]

By the time of Trilling's death in 1975, his "we" form of address had become problematical. If it once had produced a sense of intimacy between Trilling and his audience, it seemed to establish distance in the 1970s. His assumption that the public was coterminous with a homogenous audience that shared his concerns could seem off-putting in the 1970s and 1980s. For a reader like Houston A. Baker, Jr., for example, a critic who identifies with an African-American heritage that locates its hopes and fears differently, Trilling's presumption is startling.[73]

One might long for a public culture better able to sustain a general conversation than that of the present day, but the public culture of the 1940s and 1950s is beyond recall. Its very exclusionary and narrow dimensions, which we can no longer accept, are what enabled Trilling to do his work as a generalist within it. Indeed, from the perspective of the current cultural situation, one can understand the observation of Lawrence Levine: Trilling offered a cultural cosmopolitanism that was fundamentally parochial.[74] In an important respect, however, such a criticism is unfair to Trilling, whose cultural curiosity was remarkably wide and mobile. If in his reading he searched out the corners of American culture as well as its presumed mainstream, Trilling lacked an adequate rhetoric for the diverse public he confronted in the 1960s. He had no rhetorical approach, no form of address, that could reach outside of the homogeneous middle class he had defined as his audience in the 1940s. Trilling's experience marks the fate of the intellectual culture of a generation and an era.

Only when one can define differently the terrain of public culture can one begin to image a revitalization of the generalist critic. Trilling no longer provides a model. The reason is not so simple as a complaint about the limits of middle-class culture. The point here is more serious and structural. The middle-class with which Trilling identified no longer exists; it is not available, not even in the social imagination. One must construct the public out of the same plurality that is the object of contemporary cultural inquiry.[75] As Randolph Bourne understood early in this century, such a culture must respond to its internal differentiation while it transcends those differences in order to sustain an open, complex, and general conversation.[76]

Making such a public culture is hard work. Nostalgia is more tempting. That may be why those calling for a revival of the generalist— commentators as diverse as Lynne Cheney and Russell Jacoby—so easily invoke the name of Trilling. They do so without addressing the historical circumstances of his work or the different problem today of making a general conversation in a contested and fragmented public sphere. Trilling's very middle classness—by providing the perspective of distance— ends up, however paradoxically, providing contemporary American culture with a radical challenge, urging critics to find some space among nostalgia, politicized group identities, and specialized academic autonomy for the creation of a public culture.

PART III.
CONCLUSIONS AND RECONSIDERATIONS

❧[8]❧ Academic Knowledge and Political Democracy in the Age of the University

The coincidence of an invitation to give one of the 1990 Kaplan Lectures at the University of Pennsylvania and the reading of Democratic Eloquence *(1990), by Kenneth Cmiel, provided, respectively, the occasion and the immediate stimulus to reconsider the way I had been framing and valuing the historical development of the academic intellect. My current work on the meaning of a democratic public culture began to speak in new ways to my standing concern with the relation of intellect and public culture. I realized how constraining was the deeply embedded republican notion of public life. It limited access to the public, and it had, I realized, bounded my own capacity to generate a democratic conception of the public. My ongoing historical and theoretical study of the concept of a democratic public will soon, I hope, come to completion, but here I have, however sketchily, incorporated my emerging understanding of the public into my (re)interpretation of the history of academic intellect in the United States.*

An early version of this argument was delivered at Carnegie Hall in May 1990 to the graduates of NYU's Graduate School of Arts and Sciences. A fuller and more explicitly historical version was delivered under the auspices of the Kaplan Fund Lectures at the University of Pennsylvania in November 1990. What follows is an expansion of that lecture. It has not been previously published.

IN "TRUTH AND POLITICS" HANNAH ARENDT NEATLY DISTINGUISHED ACAdemic from political truth. The distinction that she drew in that notable essay had implications that she pursued with her usual insight; it implied a tension between the academy, the custodian of truth that would pass the Kantian test, and the polity, the generator of a vitally important but distinctly lesser order of truth.[1]

Most of us, I think, hold to much the same distinction, whether or not we can or wish to articulate it with the precision and eloquence that characterize Arendt's essay. Why is such a dichotomy so easily accepted, essentially without much thought on our part? Considering the difficulty of distinguishing the university from other modern, bureaucratic service institutions, public and private, an assumption that there is a profound difference in the university's culture, its type and standard of truth, is curious. The issue of institutional convergence in the modern era could be pursued, I suppose, as a problem in historical sociology. But I propose in this essay to proceed in a different fashion, relying more upon intellectual than upon social history, looking as much to epistemology as to sociology. My aim, to be clear at the outset, is to question the usefulness of the conventional distinction between academic truth and political knowledge. Conceiving the relation of culture and politics in this habitual way could isolate academic intellect. That tendency or result could in turn pose an unnecessarily formidable difficulty for any vision of academic intellect's involvement in a democratic culture and polity.

Our unreflective acceptance of this distinction hampers our ability to rethink the dilemma of the relation of expertise and democracy, a theme that runs through most studies of academic intellect, including those in this book. What I believe is a misconception of the relation of academic truth and political knowledge derives from our blindness to the contexts, contexts deeply embedded in history, that frame our consideration of the place of higher learning in our culture and polity. I hope to raise these assumptions that have surrounded academic intellect and our study of academic intellect to a greater level of critical self-awareness than has been achieved in the preceding essays. On one level the story told in the previous essays is hardly affected by this work, but the deeper contextualization I here propose forces some changes, at least in my view, in the way we value modern academic intellectual modes and in our vision of the civic ideal.

The interpretive point that I want to make here is American, but it is only by reaching back to one of the threads of America's European history that one can undertake the sort of contextualization that I am urging. I must begin, therefore, with a European prologue. Our discussions about the civic responsibility of the learned and of higher education are imperfectly embedded in the remnants of a very old set of assumptions. Often we are not aware of them, but it is important to raise these historically rooted assumptions to consciousness before we address the intellectual or public consequences of the historical rise of the modern

American research university and the disciplinary professions in the past century.

Although Renaissance Florence never had a distinguished university, that is where our effort of contextualization begins.[2] It is to the Florentine Renaissance, with its ideal of civic humanism, that we must look for the originating ideal of the Anglo-American learned man. (And it was *man*, not person.)[3] The notion that humanistic classical learning and rhetoric best prepared a man for public life was nourished in Florence; over the centuries it was incorporated into the ideal of the university, especially the Anglo-American collegiate ideal.[4] The idea was, as Quentin Skinner observed, "embarrassingly long-lived," continuing until the triumph of expertise and specialization in the modern university.[5]

This Anglo-American collegiate tradition and what has been designated in recent American historiography the "republican tradition" had the same birthplace at more or less the same moment.[6] The civic tradition of intellectual engagement and the republican tradition were not quite the same things, but they are entangled with each other. It is not their political qualities (so often discussed) that are of concern here. Rather it is the psychology and sociology that they share. Both embrace and proceed from the ideal of the undivided personality and an undifferentiated society. Jean-Jacques Rousseau was perhaps at once the most extreme and the most brutally honest advocate of this vision. Few thinkers have been so alert to the divisions that the project of modernity would entail, and no major thinker so seriously proposed forsaking such modernity in favor of the realization of a sense of oneness.[7]

Time does not permit adequate explication of Rousseau, let alone the whole tradition. Let me then assert my primary point about this tradition, even in the absence of the documentation that would be required by argument. The civic tradition is hostile to the premises and conditions of modern, interest-driven, differentiated democracy. We who worry about the condition of public life and the present chasm between academic and civic culture must be aware of how much this tradition infuses our thinking. We must be careful about nostalgic embrace of a tradition of civic engagement possessed of severe limits.[8] We especially must not allow an anachronistic set of premises to define a vision that cannot be realized, that can only present us with disappointment.

We too often overlook this European prologue when thinking about either intellect or public life. Even as historians we tend to take much too short a view of our own history. As modern academic specialists we tend to trace our institutional lineage to the founding of the first American graduate schools (at Johns Hopkins in 1876, at Columbia in

1881, at New York University in 1886, and in a few other places before 1890). We tend to be oblivious, however, to the degree that these institutions were founded within the civic tradition. We telescope too much history and we lose too much of the texture of difference when we think of these institutions as our own writ small. And if we do recognize the difference, we are too often inclined, as I am to a degree in the other essays in this book that deal with this transition, to be nostalgic.

The first graduate schools, at least at Columbia, Johns Hopkins, and NYU, were established within a distinctive context of cultural assumptions about the aims and structure of higher learning and its relation to public life, especially in cities. Our experience of the research university is quite different from what the founding generation envisioned, especially in our understanding of the relation of intellect to civic life. When the graduate school at Columbia, the Faculty of Political Science, was established in 1881, it was intended, as the name suggests, to reform our public life, our civic life, our politics. It was committed to train men in the "mental culture" that would prepare them for careers in the "civil service," for the "duties of public life" generally, or as "public journalists."[9] The curriculum was postclassical (the social sciences), but the context was classical, civic humanist.

Such expectations for the educated, the educated with advanced degrees, in public life were not realized in Gilded Age America. The Boss Tweeds and Boss Platts retained considerable power. Yet there was some success. And both the language and the expectations of the founders mark the distance of these early graduate schools from the experience of the twentieth-century research university. In the twentieth century, graduate programs have not sought to train professional gentlemen. Rather, graduate training has been focused on special fields, characterized best as presumptively autonomous disciplines organized as an academic profession.

The fullest realization of the early ambitions of the Johns Hopkins University is to be found not only in the career of a scholar (Frederick Jackson Turner, for example), but as well in the careers of Woodrow Wilson (like Turner, a product of Herbert Baxter Adams's historical seminar at Johns Hopkins) or Theodore Roosevelt (one of John W. Burgess's first students in the Columbia program in public law). Recall too Richard Ely's activism, and it is too easily forgotten that Herbert Baxter Adams was deeply involved with urban social reforms in Baltimore. This social engagement of Adams's was not simply another side of the man, what he did after hours. He understood such work to be an extension of his scholarly self. A very large number of men who became notable Progressive journalists, social workers and reformers, and political figures had passed through his historical seminar in the 1880s.[10] The institutional innovation that produced the modern structure of higher learning in the United States was born within the context of an older notion of civic culture. It anticipated neither "expertise" nor the modern pattern of academic training within disciplines that are also professions and careers.

Only in the 1890s, when higher education generally began to expand *and* the classical curriculum was displaced, did a market for academics in the social sciences emerge. At Columbia, Burgess and E.R.A. Seligman gradually noticed in the 1890s that their students were becoming academics rather than civic leaders, and they adjusted the program accordingly. The work of the graduate school faculty shifted from that of preparing men for public life and toward that of reproducing their own academic selves.[11]

This conjuncture of curricular and demographic change is important in two ways. First, the decline of the classical curriculum signaled the exhaustion of the humanist ideal of a common civic culture. Difference, diversity, and expertise became acceptable in public life. Second, the social sciences were welcomed into the American college and university. With enrollments growing and with the classical curriculum in decline, new subjects had to be taught. The growth of faculties was, therefore, in the natural sciences and the new social sciences. Here, not in the founding moment, is the origin of our academic life. With the replacement of the civic humanist ideal of public life by professionalized disciplinary communities and the academic expert, we can more properly recognize our own lineage.

Twenty-five or thirty years ago, this "revolution" in higher education, as Richard Hofstadter denoted it, was understood to usher in our own modernity and was represented in historical narrative without ambiguity as a triumph.[12] More recently, however, historians have been more critical. Or they have been, as I take the title of Bruce Kuklick's *The Rise of American Philosophy* to be, ironic.[13] My own writings belong to this revisionist mode, including those that form chapters of this book. They have assumed my generation's anti-Whig, critical stance toward professionalization. At times, my rhetoric may even have suggested both a professional self-hatred (generational rather than personal, I think) and a view of professionalization as the decline of the domain of intellect. Of course, I always gave credit to what I called the technical achievement of professionalism, but the sense of decline was associated with the negative influence that professionalization seemed to have put upon public life, upon the possibility of comfortable relations between intellect and democracy, the highest form of public life. My concern for public life is unabated, but I suspect now that the interpretive frame out of which my judgments flowed may have been faulty.

Like many others, I may have held to an anachronistic sense of both the self and the public, of knowledge and democracy. We need to escape this anachronistic vocabulary (if that be what it is) if we are going to think clearly, critically, and constructively about the relation of academic intellect to public life, to democracy.

My recent studies of the history and philosophy of the concept of the public have urged upon me a revision of the revisionist line of my writing on academic intellectuals.[14] In rethinking my position, I would not revise my account of many particulars—or even the general outline of the story of intellect's academicization in the United States. But the emergence of specialized, academic intellect in a specifically modern context changes its meaning for the human being who is an academic and for the public.[15] The legitimation of specialized intellect looks different in the context of a postrepublican (or post–civic humanist) understanding of self and the public.[16] And these two shifts bear an interesting relation to the shift in contemporary understanding of knowledge of the sort publicized (that is, I think, the right word) by the philosopher Richard Rorty.[17] Rorty's insistence that philosophical truth is to be found in history, not epistemology, has important implications for the problem of academic intellect's relation to public life, for the relation of academic and political knowledge.

The legitimation of expertise was part of a larger pattern of recognition of the complexity of modern society and the multiple identities of individuals. One need not be absolutely at one with oneself nor with others in the modern notion of the public. The implication of this shift is the opening of the public sphere to a wider range of speakers. Putting the matter rather sharply in a single illustration, let me observe that while no woman could be a civic humanist, women trained in the social sciences at the turn of the century could be and were very prominent in public life.[18] For all its limits, it is important to recognize that the rise of expertise was embedded in a transformation of the public sphere that, however imperfectly conceptualized and realized, might well be characterized as democratic in its tendencies and potential.

That new possibilities have been opened up historically does not mean, of course, that they will be realized. There have been two kinds of restraints on the academic mind in the public. One is broadly social.

It could be phrased as the problem of defining the social location, even the class affiliation, of intellect. The other is intellectual, concerning the nature of truth and authority—formally, no less than epistemology. This second point will bring us back to Arendt, and I will conclude with it—for symmetry's sake. But let me first make a few comments about the social history of academic intellect.

The social history I have in mind is developed in chapter 3, but let me make my point here by drawing upon that account for a few paragraphs, taking for my focus a key academic, E.R.A. Seligman. He was a Columbia professor, a founder of the American Economic Association, and the author of the AAUP's founding "Statement of Principles" (1915). Scion of a prominent German-Jewish banking family in the city and one of Burgess's early students in the Faculty of Political Science, he was a major figure in the city as well as a prominent member of the Columbia faculty, a noted economist, and a leader in the social sciences generally. It was this broad prominence in the social sciences that was acknowledged in his last major project in a career that extended from the 1880s to the 1930s, his editorship of the *Encyclopedia of the Social Sciences* (15 volumes, 1930–35). He was also deeply involved in public affairs, serving as an academic expert, for example, to the congressional committee that drafted the Income Tax Law.

After studying with Burgess at Columbia, Seligman went to Germany, where he was introduced to historical economics. This discipline became his vehicle for participation in public life. Academic historical economists, especially at Johns Hopkins, Wisconsin, Columbia, and the early Wharton School at Pennsylvania, rejected the formalism and absolutism that characterized the political economy of Gilded Age journalists, like E. L. Godkin, or of early academic economists, like William Graham Sumner. Against these laissez faire economists, the historical economists established the principle of intervention in the economy on the basis of observed fact. If Godkin and Sumner had addressed the "public" in the language of moral absolutes, the new economists offered a more practical language. Empirical investigation of actual conditions would justify intervention not as a general principle but on a case-by-case basis. Under the cloak of what they called the historical method, Seligman and his generation engineered an ideological victory within the profession and in public life.[19] It was also a victory *for* the profession. It assumed (and assured) a permanent and continuing role for expertise.

How would that expertise be defined and bounded? Several incidents in Seligman's career illuminate the shaping of academic expertise. One's proper audience was the political and economic elite. One should not speak directly to the masses. Expertise established authority. These propositions emerged over the years, in different incidents.

Let us begin in 1886. In that year, there were two promising young prize lecturers on the Graduate Faculty of Political Science at Columbia. One was Seligman, and the other was Daniel DeLeon. The year 1886 was also the year of Henry George's campaign for mayor of New York. It was a campaign that stirred working class hopes and provoked bourgeois terror. DeLeon supported George, actively and publicly. When DeLeon invited George to speak on campus, the president of Columbia, fearing for the future of Western civilization, demanded that Burgess fire DeLeon. Burgess, so unappealing in so many ways, believed deeply in academic freedom, and he refused. But, of course, the story does not end there. When DeLeon's three-year term expired, he was not reappointed. Seligman, who had opposed George's candidacy, was promoted into professional ranks.

DeLeon was not sorry to leave the academy. He dreamed of an alliance of intellect and working classes in the Socialist Labor party, of which he became a spokesman. He preferred direct engagement in popular political controversy. Such was not to be the model of academic intellect. Academics looked toward the institutionalization of the authority of experts. Such expertise was understood to be self-contained, monitored only by peers, by the American Economic Association. Expertise was not thought to be political. Moreover, ideas formed outside the guild of professional economists could be dismissed without argument, simply on the basis of professional authority.

An example is provided by the semipublic debate between Seligman and Henry George, held at the 1890 annual meeting of the American Social Science Association, an old-fashioned, essentially civic organization soon to be superseded by specialized disciplinary associations.

Seligman asserted that no one "with a thorough training in the history of economics" (meaning a Ph.D.) could support such radical theories (as George proposed). In biology, metaphysics, and astronomy, Seligman insisted, "we bow down before the specialist." With the expertise of the seminar room available, why, he asked, should we take seriously the ideas on economics expressed in popular books, in newspapers, and on public lecture platforms.

Henry George angrily rejected Seligman's assertion of academic authority's superiority to political debate. "Political economy," he countered, is not at all like astronomy or chemistry. It concerns "phenomena [that] lie about us in our daily lives, and enter into our most important relations, and whose laws lie at bottom of questions we are called upon to settle with our votes." If we cannot properly debate and understand them, "then democratic government is doomed to failure; and, the quicker we surrender ourselves to the government of the rich and learned, the better."[20]

In the decade of the 1890s, the bounds of professional discourse and activity were largely defined in a series of academic freedom cases. In each case, Seligman played a key role in determining the AEA response. Who should be protected? Seligman and the AEA went to the defense of academics who addressed economic issues reasonably within the purview of their supposed technical competence, even if their views on these matters were unorthodox. The custodians of the profession were also anxious to speak out against excessive and especially arbitrary trustee power over academics, arguing always that academic performance could be judged only by peers. Those academics who spoke directly to the public, as opposed to addressing peers or established political or economic elites, and who spoke for a wider range of radical proposals were not defended.

By 1900 the result of the academic freedom cases was a stronger profession and one that favored the center.[21] Academic economists were both less conservative and less radical. They were also less likely to make direct public appeals or frankly ideological statements. Investigation and objective data became more important than general ideas. The academic ideal of the unremitting search for knowledge, whether trivial or not, was born. Such was the academic envisioned and protected in the AAUP's founding "Statement of Principles."

The position taken by Seligman and his colleagues in the academic freedom cases was embedded in a larger debate within the AEA. Were social scientific experts spokesmen for the dominant classes? Or the subordinate ones? Or were they above, even beyond, the class system?

This issue was pressed forcefully by John R. Commons at the 1898 and 1899 meetings. He insisted that, like Adam Smith and Karl Marx, economists could affect society only by associating themselves with a rising class. Most economists denied the existence of classes in the United States. Seligman, however, accepted the existence of classes and even conflict of interests and classes. He offered an answer that was largely accepted by academic social science. The expert, he argued, would reconcile conflicts of class interest. Taking issue with Commons's claims that the "economists can serve the public only through the classes," Seligman argued that the economist must reject any class association. "The economist," he insisted, "tries to represent the common interest of society." Note well that for Seligman expertise, not politics, was the means of reconciling the conflicts of modern society.[22]

Not everyone was persuaded by Seligman's argument. Several of his Columbia colleagues—John Dewey, Charles Beard, and James Harvey Robinson, for example—worried that social science was tainted by class affiliation, an affiliation with the dominant classes. At least it seemed that way in Nicholas Murray Butler's Columbia University. One of their purposes in founding the New School for Social Research in 1919, after Beard had resigned from Columbia, was to free academic social science from its class affiliation.[23]

The New School experiment failed to sustain this vision of free or independent social science. But the ideal did not die with the resignations of Beard, Dewey, and Robinson from the New School. It remained at the core of Dewey's philosophy of the social sciences. His theory of social inquiry was driven by his commitment to democracy. The pragmatic, public, and democratic process of inquiry proposed by Dewey would, he thought, reduce subjectivities, including those deriving from inequalities in society.[24]

In Dewey's work, then, one finds a resistance to the social constraints that had accompanied the professionalization of social science. Moreover, in his commitment to the public realm, one finds a democratic definition of the truth that dissolves, at least in part, the distinction assumed by academics and theorized by Hannah Arendt. Let me conclude, therefore, by exploring for a moment the understanding of the relation of academic intellect and democracy in Dewey's too much neglected book, *The Public and Its Problems*, published in 1927.

Dewey devoted his long career to bringing philosophy into the world, yet he did not propose thereby to devalue the specialized and technical tasks inherent in the academic discipline of philosophy. Dewey was always anxious that public expression be well grounded in a technically viable philosophical position. In the 1920s, when he was writing *The Public and Its Problems*, he was writing some of his most important technical philosophy, including *Experience and Nature*. He regularly published in the *Journal of Philosophy* as well as the *New Republic*. The academic and the civic were for him distinct yet continuous. He did not privilege "expert" truth and devalue the truths of citizenship. He framed intellect within a conception of the public.

He sought to free values from established interests and customs. The aim was not to deny such social facts but rather to open up the truth-making process, to admit into the process of making public truths a variety of interests and emotional commitments. Dewey never fully resolved the problem of how values are created. No one, in fact, who both resists relativism and eschews appeal to some transcendent and absolute source of values can avoid some difficulty on this point. Yet the solution he proposed did have the very important effect of bringing the intellectual into the world in a way that enriched public culture. For Dewey, politics in public constituted a proper source of values, purposes, and social knowledge in a democracy. From this perspective, as James T. Kloppenberg explained, Dewey's "politics is an endless search for better truths."[25]

Such a perspective undermines the ideal of the expert envisioned by Seligman, and, even more directly, that offered by Walter Lippmann. During the war, Lippmann had been excited by the possibilities of expertise and disappointed in the capacity of the public, disturbed by how easily the masses could be manipulated. *Public Opinion* (1922) and *The Phantom Public* (1925) were his responses; they proposed a passive public and a government managed by "insiders" and experts. Dewey inverted Lippmann's formulation; he called for an active public and a responsive government. Most important for my argument here, however, he redefined the place of academic expertise in a democratic society.[26] It must be tested in the public world as well as in disciplinary communities; disciplinary truths must be entered into the conversation of the public.

Dewey called for social research, but he denied to social researchers the authority to prescribe solutions. Instead, they must bring their intelligence and their findings into the public realm. He did not fully develop a notion, nor have we, of a place off campus, so to speak, that might serve as the forum for the process of discussion and persuasion that would produce Deweyan truths and public policy. But it was to be a place, a local place—a city, even a quarter of a city. The voice, more than print, and the conversation, more than the media message, were the foundation of political discourse for Dewey.[27]

Neither of the two tendencies characteristic of academic social science were, according to Dewey, adequate to the democratic challenge. The academy could not be justified as a "refuge" for "specialism" and "scholasticism." Nor should social science be assimilated into administration. Democracy needed something else. If democracy "had its seer in Walt Whitman," then, Dewey passionately believed, "it will have its consummation when free social inquiry is indissolubly wedded to the art of full and moving communication" in public.[28]

In one respect what Dewey proposed had already been envisioned by Immanuel Kant, one of the first academic philosophers and one intensely aware of the doubleness of being a philosopher and a citizen. In his famous essay, "What Is Enlightenment?" Kant proposed that human progress would come from truth telling in public. Only in that way would humans mature.[29] Kant had anticipated the construction of truth from philosophically justified and transcendent categories. Such rational truth, being superior to other forms of understanding and knowledge, would establish political obligation. One finds this conception of the relation of truth and politics residual in Hannah Arendt's essay with which we began, "Truth and Politics." Residues of this philosophical tradition are apparent as well even in Jürgen Habermas's rather different theorization of the "public sphere."[30] Such a truth—at least as viewed from the perspective I am developing here—diminishes political truths, relegating them to an inferior order of reason. The implications for democratic theory are significant; for John Dewey this mode of understanding drove a wedge between philosophy as truth seeking and democracy as the collective search for better truths.[31]

For Dewey and (in our time) Richard Rorty, philosophies that focus on certitude, that give priority to the epistemological project of Kant, were associated in Dewey's phrase with a "metaphysics of feudalism." This program for philosophy, Dewey felt, put "democratic practice" at an "immense intellectual disadvantage." Such philosophies "have failed to furnish it [democracy] with articulation, with reasonableness, for they have at bottom been committed to the principle of a single, final and unalterable authority, from which all lesser authorities are derived."[32]

Dewey had a very different conception of philosophy—and of truth. As Rorty and others recently emphasized, Dewey rejected the epistemological project of Kant. He urged instead the grounding of truth in experience and history, emphasizing contingency and uncertainty over the quest for certainty as the foundation of democratic practice. A philosophy animated by a commitment to democracy, Dewey wrote, will propose a "universe in which there is real uncertainty and contingency, a world which is not all in, and never will be, a world which in some respect is incomplete and in the making, and which in these respects may be made this way or that according as men judge, prize, love and labor." He deeply believed that, for such a democratic philosophy, "any notion of a perfect or complete reality, finished, existing always the same without regard to the vicissitudes of time, will be abhorrent."[33]

One must be cautious in interpreting Dewey here. There is a danger that Dewey may be understood to be more radical (philosophically) than he in fact was. Richard Rorty, who has done so much to recover Dewey for our time, makes precisely this error. He misstates or overstates Dewey's position, making Dewey into a justification for his own antifoundationalism. While it is true that Dewey exchanged epistemology for history, it does not necessarily follow that he rejected metaphysics as well—a point tellingly made in Robert Westbrook's critique of Rorty.

Dewey's *Experience and Nature* is effectively a metaphysics that—in Westbrook's phrasing—makes believing in democracy possible.[34] Dewey did not expect to arrive at universal reason, at absolute truth. His truths would be contextual, specific to time and place, always experimental, rooted in history but continually refined, reduced of their subjectivities through the process of public discussion.

If Dewey developed a philosophical anthropology that accepted historical contingency and uncertainty, he did not thereby embrace subjectivity. He acknowledged the difference that social position produced in politics and philosophical outlook. He granted a role to interest and difference. But if he never denied the inevitability of subjectivity, his aim was always the reduction of subjectivity in the forming of public truths.[35] What Dewey wrote in *Experience and Nature* helps clarify both the process of truth making and its connection to social justice in a modern, differentiated society.

> The ultimate contradiction in the classic and genteel tradition is that while it made thought universal and necessary and the culminating good of nature, it was content to leave its distribution among men a thing of accident, dependent upon birth, economic, and civil status. Consistent as well as humane thought will be aware of the hateful irony of a philosophy which is indifferent to the conditions that determine the occurrence of reason while it asserts the ultimacy and universality of reason.[36]

Dewey did not offer the prospect of permanent truth, nor even rational certitude. What his participatory community of truth makers may achieve is a reasoned truth. Such truth will not be objective in any absolute sense, although the contest it implies will at once accommodate interest and reduce subjectivity. What he proposed for us is the possibility of ever more secure but never completely secure truths.

Such truth, it seems to me, is what the turn from epistemology to history is all about, and it nicely undermines the division proposed by Arendt in "Truth and Politics." Academic truth and political truth turn out not to be fundamentally different. Politics and inquiry converge in the quest for better truths. Such a notion of truth may make us uneasy— both as academics and as citizens—but it may also make it easier for us to be at once academics and citizens in a democracy.

Epilogue

THESE ESSAYS DESCRIBE AND, TO SOME EXTENT, REFLECT UPON A QUESTION asked by those American intellectuals who laid the foundations for the modern academic structure of organized knowledge. They asked themselves whether the present (then) intellectual institutions, epistemologies, and modes of discourse were adequate to the social possibilities (even responsibilities) of intellect. Did they enable the most highly trained intellect to contribute (in a democratic fashion) to the common life of the United States? These intellectuals were also interested in power and influence. If we are honest, we must acknowledge our own interests of that sort. My point is not their virtue (or ours); rather it is the use of the history they made.

The classic role for history is the denaturalization (or, in the critical vocabulary of Russian Formalists, the defamiliarization) of the present. History ought to encourage self-reflexiveness, just as it ought to enable us to imagine, if only for a moment, that things might have been and might yet be different.

The current organization of our intellectual life is just over one hundred years old; it is not a fact of nature. Nor is it inherent in the immanent unfolding of modern knowledge. The preceding essays, if they have succeeded at all, have emphasized the historical making of academic intellect in the United States, including the contingencies woven into that history. My hope is that the use of these histories will extend beyond the historical information in them. I hope that in addition they might encourage contemporary academics to reflect back upon their own relation to public life.

It would be a great error to read the present into the past and vice versa. What happened a hundred years ago to bring into existence the present organization of intellectual life is not to be repeated. Yet there is in our own time a social transformation easily comparable in magnitude (if not precisely in type) to the one that marked the late nineteenth century. Again, as was the case a century ago, the philosophical foundations of the disciplines are being seriously, if not necessarily definitively, challenged. Now is a moment, therefore, when one can imagine some rather fundamental changes in the world of intellect.

There is also today an uneasy sense of a receding capacity to achieve a compelling analytical grip on the conditions of American life. Explanatory description of social, political, and cultural circumstances, especially in our cities, seems beyond the reach of present disciplinary practice. Our universities are experiencing a serious, if not unprecedented, crisis that is not only financial but also social, intellectual, and even moral. They seem to be losing the confidence of the public. And there is a widespread and growing worry that we lack the energy, the ideas, and the institutional means to resolve our manifold problems in a political way. We are living one of those moments when one might reasonably expect both self-reflection and innovation.

It is not clear, however, that such changes will be in the direction urged in these essays. Although there have been recent laments for the decline, the near dissolution, of the public role of the intellectual, there is little in the culture of academe to suggest any lessening of the commitment to academic autonomy. There is much talk about the collapse of foundations, which might imply an opening of academic discourse out into the public realm, but the argument for the collapse of academic autonomy is utterly contained within academe. There is at least a rhetorical paradox in what many of the seemingly socially committed academics are saying and doing. Scholars who pronounce themselves uncompromising radicals have produced some of the most relentlessly academic writing. The work of these "radical" critics is informed by and builds upon important social concerns and social movements (sexism, racism, imperialism, etc.), yet there is an enormous gulf between their scholarship and the social life where men and women and children feel the effects of these evils. Perhaps this point can be better put. One cannot but be struck by the breadth of the gap between the way academics write about these issues and the way ordinary citizens think and talk about these phenomena that are so much a part of their lives.

Academics, though they draw upon the vitality and political ferment of the general culture, orient themselves nonetheless almost exclusively to professional structures and contexts, jealously defending their autonomy. They are more interested, evidently, in petty advantage in the academy, with trumping a fellow academic, than with the experience of the world. No wonder many of us harbor the cruel thought that a mystified but determined careerism animates and supplies a pattern to contemporary academic intellect.

That is a hard charge to address to one's fellow academics, and silence has been the rule. Yet the silence is being broken. As I write this epilogue, a recent essay by Richard Rorty comes to hand.[1] A slashing, even angry attack on the civic irresponsibility of intellect, especially academic intellect, Rorty's piece argues that journalists and professors have deserted democracy, or at least the notion of a democratic public. He asks, for example, why no professors of economics, nor professors of banking, nor professors of law pondered and wrote about the implications of Congress's decision in 1982 to allow savings and loan associations to invest in virtually anything with federally insured funds. What, he asks, if one professor had written about this? What if other professors had read that and decided to write similar articles for their local newspapers? Might the disaster have then become a political issue a couple of years earlier, perhaps in 1985 instead of 1988? Those three years would have saved the American people about a quarter trillion dollars. Might those dollars have done some good, somewhere?

Even more stinging is Rorty's attack on those whose work is closer to his own, those self-styled "subversive," "transgressive," postmodern intellectuals who have turned the world into a linguistic code. He asks whether radicalism is really all about language. Is radicalism simply the discussion of language in esoteric jargon? Are the injustices of our society entirely unrelated to material resources? Have politics become an academic exercise? Students seeking to change the world need not venture out into the world; rather, they can devote their energy to "getting a course on racism and sexism made compulsory for freshmen." There is much to commend such courses, but has politics shrunk to a debate over the college curriculum? How does such a politics speak for thousands of African-American single mothers and their children in our inner cities? For thousands of abused wives and children? For thousands of victims of rape? For the structurally unemployed in the Rust Belt?

The complaint that Rorty is lodging is quite the opposite of that made by conservative anti-intellectuals, like the chairwoman of the National Endowment for the Humanities. Rorty is not distressed because today's academics are tarnishing the purity of scholarship with their politics. His concern is the parochialism and triviality of that politics. He regrets the evident loss of faith in democracy; indeed, he rightly suspects a contempt for democratic public life. Academics have given up, he fears, "on the idea of democratic politics, of mobilizing moral outrage in defense of the weak, of drawing upon a moral vocabulary common to the well educated and the badly educated, to those who get paid for analyzing symbols and those who get paid for pouring concrete or dishing up cheeseburgers."

Rorty exaggerates, of course. Language is a *part* of politics, an important part. In particular contexts (and analysis must be specific), language might empower or oppress a person or a people. It is also true that some of the scholarship he has in mind *has* expanded our common language. But much—most, in fact—has not. It seems to be part of no more than an academic game that is remarkably parochial and oriented mainly to professional advance.

This academicization of intellectual life (and of politics) runs against what I take to be the current of social and cultural tides that are washing away (or at least weakening) all manner of boundaries. While other boundaries and borders become more indistinct and permeable and while academic intellectuals celebrate this, the boundary defining the border of academe has become firmer and less permeable. Interdisciplinary work thrives, but within the walls of the academy. Bridging over the walls of academe becomes rarer.

One can perhaps understand earlier worries about justifying and protecting autonomy and purity for fledgling professions. But today, when the professional project has succeeded as a social fact, when the academic disciplines and the university have been incorporated into American society—a point long since made by Daniel Bell[2]—one might have expected professional academics to be a bit less fearful of getting mixed up with ordinary life and with civic discourse. The integrity of academic intellect is not endangered by competing discourses of social inquiry. The risk now is precisely the opposite. Academe is threatened by the twin dangers of fossilization and scholasticism (of three types: tedium, high tech, and radical chic). The agenda for the next decade, at least as I see it, ought to be the opening up of the disciplines, the ventilating of professional communities that have come to share too much and that have become too self-referential.

The social history of the academy raises other questions. The recent demographic opening up of the academy is impressive, if still insufficient. The communities of the competent have incorporated a wider spectrum of scholars—broader in terms of race, ethnicity, gender, class and regional origin, religion, and educational background—than ever before. True, many groups continue to be seriously, even grossly, underrepresented, but today the social composition of the academic professions is nearer than ever before to that of the American people. We must work to continue to make it yet more representative, especially as the demography of contemporary society is changing so rapidly and profoundly. My point here, however, is that this closer fit with the civic realm might have been expected to encourage and ease movement between academe and public life, to nourish a common language, and to encourage a widened conversation about ourselves as a people. Yet demographic expansion seems to coincide with (and perhaps cause) greater professional rigidity.

If academe has been transformed, so has the public. There are now a plurality of audiences within a public culture that is essentially cosmopolitan and contested. In the past a fragment of the public, the educated middle class audience that first formed itself into a public during the era of Joseph Addison and London's eighteenth-century coffee houses, was able to pose with success as the whole. Today, the public is at once increasingly representative, and more fragmented, making it harder to find, to reach, and to define. The intellectual no longer has an unselfconscious "we" relationship to the public, although, as Michael Walzer recently argued, it may be necessary for those he calls "connected" critics self-consciously to assume such a rhetorical position.[3] But that public and the intellectual's relation to it can no longer be assumed in the way that Trilling assumed his public. It must be imagined anew, out of the same plurality that defines our modern condition.

The public is not a fixed thing, and it most certainly is not patiently awaiting the arrival of the intellectuals. The public must continually be formed and reformed. This process requires the collaboration and perhaps even the leadership of the intellectuals. The current generation of intellectuals has been hesitant to take on this work. But as Herbert Croly, the founding editor of the *New Republic*, put it in his classic *The Promise of American Life* (1909), the fact that the intellectual "is obliged to make a public instead of finding one ready made" is not so bad. That work of finding a way to win the interest of an ever more comprehensive public "will in the long run tend to keep his work vital and human."[4]

Where does one begin? Rorty's comments provide a clue. There is no better place to begin than in one's local community. One need not— ought not—be too proud to bring one's knowledge into the city where one lives and works. Jacob Burckhardt, after all, wrote more pages of notes for his public lectures for the citizens of Basel, a city smaller than most American university towns, than he ever published.[5]

If there is a rhetoric to be developed that can be spoken to a diverse public, it will be first nourished, as John Dewey understood, in the face-to-face conversation of local areas.[6] What the academic offers to his or her local culture is the intellectual power of theoretical abstraction that derives from an academic discipline. The locality, in return, offers to the academic the particularity, the concreteness, of lived experience in time and place. The language and thought of each, academic intellect and public life, would both be recognized and changed in a civic conversation. What our contemporary culture wants is the combination of theoretical abstraction and historical concreteness, technical precision and civic give-and-take, data and rhetoric. Only by entering into public life can our most highly educated intellect make for itself and for us such a rich and powerful common language of and for our democratic culture.

Notes

Preface

1. See Stephan Thernstrom, "Reflections on the New Urban History," in Felix Gilbert and Stephan R. Graubard, eds., *Historical Studies Today* (New York, 1972), 320–36.

2. See the defensiveness in John Higham and Paul Conkin, eds., *New Directions in American Intellectual History* (Baltimore, 1979), especially the essays by John Higham and by Laurence Veysey. See also the consideration of the subjective and objective standing of the field in Robert Darnton, "Intellectual and Cultural History," in Michael Kammen, ed., *The Past before Us: Contemporary Historical Writing in the United States* (Ithaca, 1980), 327–54.

3. Neil Harris, "Four Stages of Cultural Growth: The American City," in Arthur Mann, Neil Harris, and Sam Bass Warner, Jr., *History and the Role of the City in American Life* (Indianapolis, 1972), 24–49. This essay was republished in Harris's recent book, *Cultural Excursions* (Chicago, 1990), chap. 1.

4. Carl E. Schorske, *Fin-de-Siècle Vienna: Politics and Culture* (New York, 1980); Thomas Bender, *New York Intellect: A History of Intellectual Life in New York City, from 1750 to the Beginnings of Our Own Time* (New York, 1987). For a consideration of the differences between the two approaches, see Christophe Charle's review of *New York Intellect* in *Revue d'histoire moderne et contemporaine*, 39 (1992), 148–52.

5. Donald J. Olsen, *The City as a Work of Art: London, Paris, Vienna* (New Haven, 1986).

6. D. J. Olsen, "Cities and Culture: An Embarrassed Silence." Paper presented to the International Congress of Historical Sciences, Madrid, August 1990. I cited the following recent works, besides Schorske's, which I mentioned above: Jerrold Seigel, *Bohemian Paris* (New York, 1986); T. J. Clark, *The Painting of Modern Life* (New York, 1984); Marshall Berman, *All That is Solid Melts into Air* (New York, 1982) Richard Sennett, *The Fall of Public Man* (New York, 1977); Raymond Williams, *The Country and the City* (New York, 1973); Jeffrey Needel, *A Tropical Belle Epoch: Elite Culture and Society in Turn-of-the-Century Rio de Janeiro* (New York, 1987); Beatriz Sarlo, *Una modernidad periferica: Buenos Aires, 1920 y 1930* (Buenos Aires, 1988). With its recent publication, I would now add Gwendolyn Wright, *The Politics of Design in French Colonial Urbanism* (Chicago, 1991).

7. See Morton and Lucia White, *Intellectuals versus the City* (New York, 1964).

In my book, *Toward an Urban Vision: Ideas and Institutions in Nineteenth Century America* (Baltimore, 1982, orig. ed. 1975), I challenged the particular formulation of American urban attitudes proposed by the Whites, but both their book and mine would sustain this interpretation.

8. Jefferson was quite precise on this point. See Bender, *Toward an Urban Vision*, 21.

9. See Andreas Huyssen, *After the Great Divide: Modernism, Mass Culture, and Postmodernism* (Bloomington, Ind., 1986), esp. vii–xii, 178–221.

10. An important book that assays these issues—Lawrence Levine, *Highbrow/ Lowbrow: The Emergence of Cultural Hierarchy in America* (Cambridge, Mass., 1988)— fails because it assumes more purity and autonomy than existed and because it does not attend sufficiently to the complexity of the internal history of art forms.

11. Clifford Geertz, *Local Knowledge* (New York, 1983).

12. Elizabeth Kendall, *Where She Danced* (New York, 1979); Peter Jelavich, "Popular Dimensions of Modernist Elite Culture: The Case of Theatre in Fin-de-Siècle Munich," in Dominick La Capra and Steven L. Kaplan, eds., *Modern European Intellectual History* (Ithaca, 1982), 220–50; Svetlana Alpers, *The Art of Describing: Dutch Art in the Seventeenth Century* (Chicago, 1983). See also the remarkable book by Michael Baxandall, *Painting and Experience in Fifteenth Century Italy* (New York, 1972).

13. See Wilson Smith, "John Locke in the Great Unitarian Controversy," in Harold M. Hyman and Leonard W. Levy, eds. *Freedom and Reform: Essays in Honor of Henry Steele Commager* (New York, 1967), 78–100, and Daniel H. Calhoun, *Professional Lives in America: Structure and Aspiration, 1750–1850* (Cambridge, Mass., 1965).

14. See Thomas Bender, ed., *The University and the City: From Medieval Origins to the Present* (New York, 1988).

15. Here I have found Alfred D. Chandler, Jr., *The Visible Hand: The Managerial Revolution In American Business* (Cambridge, Mass., 1977), to be of enormous heuristic value and, likewise, the polemical and often penetrating book by Jane Jacobs, *Cities and the Wealth of Nations* (New York, 1984).

16. The whole work of revisionism owed an enormous debt to Bernard Bailyn's brilliant critique of the historiography of education in his *Education in the Forming of American Society* (New York, 1960).

17. Thomas S. Kuhn, *The Structure of Scientific Revolutions*, 2d ed. (Chicago, 1962).

18. See David A. Hollinger, *In the American Province* (Baltimore, 1989), chap. 7.

19. Somewhat later the literary critic Stanley Fish would write in equally suggestive ways about "interpretive communities." See Stanley Fish, *Is There a Text in This Class?* (Cambridge, Mass. 1980). Lest a false conclusion be drawn here by anyone unfamiliar with the work of Fish and Kuhn, they hold quite different positions on the foundations of knowledge.

20. In this formulation, I drew upon a passage in William James, *Pragmatism* (London, 1927), 59–60. My first recognition of the usefulness of the concept was recorded in Thomas Bender, "James Fenimore Cooper and the City," *New York History* 51 (1970): 305.

21. For my general critique of modernization theory, see my *Community and Social Change in America* (Baltimore, 1982; orig. ed. 1978). See also Thomas Bender, Peter Dobkin Hall, and Thomas L. Haskell, "Institutionalization and Education in the Nineteenth and Twentieth Centuries," *History of Education Quarterly* 20 (1980): 449–72.

22. The sources of this approach were diverse and metaphorical rather than methodological. Most important to me then, though these works now seem distant, were Kurt Lewin, *Field Theory in Social Science* (New York, 1951), and Georges Gurvitch, *The Social Frameworks of Knowledge* (Oxford, 1971). More recently, this way of

conceiving the problem has been reinforced in my mind by Pierre Bourdieu, *Homo Academicus* (Stanford, 1988).

23. I raised these issues in the first essay published here, but I regret that I never pursued them. Since I wrote that essay, Roger Chartier and others, writing in a very different tradition of French scholarship, *l'histoire du livre*, explored these dimensions of cultural history with great imagination and effect. For convenient access to this work, see Roger Chartier, "Texts, Printings, Readings," in Lynn Hunt, ed. *The New Cultural History* (Berkeley, 1989), 154–75.

24. Dorothy Ross, *The Origins of American Social Science* (New York, 1991); Peter Novick, *That Noble Dream: The 'Objectivity Question' and the American Historical Profession* (New York, 1988); Mary O. Furner, *Advocacy and Objectivity: A Crisis in the Professionalization of American Social Science, 1865–1905* (Lexington, Ky., 1975); Robert C. Bannister, *Sociology and Scientism: The American Quest for Objectivity, 1880–1940* (Chapel Hill, 1987). Two other works that do not precisely fit this category might be included here: Edward A. Purcell, *The Crisis of Democratic Theory: Scientific Naturalism and the Crisis of Value* (Lexington, Ky. 1973); Steven A. Diner, *A City and Its Universities: Public Policy in Chicago, 1892–1919* (Chapel Hill, 1980).

25. Thomas L. Haskell, *The Emergence of Professional Social Science* (Urbana, Ill. 1977); Burton J. Bledstein, *The Culture of Professionalism* (New York, 1976).

26. Samuel Haber, *The Quest for Authority and Honor in the American Professions, 1750–1900* (Chicago, 1991).

27. Charles Lindblom and David K. Cohen, *Usable Knowledge: Social Science and Social Problem-Solving* (New Haven, 1979); Charles E. Lindblom, *Inquiry and Change: The Troubled Attempt to Understand and Shape Society* (New Haven, 1990).

28. This point is well made by Haskell, *Emergence of Professional Social Science.*

29. Peter Dobkin Hall, *The Organization of American Culture, 1700–1900: Private Institutions, Elites, and the Origins of American Nationality* (New York, 1982).

30. See Lee Benson, *The Concept of Jacksonian Democracy* (Princeton, 1961); Patricia U. Bonomi, "The Middle Colonies: Embryo of the New Political Order," in Alden Vaughn and George A. Billias, eds. *Perspectives on Early American History* (New York, 1973) 63–92; Jack P. Greene, *Pursuits of Happiness: The Social Development of Early Modern British Colonies and the Formation of American Culture* (Chapel Hill, 1988).

1. The Cultures of Intellectual Life

1. Thomas Kuhn's discussion of the paradigm in *The Structure of Scientific Revolutions*, rev. ed. (Chicago, 1970), suggests but does not quite say that a paradigm's significance flows from its institutionalization. See also Stephen E. Toulmin, *Human Understanding*, vol. 1 (Princeton, 1972). For an example, see Frank Manuel's discussion of Newtonian science in his *Portrait of Isaac Newton* (Cambridge, Mass., 1968).

2. Daniel Bell writes, "Reality is a confirmation by 'significant others' " (*The Cultural Contradictions of Capitalism* [New York, 1976], 90). More generally, see Bukart Holzner, *Reality Construction in Society* (Cambridge, Mass., 1968), and Peter L. Berger and Thomas Luckmann, *The Social Construction of Reality: A Treatise in the Sociology of Knowledge* (Garden City, N.Y., 1966).

3. Robert K. Merton, *Social Theory and Social Structure*, rev. ed. (New York, 1957), 482–83.

4. Quoted phrase from Georges Gurvitch, *The Social Frameworks of Knowledge*, trans. M. Thompson and K. Thompson (Oxford, 1971).

5. Haskell, *Emergence of Professional Social Science*; Bruce Kuklick, *The Rise of American Philosophy: Cambridge, Massachusetts, 1860–1930* (New Haven, 1977); Bledstein, *Culture of Professionalism*; Furner, *Advocacy and Objectivity*; Sally G. Kohlstedt, *The Formation of the American Scientific Community: The American Association for the*

Advancement of Science, 1848–1860 (Urbana, Ill., 1976); Calhoun, *Professional Lives.* See also two excellent review essays of some of this recent literature: Bari Watkins in *History and Theory* 15 (1976), 57–66; and Henrika Kuklick in *American Quarterly* 28 (1976): 124–41. Twenty-five years ago Donald Fleming wrote a brief (and not entirely successful) study that he presented as a model for further studies of the relationship of science and local communities, but the study seems to have been forgotten rather than built upon. See Donald Fleming, *Science and Technology in Providence, 1760–1914: An Essay in the History of Brown University in the Metropolitan Community* (Providence, R.I., 1952). Some provocative questions concerning the American city as a context for intellectual life are posed in Perry Miller, *The Raven and the Whale* (New York, 1956), and Martin Green, *The Problem of Boston* (New York, 1966). Although his focus is not quite on intellectual life, many stimulating perceptions on the changing character of urban culture can be gleaned from Neil Harris, "Four Stages of Cultural Growth: The American City," in Arthur Mann et al., eds., *The History and Role of the City in American Life,* (Indianapolis, 1972), 24–49. Manchester, England, is the subject of two interesting recent attempts to study intellectual history from an urban perspective, and Vienna is the subject of another. See Arnold Thackray, "Natural Knowledge in a Cultural Context: The Manchester Model," *American Historical Review* 79 (1974): 672–709; Robert H. Kargon, *Science in Victorian Manchester* (Baltimore, 1977); Allan Janik and Stephen Toulmin, *Wittgenstein's Vienna* (New York, 1973).

6. On this process, see Thomas Bender, "Science and the Culture of American Communities: The Nineteenth Century," *History of Education Quarterly* 16 (1976): 67–77 (Chap. 2 in this volume).

7. These issues are raised, in far broader contexts, in Gurvitch, *Social Frameworks of Knowledge,* and in Jürgen Habermas, *Knowledge and Human Interests* (Boston, 1971).

8. Felix Gilbert, "Intellectual History: Its Aims and Methods," *Daedalus* 100 (Winter 1971): 80–97. Other conventional examples might be noted, including London coffee houses, Paris salons, or, later, cafés. See Lewis Coser, *Men of Ideas* (New York, 1965).

9. Walter J. Ong is suggestive here. See his "Agonistic Structures in Academia: Past to Present," *Daedalus* 103 (Fall 1974): 229–38.

10. Nathan Reingold, "Definitions and Speculations: The Professionalization of Science in America in the Nineteenth Century," in Alexandra Oleson and Sanborn C. Brown, eds., *The Pursuit of Knowledge in the Early Republic,* (Baltimore, 1976), 48. Compare the assumption of continuity in Samuel Harber, "The Professions and Higher Education in America: A Historical View," in Margaret Gordon, ed., *Higher Education and the Labor Market* (New York, 1974) 237–80, with the argument of a distinctive form of professionalism in the era of industrial and corporate capitalism in Magali Sarfatti Larson, *The Rise of Professionalism: A Sociological Analysis* (Berkeley, 1977).

11. Florence provides the baseline for assessing civic culture; hence my notion of "civic professionalism" is intentionally reminiscent of the "civic humanism" so prominent in Florentine historiography. See especially Lauro Martines, *The Social World of the Florentine Humanists, 1390–1460* (Princeton, 1963); Eugenio Garin, *Italian Humanism,* trans. Peter Munz (Oxford, 1965); Gene Brucker, *Renaissance Florence* (New York, 1969), esp. chaps. 3, 6. J.G.A. Pocock's recent book demonstrating the persistence of certain Florentine categories in early American republican thought suggests an interesting possibility for urban history; perhaps Florence also provided the central example for the basic social organization of intellectual life in a republic. See *The Machiavellian Moment: Florentine Political Thought and the Atlantic Republican Tradition* (Princeton, 1975).

12. What follows is based upon my unpublished essay, "New York Hospital and the Culture of Cities." The most important secondary references are Calhoun, *Profes-*

sional Lives, chap. 2, and Donald H. Fleming, *William H. Welch and the Rise of Modern Medicine* (Boston, 1954).

13. Eric Larrabee, *The Benevolent and Necessary Institution: The New York Hospital, 1771–1971* (Garden City, N.Y., 1971), 2.

14. To some extent this movement reflects a quest for identity by a provincial elite. An essay that makes this point about Edinburgh, a city whose civic culture had deeply impressed Bard, is N. T. Phillipson's "Culture and Society in the Eighteenth Century Province: The Case of Edinburgh and the Scottish Enlightenment," In Lawrence Stone, ed., *The University in Society*, 2 vols. (Princeton, 1974), 2:407–48.

15. David B. Tayck, *George Ticknor and the Boston Brahmins* (Cambridge, Mass., 1967), 27 and passim; Green, *Problem of Boston*, chap 4. For Harvard as a local institution, see Ronald Story, "Harvard and the Boston Brahmins: A Study in Institutional and Class Development, 1800–1865," *Journal of Social History* 8 (1975): 94–121. Much the same can be said in the case of Boston for James Russell Lowell's slightly later generation. See Edward Everett Hale, *James Russell Lowell and His Friends* (Boston, 1899), chap. 5.

16. Even in French intellectual history, where a concentration on Paris seems more justifiable, the data available on provincial intellectual life are beginning to force broader conceptions of French intellectual history. See Theodore Zelden, *France, 1848–1945*, 2 vols. (Oxford, 1973–77), 2:29–43.

17. Daniel Boorstin, *The Americans: The National Experience* (New York, 1965), 113–68; Richard Wade, *The Urban Frontier* (Chicago, 1964); Robert Wiebe, *The Segmented Society* (New York, 1976), 37.

18. Charles P. Cist, *Cincinnati in 1841* (Cincinnati, 1841), 129.

19. William Dean Howells, *Years of My Youth* [1916] (Bloomington, 1975), 77, 92.

20. Charles Lyell, *Travels in North America*, 2 vols. (London, 1855), 1:106–9. See also Alex de Tocqueville, *Democracy in America*, 2 vols. (New York, 1945), 2:47; Harriet Martineau, *Retrospect of Western Travel* 2 vols. (London, 1838), 2:91.

21. Henry D. Shapiro and Zane L. Miller, eds., *Physician to the West: Selected Writings of Daniel Drake on Science & Society* (Lexington, Ky., 1970), 59.

22. On the tariff function of poor transportation, see Julius Rubin, "Urban Growth and Regional Development," in David Gilchrist, ed., *The Growth of Seaport Cities, 1790–1825* (Charlottesville, Va., 1967), 3–21. Antebellum communication patterns are discussed in relation to urban development in Allen R. Pred, *Urban Growth and the Circulation of Information, 1790–1840* (Cambridge, Mass., 1973).

23. Henry W. Bellows, "The Townward Tendency," *The City* (1872), 38. For some general observations on the changing significance of locality in American culture, see Thomas Bender, *Community and Social Change in America* (New Brunswick, N.J., 1978), chap. 3.

24. Kohlstedt, *Formation of the American Scientific Community*, 83–84. See also Henry D. Shapiro, "The Western Academy of Natural Sciences of Cincinnati and the Structure of Science in the Ohio Valley, 1810–1850," in Oleson and Sanborn, *Pursuit of Knowledge*, 237–42, and Hamilton Cravens, "American Science Comes of Age: An Institutional Perspective, 1850–1930," *American Studies* 17 (1976): 49–70.

25. Quoted in Bledstein, *Culture of Professionalism*, 159.

26. Holzner, *Reality Construction in Society*, 68–69.

27. See Haskell, *Emergence of Professional Social Science*, and Furner, *Advocacy and Objectivity*, chap. 1.

28. See J. Kirkpatrick Flack, *Desideratum in Washington: The Intellectual Community in the Capital City, 1870–1900* (Cambridge, Mass., 1975).

29. Massachusetts Board of Education, *Third Annual Report* (Boston, 1839), 78–79.

30. See, for example, Miller, *Raven and the Whale*; Calhoun, *Professional Lives*;

idem, *The Intelligence of a People* (Princeton, 1973); Neil Harris, *Humbug: The Art of P. T. Barnum* (Boston, 1973); Green, *Problem of Boston*; Ann Douglas, *The Feminization of American Culture* (New York, 1977).

31. Calhoun, *Intelligence of a People*, 229–30 and passim. See also David Hall, "The World of Print and Collective Mentality in Seventeenth-Century New England," in John Higham and Paul Conkin, eds., *New Directions in American Intellectual History* (Baltimore, 1979), 166–80.

32. Douglas, *Feminization of American Culture*, 142. More generally, see Richard Sennett, *The Fall of Public Man* (New York, 1977). On the problem writers had in defining their audience, see William Charvat, *Literary Publishing in the United States, 1790–1850* (Philadelphia, 1959).

33. Douglas, *Feminization of American Culture*, pt. 1.

34. On Beecher's intellectual style, see the comments in Douglas, *Feminization of American Culture*, 81–84, 132–41, 153–61, and Calhoun, *Intelligence of a People*, 256–91. On Barnum, see Harris, *Humbug*.

35. Edwards A. Park, *Discourse Delivered in Boston . . .* (Andover, Mass., 1844), 5–7; Kuklick, *Rise of American Philosophy*, esp. 560–72.

36. See, for example, Larson, *Rise of Professionalism*.

37. Surely after the Tilton affair, the moral and intellectual authority symbolized by Beecher's style was suspect. E. L. Godkin points this out in "Chromo-civilization," *Nation* 19 (1874): 201–2. The embarrassingly frequent collapses of built structures— from factories to bridges—called other types of competence into question.

38. See Bender, "Science and the Culture of Communities," 70–71.

39. See Calhoun, *Intelligence of a People*, 319–22, and Haskell, *Emergence of Professional Social Science*.

40. Alfred North Whitehead, *Science and the Modern World* (New York, 1948; orig. ed. 1925), 196–97.

41. Merle Curti, *The Growth of American Thought*, 2d ed. (New York, 1951), vi.

42. See Robert Darnton, "In Search of the Enlightenment: Recent Attempts to Create a Social History of Ideas," *Journal of Modern History* 43 (1971): 113–32. A dominant response of intellectual historians to social history is reflected in the concern for quantitative data on social structures and book distribution in Henry F. May, *The Enlightenment in America* (New York, 1976). The desire for rapprochement is clear in May's comment in p. 364n. The current concern for grounding ideas in the work of quantitative social history does not, however, produce a clear sense of the structure of discourse.

43. While the customary practice of studying ideas in a national context is difficult to defend, a study of intellectual life as a cultural activity within a given society is easily justified.

44. The phrase is originally from Paul Goodman; I have taken it from Thomas L. Haskell, "Power to the Experts," *New York Review of Books* 24 (13 October 1977): 28–33.

2. Science and the Culture of American Communities

1. Science has fared considerably better in studies of colonial education. See Lawrence Cremin, *American Education: The Colonial Experience* (New York, 1970).

2. On their pervasiveness in the nineteenth century, see Ralph S. Bates, *Scientific Societies in the United States* (Cambridge, Mass., 1965). Their role in the eighteenth century is assessed in Brooke Hindle, *The Pursuit of Science in Revolutionary America, 1735–1789* (Chapel Hill, 1956), and Raymond P. Stearns, *Science in the British Colonies of America* (Urbana, Ill., 1970), 506–13. For an example of how one might study the role of one of these nineteenth-century urban educational institutions in the

transmission of scientific ideas, see Margaret W. Rossiter, "Benjamin Silliman and the Lowell Institute: The Popularization of Science in Nineteenth Century America," *New England Quarterly* 44 (December 1971): 601–26.

3. A. Hunter Dupree, *Asa Gray* (Cambridge, Mass., 1959); Edward Lurie, *Louis Agassiz: A Life in Science* (Chicago, 1960). On moral philosophers, see Wilson Smith, *Professors and Public Ethics: Studies of Northern Moral Philosophers before the Civil War* (Ithaca, 1956); Daniel Walker Howe, *The Unitarian Conscience: Harvard Moral Philosophy, 1805–1861* (Cambridge, Mass., 1970); and Donald H. Meyer, *The Instructed Conscience: The Shaping of the American National Ethic* (Philadelphia, 1972). A beginning has been made, however, in Stanley M. Guralnick, "Science and the American College, 1828–1860" (Ph.D. diss., University of Pennsylvania, 1969).

4. Allan Stanley Horlick's study of New York City's mercantile elite, which includes a discussion of the uses of phrenology for that social group, provides an example of what can be done in this area. See his *Country Boys and Merchant Princes: The Social Control of Young Men in New York* (Lewisburg, Pa., 1975), chap. 8. Although it deals with an English case, Arnold Thackray's "Natural Knowledge in Culture Context: The Manchester Model," *American Historical Review* 79 (1974): 672–709, provides a stimulating example.

5. Nathan Reingold, ed., *The Papers of Joseph Henry*, vol. 1 (Washington, D.C., 1972), xxiii, xix.

6. Incidentally, such specific explorations of urban contexts will be more valuable than those purely quantitative studies that find urban areas, using simple census definitions, producing the bulk of nineteenth-century American scientists. See Ronald C. Tobey, "How Urbane is the Urbanite? An Historical Model of the Urban Hierarchy and the Social Motivation of Service Classes," *Historical Methods Newsletter* 7 (1974): 259.

7. Shapiro and Miller, *Physician to the West*, 324.

8. See, for example, Richard Wade, *The Urban Frontier* (Chicago, 1964).

9. Twenty-five years ago Donald Fleming wrote a brief (and not entirely successful) study that he presented as a model for further studies of the relationship of science and local communities, but the study seems to have been forgotten rather than built upon. See Fleming, *Science and Technology in Providence*.

10. Richard Shryock, "American Indifference to Basic Science during the Nineteenth Century," *Archives internationales d'histoire des sciences*, no. 5 (1948): 50–65.

11. See Nathan Reingold, "American Indifference to Basic Research: A Reappraisal," in George H. Daniels, ed., *Nineteenth-Century American Science* (Evanston, Ill., 1972), 38–62.

12. Put differently, most history of American science reveals a commitment, not always articulated, to the developmental philosophy of science that is best exemplified in Charles C. Gillispie, *The Edge of Objectivity* (Princeton, 1960), rather than the more relativistic approach of Thomas Kuhn in *Structure of Scientific Revolutions*.

13. This ahistorical approach to higher education is now being challenged. The *History of Education Quarterly* recently devoted a whole issue to a critical reappraisal of the history of the liberal arts college. Two articles from that issue are directly relevant to this point: James Axtell, "The Death of the Liberal Arts College," *History of Education Quarterly* 11 (1971): 339–52; Hugh Hawkins, "The University-Builders Observe the Colleges," ibid.: 353–62: See also Wilson Smith, "Apologia pro Alma Mater: The College as Community in Ante-Bellum America," in Stanley Elkins and Eric McKitrick, eds., *The Hofstadter Aegis* (New York, 1974), 125–83; Stanley M. Guralnick, "Sources of Misconception on the Role of Science in the Nineteenth-Century American College," *Isis* 65 (1974): 352–66; and Douglas Sloan, "Harmony, Chaos, and Consensus: The American College Curriculum," *Teacher's College Record* 73 (1971): 221–51.

14. This is suggested by Reingold, "American Indifference to Basic Research," 39.

15. Current skepticism about science may have just now made this possible. I am certain that my interest in reexamining the community-oriented science that was destroyed by professionalism proceeds at least in part from a concern about the place and function of "science" in modern American society. On this point I think it is significant that the reappraisals of the old-time college by Sloan and Smith, cited above, both begin with a discussion of the current problems of higher education.

16. Kuhn, *Structure of Scientific Revolutions*. While Kuhn's notion of "paradigms" has become well known, even faddish, among historians, his second idea, which I want to stress here, has been much less remarked upon. For a fuller discussion of Kuhn's ideas and their relationship to historical scholarship, see M. D. King, "Reason, Tradition, and the Progressiveness of Science," *History and Theory* 10 (1971): 3–32, and David A. Hollinger, "T. S. Kuhn's Theory of Science and Its Implications for History," *American Historical Review* 78 (1973): 376–93.

17. Charles Rosenberg, "On Writing the History of American Science," in Herbert J. Bass, ed., *The State of American History* (Chicago, 1970), 185.

18. Although they are general studies, two books by Robert H. Wiebe are relevant here: *The Segmented Society* and *The Search for Order, 1877–1920* (New York, 1967).

19. Alfred North Whitehead, *Science and the Modern World* (New York, 1948; orig. ed. 1925), 91–92.

20. See Sloan, "Harmony, Chaos, and Consensus," 223–27.

21. See Smith, "Apologia pro Alma Mater," 131–32; David B. Potts, "American Colleges in the Nineteenth Century: From Localism to Denominationalism," *History of Education Quarterly* 11 (1971): 367–69, 371–73; and Christopher Jencks and David Riesman, *The Academic Revolution* (New York, 1968), chaps. 1, 4.

22. For Daniels's argument, see his *American Science in the Age of Jackson* (New York, 1968). On Drake's publications, see the list in Shapiro and Miller, *Physician to the West*, 381–419, where I count 728. Drake's teaching duties at the medical school in Louisville during the 1840s were related more to a regional identification than a professional one.

23. de Tocqueville, *Democracy in America*, (1945), 2:47; Harriet Martineau, *Retrospect of Western Travel*, 2 vols. (London, 1838), 2:91; Charles Lyell, *A Second Visit to the United States of North America*, 2 vols. (New York, 1849), 1:57, 153.

24. Clifford K. Shipton, "The Museum of the American Antiquarian Society," in Whitfield J. Bell, Jr., ed., *A Cabinet of Curiosities* (Charlottesville, Va., 1967), 36–38; John M. Kennedy, "Philanthropy and Science in New York City: The American Museum of Natural History, 1868–1968" (Ph.D. diss., Yale University, 1968), 46.

25. The starting point for any consideration of the culture of American cities is Neil Harris, "Four Stages of Cultural Growth: The American City," in Arthur Mann, Neil Harris, and Sam Bass Warner, *History and the Role of the City in American Life* (Indianapolis, 1972), 24–49.

26. See Daniel Boorstin, *The Americans: The National Experience* (New York, 1965), 113–68.

27. On the "sublime" in American romantic thought generally and science in particular, see Perry Miller, *The Life of the Mind in America: From the Revolution to the Civil War* (New York, 1965), esp. 3.

28. Shapiro and Miller, *Physician to the West*, 146–59: Charles Cist, *Cincinnati in 1841* (Cincinnati, 1841), 129, 134.

29. Shapiro and Miller, *Physician to the West*, 133.

30. See Louis L. Tucker, " 'Ohio Show-Shop': The Western Museum of Cincinnati, 1820–1867," in Bell, *Cabinet of Curiosities*, 73–105.

31. Carl Bode, *The American Lyceum* (New York, 1956), 92, 250.

32. Reingold, *Papers of Joseph Henry*, 75. My italics.

33. See, for example, ibid., 354–55, 407–9.

34. Ibid., 349.

35. Ibid., 435.

36. This point is made in more detail by Edward Lurie, "Science in American Thought," *Cahiers d'histoire mondiale* 8 (1965): 656–57.

37. Shapiro and Miller, *Physicians to the West*, 170–71.

38. Harris, *Humbug*, 57, 79. This superficial empiricism is explored more systematically and with similar conclusions in Calhoun, *Intelligence of a People*.

39. Harris, *Humbug*, 65.

40. Reingold, *Papers of Joseph Henry*, 409.

41. See Calhoun, *Intelligence of a People*.

42. Quoted in Daniels, *American Science in Age of Jackson*, 38.

43. For the conflict between scientists and donors at the American Museum of Natural History, see Kennedy, "Philanthropy and Science in New York," 4 and passim.

44. For an interesting and valuable consideration of the problem of community and esoteric culture in an entirely different context, see Gene Brucker, *Renaissance Florence* (New York, 1969), esp. chaps. 3, 6.

45. On this problem, see Howard S. Miller, *Dollars for Research: Science and its Patrons in Nineteenth-Century America* (Seattle, 1970), and A. Hunter Dupree, *Science in the Federal Government: A History of Policies and Activities to 1940* (Cambridge, Mass. 1957).

46. I. Bernard Cohen, "Some Reflections on the State of Science in America during the Nineteenth Century," *Proceedings of the National Academy of Sciences of the United States of America* 45 (1959): 671–72. The conflicting goals for higher education during this period are surveyed by Laurence R. Veysey, *The Emergence of the American University* (Chicago, 1965), pt. 1.

47. See Lurie, "Science in American Thought," 656, and Rossiter, "Benjamin Silliman," 625.

48. In fact, the need was if anything greater. See A. Hunter Dupree, "Public Education for Science and Technology," *Science* 134 (15 September 1961): 716–18.

49. Some of the intellectual, political, and social implications of the integration of scientists into the major institutional structures of the United States in the twentieth century are discussed by Edward A. Purcell, Jr., "Service Intellectuals and the Politics of 'Science,' " *History of Education Quarterly* 15 (Spring 1975): 97–110.

50. Although professional science defines what is legitimately "science" in the late twentieth century, it is important to recognize that a weakened vernacular science still survives, without prestige, in American popular culture. The key point I want to emphasize here, however, is the loss of legitimacy which forms a contrast with the midnineteenth century situation.

51. For this incident, I have relied upon the account in Miller, *Dollars for Research*, 39–47.

3. The Erosion of Public Culture

1. Of a vast literature, see especially Richard Hofstadter, "The Revolution in Higher Education," in Morton White and Arthur Schlesinger, Jr., eds., *The Paths of American Thought* (Boston, 1970), 269–90; Walter P. Metzger, *Academic Freedom in the Age of the University* (New York, 1955); Veysey, *Emergence of the American University*; Richard Storr, *The Beginnings of Graduate Education in America* (Chicago, 1953); Haskell, *Emergence of Professional Social Science*; Kuklick, *Rise of American Philosophy*; Bledstein, *Culture of Professionalism*; Furner, *Advocacy and Objectivity*; Kohlstedt, *For-*

mation of the American Scientific Community; Calhoun, *Professional Lives*; Larson, *Rise of Professionalism*; Edward Shils, "The Order of Learning in the United States from 1865 to 1920: The Ascendancy of the Universities," *Minerva* 16 (1978): 159–95; Jurgen Herbst, *The German Historical School in American Scholarship* (Ithaca, 1965); Carl Diehl, *Americans and German Scholarship, 1770–1870* (New Haven, 1978).

2. For an expanded discussion of the issues in this paragraph, see chap. 1, this volume.

3. See Paul Farmer, "Nineteenth Century Ideas of the University: Continental Europe," in Margaret Clapp, ed., *The Modern University* (Ithaca, 1950), 1–24. See also Robert Mandrou, *From Humanism to Science, 1480–1700* (New York, 1978); Edward Shils, "British Intellectuals in the Mid-Twentieth Century," in his *The Intellectuals and the Powers and Other Essays* (Chicago, 1972), 135–53; Reinhard Bendix, "Province and Metropolis: The Case of Eighteenth-Century Germany," in Joseph Ben-David and T. N. Clark, eds., *Culture and Its Creators* (Chicago, 1977), 119–49; N. T. Phillipson, "Culture and Society in the Eighteenth Century Province: The Case of Edinburgh and the Scottish Enlightenment," in Lawrence Stone, ed., *The University in Society*, 2 vols. (Princeton, 1974), 2:407–48.

4. Johan Wolfgang von Goethe, *Conversations with Eckermann*, trans. John Oxenford (London, 1909), 252. From a nearer perception and experience, compare Honore de Balzac, *Lost Illusions* (Baltimore, 1971; orig. ed. 3 vols., 1837–43). Theodore Zeldin has recently shown that the dominance of Paris has been somewhat exaggerated. See his *France, 1848–1945*, 2 vols. (Oxford, 1973–77), 2:29–43.

5. On denominational discourse, see Howard Miller, *The Revolutionary College: American Presbyterian Higher Education, 1707–1837* (New York, 1976); Theodore D. Bozeman, *Protestants in an Age of Science* (Chapel Hill, 1977).

6. On the lesser cities, see chapter 2, this volume.

7. Sam Bass Warner, Jr., *The Private City: Philadelphia in Three Periods of Its Growth* (Philadelphia, 1968).

8. See the suggestive essay by Brooke Hindle, "The Underside of the Learned Society in New York, 1754–1854," in Oleson and Brown, *Pursuit of Knowledge*, 84–116.

9. The best way to grasp the meaning of learning and culture for these early American cultural leaders is by examining, in addition to Franklin's autobiography, some key diaries. See, for example, Dorothy Barck, ed., *Letters of John Pintard to His Daughter*, 4 vols. (New York, 1937–40); James Cronin, ed., *The Diary of Elihu Hubbard Smith, 1771–1798* (Philadelphia, 1973); Dorothy Barck, ed., *Diary of William Dunlap, 1786–1834*, 3 vols. (New York, 1929–31).

10. For some indication of what these numbers meant for urban experience, see Warner, *Private City*; Oscar Handlin, *Boston's Immigrants* (New York, 1959); and Carroll Smith Rosenberg, *Religion and the Rise of the American City: The New York City Mission Movement, 1812–1870* (Ithaca, 1971).

11. Warner, *Private City*, 62. See also Wiebe, *The Segmented Society*.

12. For a recent survey of the quest for social order, see Paul Boyer, *Urban Masses and Moral Order in Urban American, 1820–1920* (Cambridge, Mass., 1978).

13. Charles Eliot Norton, "The Intellectual Life of America," *New Princeton Review* 6 (1888): 312–13, 321.

14. The intellectual was in a circumstance similar to that of the wholesale merchant of the era. E. L. Godkin observed that "it is not the dry goods man or the grain merchant only who has goods for sale, but the poet, the orator, the scholar, the philosopher, and the politician. We are all in a measure seeking a market for our wares. What we desire, therefore . . . is a good means of making known to all the world where our store is and what we have to sell." (E. L. Godkin, *Reflections and Comments, 1865–1895* [New York, 1895], 53.) Godkin recognized the value of

professional communities in solving this problem. See his "Professional Guilds," *American Institute of Architects, Proceedings* (1870): 186–94. On the fragmented and anonymous character of the wholesale market at midcentury and the organizational resolution to the problem, see P. Glenn Porter and Harold Livesay, *Merchants and Manufacturers: Studies in the Changing Structure of Nineteenth-Century Marketing* (Baltimore, 1971), and Chandler, *Visible Hand.*

15. Edith Wharton, *The Age of Innocence* (New York, 1948; orig., 1920). This separation was not so drastic in Boston. See Green, *Problem of Boston* (New York, 1966).

16. de Tocqueville, *Democracy in America* (1945) 2:62.

17. Of course, Melville's novel is set on a riverboat, but Melville often treated boats as microcosms of the city, and he explicitly identifies his characters with urban types in *The Confidence Man* (New York, 1955), 278. For a discussion of "confidence" in this age of moral, social, and intellectual chaos, see Harris, *Humbug.* For the collapse of traditional methods of recruitment into the professions and into the urban elite, see Calhoun, *Professional Lives;* Larson, *Rise of Professionalism;* and Allan S. Horlick, *Country Boys and Merchant Princes: The Social Control of Young Men in New York* (Lewisburg, Pa., 1975).

18. Massachusetts Board of Education, *Third Annual Report* (Boston, 1839), 78–79. On the importance and pervasiveness of the public lecture in midcentury, see Donald M. Scott, "The Popular Lecture and the Creation of a Public: Professionals and Their Audiences in Mid-Nineteenth Century America" (paper presented to Davis Center Seminar, Princeton University, February 1979).

19. C. W. Eliot, "Popularizing Science," *Nation* 4 (10 January 1867), 32–33.

20. I am here emphasizing the intellectual aspects of the crisis; for those in traditional professions, questions of power, prestige, and control were also involved. On these issues, see the excellent studies by Calhoun, *Professional Lives,* and Larson, *Rise of Professionalism.*

21. Several critics have centered their attention on Beecher as an example of the weaknesses of mid-nineteenth-century intellectual life. I have in mind particularly the extremely perceptive studies by Calhoun, *Intelligence of a People,* and Douglas, *Feminization of American Culture.*

22. Henry Ward Beecher, *Oratory* (Philadelphia, 1876), 6; idem, *Yale Lectures on Preaching,* first series (3 vols. bound in one, separately paged; New York, 1881), 209.

23. Beecher, *Yale Lectures on Preaching,* first series, 59; Beecher, *Oratory,* 6.

24. Beecher, *Yale Lectures on Preaching,* first series, 94, 96.

25. Beecher, *Yale Lectures on Preaching,* second series, 33; Beecher, *Oratory,* 1, 66.

26. Beecher, *Yale Lectures on Preaching,* first series, 70–74.

27. His father, Lyman Beecher, representing an earlier, small-town version of professional and intellectual life, had emphasized that trust and authority depended upon "character and deeds." Quoted in Sidney Mead, "The Rise of an Evangelical Conception of the Ministry in America, 1607–1850," in H. Richard Niebuhr and Daniel Williams, eds., *The Ministry in Historical Perspective* (New York, 1956), 218.

28. H. W. Bellows; quoted in Clifford E. Clark, *Henry Ward Beecher* (Urbana, 1978), 122.

29. Godkin, *Reflections and Comments,* 191–204; quotes from 203–4.

30. Even after he went to Michigan, he maintained his interest in a university in New York. But his did not prevent him from articulating a vision of a nonurban university. At Michigan he proposed that all the intellectual auxiliaries available in the city be brought together not in a city but at a campus. See Henry P. Tappan, *Discourse . . . on the Occasion of his Inauguration as Chancellor of the University of Michigan*

(Detroit, 1853), 14–16, 38. Andrew Dickson White credits Tappan at Michigan for the real beginning of the American university. See White's *Autobiography*, 2 vols. (New York, 1905), 1:292.

31. Henry P. Tappan, *University Education* (New York, 1951), 60, 68, 60.

32. Henry P. Tappan, *The Growth of Cities* (New York, 1855), 7–8, 31–35.

33. Ibid., 17–19.

34. Ibid., 45.

35. Tappan, *University Education*, 89–90.

36. Ibid., 95.

37. Ibid., 93.

38. Alexander Dallas Bache, *Anniversary Address before the American Institute of the City of New York* (New York, 1857), 44, 59. See also Benjamin Peirce, *Working Plan for the Foundation of a University* (Cambridge, Mass., 1856).

39. For this terminology, see Nathan Reingold, "Definitions and Speculations: The Professionalization of Science in America in the Nineteenth Century," in Oleson and Brown, *Pursuit of Knowledge*, 33–69. For an application of the terminology in an urban context, see the fine article by Douglas Sloan, "The Organization of Science: Natural History in New York City, 1867–1907," *Isis* 71 (1980): 35–76.

40. [E. L. Godkin,] "The Organization of Culture," *Nation* 6 (18 June 1868), 486–88. The idea obviously derives from the Institute de France; for a brief account of it at midcentury, see T. N. Clark, *Prophets and Patrons: The French University and the Emergence of the Social Sciences* (Cambridge, Mass., 1973), 55–60.

41. Sanborn, "The Social Sciences, 6. The aims, accomplishments, and ultimate failure of the ASSA are perceptively discussed by Haskell, *Emergence of Professional Social Science*. Cf. William Leach, *True Love and Perfect Union* (New York, 1980), chaps. 11–12.

42. At the tenth annual meeting in 1879, for example, only ten of twenty-seven papers were the work of academics.

43. For a clarifying discussion of how the "scholarly question" differs from general cultural discourse, see Diehl, *Americans and German Scholarship*, chap. 2.

44. Hugh Hawkins, *Pioneer: A History of the Johns Hopkins University, 1874–1889* (Ithaca, 1960), 73.

45. On this proposal and Gilman's rejection of it, see Haskell, *Emergence of Professional Social Science*, chap. 7. The proposal is no doubt an updated version of the proposal Peirce and Bache developed in the 1850s.

46. Daniel Coit Gilman, "The Utility of Universities," in his *University Problems in the United States* (New York, 1898), 45–52.

47. Gilman, "The Characteristics of a University," in ibid., 93, 99. See also the extremely interesting observations on Harvard in 1904 in Henry James, *The American Scene* (New York, 1967), 57–58.

48. See Neil Harris, *The Land of Contrasts, 1880–1901* (New York, 1970), 17; Harris, "Four Stages of Cultural Growth: The American City," in Mann, Harris, and Warner, *History and Role of the City*, 24–49; Richard Sennett, *Families against the City* (Cambridge, Mass., 1970); Sam Bass Warner, *The Urban Wilderness* (New York, 1972).

49. Haskell, *Emergence of Professional Social Science*, 52.

50. George William Curtis, *Opening Address at the New York Meeting [of the ASSA] 1874* (Cambridge, Mass., 1874), 4. See also Sanborn's description of the course on "social science" that he offered at Cornell. It was designed, he said, to teach ethics inductively by having students observe some charity or reform so they might achieve "a living interest in the subjects"—something that would make them "more public-spirited as citizens." (Sanborn, "The Social Sciences," 7–12; quotes 8.)

51. See Haskell, *Emergence of Professional Social Science*; Nathan Glazer, "The Rise of Social Research in Europe," in Daniel Lerner, ed., *The Human Meaning of the Social Sciences* (Cleveland, 1959), 43–72; and Clark, *Prophets and Patrons*, esp. 123–24.

52. Albion W. Small, *The Origins of Sociology* (Chicago, 1924), 335–37, 326.

53. Franklin H. Giddings, "The Relation of Sociology to Other Scientific Studies," *Journal of Social Science* 32 (1894): 145, 146.

54. See Diner, *A City and Its Universities*.

55. For a different perspective on this process, see Michael Frisch, "Urban Theorists, Urban Reform, and American Political Culture in the Progressive Period," *Political Science Quarterly* 97 (1982): 295–315. See also R. S. Lynd, *Knowledge for What? The Place of Social Science in American Culture* (New York, 1964; orig. ed. 1939), 19.

56. James Bryce, *The American Commonwealth*, rev. ed. (New York, 1889), 660. For accounts of such aspirations in Boston and Washington, see Green, *Problem of Boston* and Flack, *Desideratum in Washington*.

57. Shils, *Intellectuals and the Powers*, 118, 124; Clark, *Prophets and Patrons*.

58. See Lynd, *Knowledge for What?* 118, 165.

59. This may partially explain the "two Chomsky" problem. See Paul Robinson, "The Chomsky Problem," *New York Times Book Review* (25 February 1979), 3, 37.

4. E.R.A. Seligman and the Vocation of Social Science

1. John Milton Cooper, Jr., *The Warrior and the Priest: Woodrow Wilson and Theodore Roosevelt* (Cambridge, Mass., 1983).

2. I made this argument more fully in *New York Intellect*, 265–78. See also chap. 3 in this volume.

3. Columbia College, *Outline of a Plan for the Instruction of Graduate Classes* (New York, 1880) 4, 11, 12, 15.

4. See Marvin Gettleman, *An Elusive Presence: John H. Finley and His America* (Chicago, 1979), bk. 2. It is also worth noting that there were serious proposals to consolidate the new Johns Hopkins University with the civic reform organization, the American Social Science Association. See Haskell, *Emergence of Professional Social Science*, chap. 7. See also chap. 3 in this volume.

I have sought to develop a statistical base for this generalization, but the task has proven to be more difficult than was expected. The needed data for Columbia, the institution about which I have the greatest qualitative evidence, are not available in either published or archival form. Some data are available for Johns Hopkins, however. Tracy Tullus, a graduate student in history at NYU, has been able to identify the careers of the cohort of the Johns Hopkins graduates of the 1880–90 period. She tracked twenty-five of the twenty-six scholars who received a Ph.D. in history during that decade. Sixty-four percent of them went on to academic careers, while 36 percent went into business, government, or some form of social activism. Somewhat surprisingly, the cohort of 1900–1920 is only a bit more academic, with 70 percent pursuing academic careers and 30 percent following social/civic leadership careers. She obtained her data from W. Norman Brown, comp. *Johns Hopkins Half-Century Directory, 1876–1926* (Baltimore, 1926).

5. Quoted in Veysey, *Emergence of the American University*, 149. Italics added.

6. Furner, *Advocacy and Objectivity*; Haskell, *Emergence of Professional Social Science*; Novick, *That Noble Dream*; Ross, *Origins of American Social Science*. I should note also a very recent essay not within the historiography of the professionalization of the social sciences but both bearing directly upon it and speaking very much to the issue of this essay. It touches the themes of this essay (and even considers some of the

same figures and evidence). Leon Fink, " 'Intellectuals' versus 'workers': Academic Requirements and the Creation of Labor History," *American Historical Review* 96 (1991): 395–421.

7. Roger L. Geiger, *To Advance Knowledge: The Growth of American Research Universities, 1900–1940* (New York, 1986), 27.

8. On the older gentry, see Bender, *New York Intellect*, chap. 5; John G. Sproat, *The Best Men: Liberal Reformers in the Gilded Age*. (New York, 1968); George Fredrickson, *The Inner Civil War: Northern Intellectuals and the Crisis of the Union* (New York, 1965).

9. For a different view, one that argues that a new societal *acceptance* of hierarchy between 1880–1900 facilitated academic professionalization, see Haber, *Quest for Authority and Honor*, pt. 3.

10. Karl Mannheim, *Ideology and Utopia* (New York, 1936); idem, *Essays on the Sociology of Knowledge* (London, 1952).

11. The best recent account is David Scobey, "Boycotting the Politics Factory: Labor Radicalism and the New York City Mayoral Election of 1886," *Radical History Review* 28–30 (1984): 280–325.

12. (E. L. Godkin,) "The Real Objection to the Candidacy of Henry George," *Nation* (30 September 1886): 264–65.

13. On DeLeon, see L. Glen Seretan, *Daniel DeLeon: The Odyssey of an American Marxist* (Cambridge, Mass., 1979). There is no biography of Seligman, but Joseph Dorfman's brief sketch in *The Dictionary of American Biography* contains the basic facts and well characterizes him.

14. John W. Burgess, *Reminiscences of an American Scholar* (New York, 1934), 182.

15. *Ibid.*, 182.

16. The phrase "quasi-public" is from E.R.A. Seligman to Henry Bruere, 22 November 1915, Seligman Papers, Butler Library, Columbia University. There is, of course, a great deal of variation contained within the phrase *German professor*. And there was a good deal of misunderstanding on the American side. Recent scholarship on Max Weber and his generation of social and political analysts is helpful. See Wolfgang Mommsen and Jurgen Osterhammeld, eds. *Max Weber and His Contemporaries* (London, 1987). See also Charles McClelland, *State, Society, and University in Germany, 1700–1914* (New York, 1980). American understanding (and misunderstanding) of their German model can be tracked in Lenore O'Boyle, "Learning for Its Own Sake: the German University as Nineteenth Century Model," *Comparative Studies in Society and History* 25 (1983): 3–25; Fritz Ringer, "The German Academic Community," in Alexandra Oleson and John Voss, eds. *The Organization of Knowledge in America, 1860–1920* (Baltimore, 1979), 409–29.

17. Quoted in Seretan, *DeLeon*, 15, 16.

18. R. Gordon Hoxie, *A History of the Faculty of Political Science, Columbia University* (New York, 1955), 30–31.

19. Quoted in Seretan, *DeLeon*, 17.

20. Defending such power for professors was in the interest of the administrators in their own contest for autonomy from trustees. On this, see Haber, *Quest for Authority and Honor*, 286.

21. "The Single Tax Debate," *Journal of Social Science* 27 (1890): 44, 85.

22. For the best and most comprehensive history of American Social Science— and one that attends to the issue of generational sequences or phasing of development—see Ross, *Origins of American Social Science*.

23. Seligman's papers are at Columbia University. A small but revealing selection was published by Joseph Dorfman, "The Seligman Correspondence," *Political Science Quarterly* 56 (1941): 107–24, 270–86, 392–419, 573–99.

24. This statement is conveniently reprinted in Richard Hofstadter and Wilson Smith, eds., *American Higher Education: A Documentary History*, 2 vols. (Chicago, 1961), 2:860–78.

25. E.R.A. Seligman, "Economics and Social Progress," *Publications of the American Economic Association*, 3rd series, 4 (1903): 6; Morton White, *Social Thought in America: The Revolt against Formalism* (Boston, 1957).

26. Furner, *Advocacy and Objectivity*, 97, 109. See also Edward Silva and Sheila Slaughter, *Serving Power: The Making of the Academic Social Science Expert* (Westport, Conn., 1984).

27. See Benjamin G. Rader, *The Academic Mind and Reform: The Influence of Richard T. Ely in American Life* (Lexington, Ky., 1966), chap. 6. The Wisconsin statement is reprinted in Hofstadter and Smith, *American Higher Education*, 2:859–60.

28. Silva and Slaughter, *Serving Power*, 89.

29. Furner, *Advocacy and Objectivity*, 259.

30. On literary intellectuals, see Bender, *New York Intellect*, chap. 6; Christopher Lasch, *The New Radicalism in America, 1889–1963: The Intellectual as a Social Type* (New York, 1965).

31. John R. Commons et al., "Discussion of the President's Address," *Publications of the American Economic Association*, 3rd series, 1 (1900): 62–88.

32. E.R.A Seligman et al., "Discussion on the President's Address," *Economic Studies Supplement . . . Together with The Report of the Eleventh Annual Meeting, New Haven, Conn., December 27–29, 1898*, 4 (1899): 110–12.

33. This ideal informed one of the most influential efforts to institutionalize economic expertise, Wesley Clair Mitchell's National Bureau of Economic Research, established in New York in 1920. See Arthur F. Burns, ed., *Wesley Clair Mitchell* (New York, 1952).

34. John R. Commons, *Myself* (New York, 1934), 87, 88.

35. On Chicago, see Diner, *A City and Its Universities*, and Edward Shils, "The University, the City, the World: Chicago and the University of Chicago," in Bender, *University and the City*, 210–30. On Wisconsin, see Merle Curti and Vernon R. Cartensen, *University of Wisconsin, 1848–1925*, 2 vols. (Madison, 1949). On Columbia, see Hoxie, *Faculty of Political Science*.

36. Diner, *A City and Its Universities*, 3.

37. For Beard's statement, see Hofstadter and Smith, *American Higher Education*, 2:883.

38. Many of these modernizing leaders have in fact been designated *corporate liberals*. For the term, which was developed in the context of a critique of such liberal reform, see James Weinstein, *The Corporate Ideal and the Liberal State, 1900–1918* (Boston, 1968).

39. This issue—as well as the problem of the relation of stated professional or bureaucratic goals to practice—in the professions is illuminated by Eliot Freidson, *Professional Powers* (Chicago, 1986).

40. Jurgen Herbst, *The German Historical School in American Scholarship* (Ithaca, 1965), 162.

41. White, *Social Thought in America*, 128.

42. Richard Hofstadter, "The Department of History," in Hoxie, *Faculty of Political Science*, 225.

43. Thorstein Veblen, *The Higher Learning in America* (Chicago, 1918).

44. Carol S. Gruber, *Mars and Minerva: World War I and the Uses of Higher Learning in America* (Baton Rouge, 1975).

45. Dewey quoted in White, *Social Thought in America*, 53.

46. Edwin Slosson, *The Great American Universities* (New York, 1910), 453.

47. Charles A. Beard, *Politics* (New York, 1908), 5–6; James Harvey Robinson,

History (New York, 1908), 28–29; idem, *The New History* (New York, 1912); Franz Boas, *Anthropology* (New York, 1908), 26.

48. John Dewey, *Ethics* (New York, 1908), 8, 21, 12, 26.

49. This document is in the Columbiana Room, Low Library, Columbia University.

50. The reference is to Ross's biographical sketch of Cattell in the *Dictionary of American Biography*, Supplement 3.

51. James McKeen Cattell, *University Control* (New York, 1913), v, 5, 14, 32, 18, 62.

52. James McKeen Cattell to John Dewey, 14 May 1913, 15 May 1913; "Confidential Memorandum," James McKeen Cattell Papers, Butler Library, Columbia University.

53. See E.R.A. Seligman to John Erskine, 5 June 1917; E.R.A. Seligman, "Memorandum," 5 March 1917, Seligman Papers. The best account of this complex affair is Carol S. Gruber, "Academic Freedom at Columbia University, 1917–1918: The Case of James McKeen Cattell," *AAUP Bulletin* 58 (1972): 297–305.

54. E.R.A. Seligman to James McKeen Cattell, 5 June 1917, Cattell Papers.

55. For some evidence of this, see Nicholas Murray Butler to William Lawson, 13 February 1917, Seligman Papers.

56. Columbia University, *Report of Special Committee . . . to Inquire into the State of Teaching* (1917), 2.

57. Quoted in Gruber, *Mars and Minerva*, 166, 171–72.

58. James McKeen Cattell to Honorable Julius Kahn, 23 August 1917, Cattell Papers.

59. E.R.A. Seligman to G. L. Ingraham, 24 September 1917, Seligman Papers.

60. Hofstadter and Smith, *American Higher Education*, 2:887–92. Columbia University, *Annual Report of the President* (1918), 42.

61. *New York Times*, 10 October 1917; Dewey's opinion quoted in the *New York American*, 10 October 1917.

62. John Dewey to E.R.A. Seligman, 25 September 1917, 3 October 1917, Seligman Papers.

63. John Dewey to E.R.A. Seligman, 10 October 1917, Seligman Papers.

64. On Dewey's withdrawal from University affairs, see Jacques Barzun, ed., *A History of the Faculty of Philosophy* (New York, 1957), 126–27. I could locate no correspondence to or from Dewey in the Central Files of Columbia after 1917, save for an annual bureaucratic inquiry about his possible retirement plans.

65. Hofstadter and Smith, *American Higher Education*, 2:883–84.

66. Columbia University, *Annual Report of the President* (1917), 49–50. See also Columbia University, *Annual Report of the President* (1918), 42, 48.

67. John W. Burgess to E.R.A. Seligman, 17 February 1917, 29 August 1918, Seligman Papers.

68. This motivated even Wesley Clair Mitchell, the least "radical" of the founders. See Lucy Sprague Mitchell, *Two Lives: The Story of Wesley Clair Mitchell and Myself* (New York, 1953), 340. On the original name, see ibid., 333. On the École Libre model, see Herbert Croly, "A School of Social Research," *New Republic* 15 (8 June 1918), 167. More generally, see Peter M. Rutkoff and William B. Scott, *New School: A History of the New School for Social Research* (New York, 1986), chap. 1.

69. Bertha Mailly, "The Rand School of Social Science," *Report of Proceedings, First National Conference on Workers Education in the United States* (New York, 1921), 25–27; Margaret Hodgen, *Workers' Education in England and the United States* (New York, 1925), 216–217; Morris Hilquit, *Loose Leaves from a Busy Life* (New York, 1934), 66; Charles F. Howlett, "More than Business Unionism: Brookwood Labor College and Worker Commitment to Peace and Social Justice, 1919–1937" (master's thesis, Teacher's College, Columbia University, 1983).

70. Mitchell, *Two Lives*, 333.

71. James T. Shotwell, *Autobiography* (Indianapolis, 1961), 42.

72. Luther V. Hendricks, "James Harvey Robinson and the New School for Social Research," *Journal of Higher Education* 20 (1949): 5; James Harvey Robinson, "The New School," *School and Society* 11 (31 January 1920): 130–31; Croly, "A School of Social Research," 168.

73. Alvin Johnson, *Pioneer's Progress: An Autobiography* (New York, 1952), 273.

74. Quoted in Ellen Nore, *Charles A. Beard: An Intellectual Biography* (Carbondale, Ill., 1983), 89.

75. On the other attacks, see David W. Levy, *Herbert Croly of the New Republic* (Princeton, 1985), 271; Hendricks, "James Harvey Robinson," 9–10.

76. Its principal value—and a crucially important contribution to the city's cultural life—was as center for the sustenance and diffusion of the modernist movement in the arts in New York City in the 1920s and early 1930s. Later, of course, it became notable as the home of exile scholars after 1933. On both phases, see Rutkoff and Scott, *New School*.

77. Charles A. Beard, "A Suggestion from Professor Beard," *Freeman* 3 (20 July 1921); 450–51.

78. For an outstanding account of this process, see Barry Karl, *Charles E. Merriam and the Study of Politics* (Chicago, 1974).

79. For a fuller discussion of Beard and Mitchell, see Bender, *New York Intellect*. 302–8. For Beard's shifting perspectives on these issues, see chap. 5 of this volume.

80. Wesley Clair Mitchell et al., *A Quarter Century of Learning, 1904–1929* (New York, 1931), 5.

81. Ibid., 9–30, for Hayes; ibid., 31–61, for Mitchell.

82. A comparative study of the shaping of British and American social science and the different relations to the organized working classes (trade unions) would, I think, be quite illuminating.

83. Bender, *New York Intellect*, chap. 8.

84. Shils, "The University, the City, the World," 225–26.

85. For relevant characterizations—and perceptive ones as well—of the different roles played by Columbia, the University of Michigan, and the University of California, Berkeley, in mid-twentieth-century American social science and intellectual life, see David A. Hollinger, "Academic Culture at Michigan, 1938–1988: Apotheosis of Pluralism," *Rackham Reports*, The Horace H. Rackham School of Graduate Studies, The University of Michigan (1988–89), 58–101.

5. The Emergence of the New York Intellectuals

1. Thomas Bender, "Metropolitan Culture: Brooklyn Bridge and the Transformation of New York City," *Annals of the New York Academy of Science* 424 (1984): 325–32.

2. On Budapest, I rely on Mary Gluck's comments in her *Georg Lukács and His Generation, 1900–1918* (Cambridge, Mass., 1987), esp. 48.

3. On the theme of the Civil War as America's war of national unification on liberal as opposed to Bismarckian terms, see David Potter, "Civil War," in C. Vann Woodward, ed., *The Comparative Approach to American History* (New York, 1968), 135–45.

4. The best evocation of this culture is Henry F. May, *The End of American Innocence* (New York, 1959), pt. 1.

5. Gluck, *Georg Lukacs*, 74, indicates that this conceptualization was complete in Mannheim's thought by 1918. Randolph Bourne in New York called for a "declassed mind" in 1918. See Randolph Bourne, *War and the Intellectuals*, ed. C. Resek (New York, 1964), 182.

6. See Robert Wohl, *The Generation of 1914* (Cambridge, Mass., 1979), and Carl

E. Schorske, "Generational Tensions and Cultural Change: Reflections on the Case of Vienna," *Daedalus* 107 (1978): 111–22.

7. Max Eastman, *Enjoyment of Living* (New York, 1948), 399.

8. James Kloppenberg, *Uncertain Victory: Social Democracy And Progressivism in European and American Thought, 1870–1920* (New York, 1987), chaps. 1–5.

9. See Neil Coughlin, *Young John Dewey* (Chicago, 1975), 155.

10. Cf. Lionel Trilling, *Beyond Culture* (New York, 1965), esp. 3–30, 209–33, with Peter Gay, *Freud, Jews, and Other Germans* (New York, 1978), 22–26, and Daniel J. Singal, *The War Within* (Chapel Hill, 1982), chap. 1.

11. Herbert C. Croly to R. S. Bourne, 15 September 1914, Bourne Papers, Columbia University.

12. Lewis Mumford, *Sketches from Life* (New York, 1982), 357.

13. May, *End of American Innocence*, 322.

14. Nearly every article in the first issue, including those by foreign writers, invoked Whitman.

15. Eric J. Sandeen, ed., *The Letters of Randolph Bourne* (Troy, N.Y., 1981), 163.

16. James Oppenheim, "The Story of the *Seven Arts*," *American Mercury* 20 (1930): 156. On the Budapest group, see Gluck, *Georg Lukacs*.

17. Oppenheim, "Story of the Seven Arts," 158.

18. Ibid.

19. *Seven Arts* 1 (November 1916): 52–53.

20. Randolph Bourne, "Twilight of Idols," in Bourne, *War and the Intellectuals*, 53–64.

21. Sandeen, *Letters of Randolph Bourne*, 412.

22. Bourne, "Twilight of Idols," 59–64.

23. Bourne, *War and the Intellectuals*, 108, 114, 108.

24. David A. Hollinger, "Ethnic Diversity, Cosmopolitanism, and the Emergence of the American Liberal Intelligentsia," *American Quarterly* 27 (1975): 142.

25. Ellery Sedgwick to Randolph Bourne, 30 March 1916, Bourne Papers, Columbia University.

26. Henry James to Thomas Sergeant Perry, 20 September [1867], in Leon Edel, ed., *Henry James: Selected Letters* (Cambridge, Mass., 1987), 15–16.

27. Henry James, *The American Scene* (Bloomington, Ind., 1988), 138–39.

28. Bourne, *War and the Intellectuals*, 179–83; Harriet Monroe, "Mr. Bourne on Traps," *Poetry* 12 (May 1918): 90–94; Randolph Bourne and Van Wyck Brooks, "The Retort Courteous," *Poetry* 12 (September 1918): 341–44.

29. Edmund Wilson, *Classics and Commercials* (New York, 1950), 114; Elena Wilson, ed., *Letters [of Edmund Wilson] on Literature and Politics* (New York, 1977), 151, 212.

30. Wilson, *Classics and Commercials*, 115.

6. The Historian and Public Life

1. John Higham, "Herbert Baxter Adams and the Study of Local History," *American Historical Review* 89 (December 1984): 1225–39.

2. Mary Ritter Beard, *The Making of Charles A. Beard* (New York, 1955), 14–15. Ellen Nore rejected this view of the importance of Chicago in her useful book *Charles A. Beard* (Carbondale, Ill., 1983), 12.

3. See Harlan B. Phillips, "Charles Beard: The English Lectures, 1899–1901," *Journal of the History of Ideas* 14 (1953): 451–56; idem, "Charles Beard, Walter Vrooman, and the Founding of Ruskin Hall," *South Atlantic Quarterly* 50 (1951): 186–91. See also John Braeman, "Charles A. Beard: The English Experience," *Journal of American Studies* 15 (1981): 165–89.

4. Charles A. Beard, *The Industrial Revolution*, 2d ed. (London, 1902), xvi.

5. Ibid., 91.

6. Charles A. Beard, *American Government and Politics* (New York, 1910), 48. In all of the political science text-books he wrote, including *American Citizenship* (1914), which he wrote with Mary Beard, the discussion began with human needs and wants to which the state must be able to respond.

7. Charles A. Beard, *Politics* (New York, 1908), 6–7.

8. Karl, *Charles Merriam*; Diner, *A City and Its Universities*; Haskell, *Emergence of Professional Social Science*; Furner, *Advocacy and Objectivity*; Veysey, *Emergence of the American University*.

9. Diner, *A City and Its Universities*, 25.

10. Merle Curti, *American Scholarship in the Twentieth Century* (Cambridge, Mass., 1953), 19.

11. For Beard's own positive assessment of the role of the scholar in politics, see Charles A. Beard, "The Study and Teaching of Politics," *Columbia University Quarterly* 12 (June 1910): 268–74.

12. *Political Science Quarterly* 23 (1908): 739–41.

13. See Michael Frisch, "Urban Theorists, Urban Reform, and American Political Culture in the Progressive Period," *Political Science Quarterly* 97 (1982): 295–315.

14. Charles A. Beard, *American City Government* (New York, 1912), ix. See also 385–86.

15. Charles A. Beard, "Political Parties in City Government: A reconsideration of Old View Points," *National Municipal Review* 6 (March 1917): 202.

16. See Karl's excellent study, *Charles Merriam*.

17. Ibid., 211.

18. Jane Dahlberg, *The New York Bureau of Municipal Research* (New York, 1966), 30 n. 41.

19. Matthew Josephson, "Charles A. Beard: A Memoir," *Virginia Quarterly Review* 25 (1949): 585.

20. Ray Allen Billington, *Frederick Jackson Turner* (New York, 1973).

21. John Braeman, "Charles A. Beard, Historian and Progressive," in Martin C. Swanson, Ed., *Charles A. Beard: An Observance of the Centennial of His Birth* (Greencastle, Ind., 1976), 57.

22. Charles A. Beard, "Note to the Student," in *A Syllabus of American Government and Politics* (New York, 1908).

23. Charles A. Beard, "The City's Place in Civilization," *American City* 39 (November 1928): 103.

24. Charles A. Beard, "Grounds for a Reconsideration of Historiography," in *Theory and Practice in Historical Study: A Report of the Committee on Historiography* (New York, 1946), 12.

25. Barry D. Karl, *Executive Reorganization and Reform in the New Deal* (Cambridge, Mass., 1963), 139.

26. The best account of Beard in this context is the essay by Luther Gulick, "Beard and Municipal Reform," in Howard K. Beale, ed., *Charles A. Beard* (Lexington, Ky., 1954), 47–60.

27. Dahlberg, *New York Bureau*, 95.

28. Bureau of Municipal Research, *Purposes and Methods of the Bureau of Municipal Research* (New York, 1907), 1 (quote), 19–25.

29. Charles A. Beard, *Government Research* (New York, 1926), 3–4.

30. Beard, *American City Government*, 129.

31. The founder who most influenced the definition of the bureau's work was Frederick A. Cleveland, a professor of accounting at New York University.

32. Quoted in Martin J. Schiesl, *The Politics of Efficiency: Municipal Administration and Reform in America, 1900–1920* (Berkeley, 1977), 115–16.

33. Beard, *American Government and Politics*, 458, 480.

34. Charles A. Beard, "Training for Efficient Public Service," *Annals of the American Academy of Political and Social Science* 64 (March 1916): 215–17.

35. Robert Westbrook, "Dewey's Truth," *History of Education Quarterly* 20 (1980): 345–53. See also idem, *John Dewey and Democracy* (Ithaca, 1991).

36. Braeman, "Charles Beard: Historian and Progressive," 57.

37. Beard, *Government Research*, 5.

38. Gulick, "Beard and Municipal Reform," 58.

39. Charles A. Beard, review in *Political Science Quarterly* 26 (1911): 714.

40. See Charles A. Beard, "Politics and Education," *Teachers College Record* 17 (May 1916): 215–16; idem, *The Economic Basis of Politics* (New York, 1922, 1934), iii, and idem, "Conflicts in City Planning," *Yale Review* 17 (October 1927): 65–77.

41. Charles A. Beard, "Some Aspects of Regional Planning," *American Political Science Review* 20 (May 1926): 276–78.

42. Beard, "Conflicts in City Planning," 67.

43. For an impressive essay demonstrating the difference between a Beardian and a class analysis, see Eugene Genovese, "Charles Beard and the Economic Interpretation of History," in Swanson, *Charles A. Beard*, 25–44.

44. Theodore Lowi, "Machine Politics—Old and New," *Public Interest* (Fall 1967): 83–92.

45. See Edward Purcell, *The Crisis of Democratic Theory: Scientific Naturalism and the Problem of Value* (Lexington, Ky., 1973), 191–92.

46. Charles A. Beard, *The Open Door at Home* (New York, 1934), 138.

47. Purcell, *Crisis of Democratic Theory*, 26.

48. See Charles A. Beard, "Historian and Society," *Canadian Historical Review* 14 (March 1933): 1–4.

49. Charles A. Beard, "Written History as an Act of Faith," *American Historical Review* 39 (1934): 219–27.

50. Charles A. Beard, "Fact, Opinion, and Social Values," *Yale Review* 22 (March 1933): 595–97.

51. Ibid.

52. Charles A. Beard, "Limitations to the Application of Social Science Implied in *Recent Social Trends*," *Social Forces* 11 (May 1933): 510.

53. Charles A. Beard, "That Noble Dream," *American Historical Review* 41 (1935): 74–87.

54. See Thomas Bender, "The New History—Then and Now," *Reviews in American History* 12 (1984): 612–22.

7. Lionel Trilling and American Culture

1. On the *Partisan Review*, see James Gilbert, *Writers and Partisans: A History of Literary Radicalism in America* (New York, 1968); Terry A. Cooney, *The Rise of the New York Intellectuals* (Madison, Wis., 1986); Alexander Bloom, *Prodigal Sons: The New York Intellectuals and Their World* (New York, 1986).

2. Trilling had a fascination with writers who became figures. This fascination is most apparent in two essays written at moments in his career when such an interest is suggestive. I refer to his essay "George Orwell and the Politics of Truth" (1952) and the essay he left unfinished at his death, "Why We Read Jane Austen." The Orwell essay appears in Trilling's *The Opposing Self* (New York, 1955), 151–72; the Austen essay in his *The Last Decade*, ed. Diana Trilling (New York, 1979), 204–25.

3. Lionel Trilling, *Speaking of Literature and Society*, ed. Diana Trilling (New York, 1980), 120–21.

4. Richard Rorty, "The Humanistic Intellectual: Eleven Theses," in *Viewpoints*,

American Council of Learned Societies Occasional Paper No. 10 (New York, 1989), 9.

5. I refer to the powerful fifth chapter in John Stuart Mill's *Autobiography* (London, 1873).

6. On Niebuhr, see Richard W. Fox, *Reinhold Niebuhr* (New York, 1985).

7. Lionel Trilling, *The Liberal Imagination* (Garden City, N.Y., 1950), 213–15.

8. Lionel Trilling, letter to the editor, *Partisan Review* 16 (June 1949): 655.

9. See especially Trilling, *Speaking of Literature*, 121–34, 186–91.

10. For recent histories of American literary criticism, see Grant Webster, *The Republic of Letters: A History of Postwar Literary Opinion* (Baltimore, 1979); Gerald Graff, *Professing Literature: An Institutional History* (Chicago, 1987); and Vincent B. Leitch, *American Literary Criticism from the 30s to the 80s* (New York, 1988).

11. It should be no surprise, therefore, that Trilling served on the editorial board of the *Kenyon Review*, the principal journal of the New Critics, and that two of the essays included in *The Liberal Imagination* were originally published in the *Kenyon Review*.

12. Denis Donoghue, "The Critic in Reaction," *Twentieth Century* 158 (October 1955): 378–79.

13. Cornell West, *The American Evasion of Philosophy* (Madison, Wis., 1989), 169.

14. Trilling, *The Last Decade*, 228.

15. Lionel Trilling, "Contemporary American Literature in Its Relation to Ideas," *American Quarterly* 1 (Fall 1949): 195–208. In *The Liberal Imagination* the title was changed to "The Meaning of a Literary Idea."

16. Trilling, *Liberal Imagination*, 275, 283, 284. T. S. Eliot said that "Henry James had a mind so fine that no idea could violate it," ibid., 276.

17. Trilling, *Liberal Imagination*, 293.

18. See René Wellek, *A History of Modern Criticism, 1750–1950*, 7 vols. (New Haven, 1986), 6:141. See also Joseph Frank's charge that Trilling misread or misunderstood Hegel. Joseph Frank, "Lionel Trilling and the Conservative Imagination," reprinted with an appendix in *Salmagundi* 41 (Spring 1978): 33–54.

19. Trilling, *The Last Decade*, 228.

20. Lionel Trilling, *Beyond Culture: Essays on Literature and Learning* (New York, 1965), 13.

21. Lionel Trilling, "Elements That Are Wanted," *Partisan Review* 7 (1940): 374. Diana Trilling notes that Lionel Trilling apparently intended to include this essay in *The Liberal Imagination* but for some reason in the end did not. See Trilling, *Speaking of Literature*, 156n.

22. The papers are deposited at Columbia University, but Diana Trilling retains the power to permit or not permit access to individual scholars. Although she has allowed several scholars access, she declined my request.

23. Alfred Kazin, *On Native Grounds* (Garden City, N.Y., 1956; orig. ed. 1942); idem, *A Walker in the City* (New York, 1951); idem, *New York Jew* (New York, 1978). Compare also Clement Greenberg, *Art and Culture* (Boston, 1961).

24. Trilling, *Speaking of Literature*, 199.

25. This problem will be resolved, one hopes, with the publication of Diana Trilling's account of her and Lionel's early careers, *The Beginning of the Journey*.

26. Lionel Trilling, *Of This Time, of That Place and Other Stories*, ed. Diana Trilling (New York, 1979), 72–116.

27. The place of Marxism in the formation of Trilling and his circle may be clearer if we distinguish between the group's *intellectual* and *social* formation. The *community* of the New York Intellectuals was formed by their battles over Stalinism, a point made by Trilling and endorsed by David A. Hollinger, *In the American Province* (Baltimore, 1989), 67.

28. See O'Hara, *Lionel Trilling: The Work of Liberation* (Madison, Wis., 1988), 63. Trilling himself later remarked that the Jewish middle and upper classes were "too provincial and parochial" to give "sustenance to the American artist or intellectual who is born a Jew." Trilling, *Speaking of Literature*, 201.

29. See Trilling, *The Last Decade*, 160–76.

30. Lionel Trilling, *A Gathering of Fugitives* (New York, 1978; orig. ed. 1956), 53; Trilling, *The Last Decade*, 229.

31. Hollinger, *In the American Province*, chap. 4. See also Cooney, *New York Intellectuals*.

32. Trilling, *A Gathering*, 229. On the earlier group, see Bender, *New York Intellect*, chap. 6, esp. 228–41.

33. Trilling, *Liberal Imagination*, ix. For Bourne, see his *War and the Intellectuals*, and for Brooks, see especially his *Letters and Leadership* (1918), reprinted in *Three Essays on America* (New York, 1934), 113–90.

34. Lionel Trilling, "A Young Critic in a Younger America," *New York Times Book Review* (7 March 1954): 28.

35. Bourne published a second version of his famous essay, "Trans-National America," the charter of the cosmopolitanism of the New York Intellectuals, in the *Menorah Journal* as "Jews and Trans-National America." And in a reminiscence about his days at the *Menorah Journal* Trilling remembered Lewis Mumford, who then very much associated himself with the legacy of Bourne, as one of the established or senior writers associated with the magazine.

36. Trilling, *The Last Decade*, 7–15. He wrote twenty-five articles, stories, and reviews for the *Menorah Journal* in the 1920s.

37. Trilling, *Speaking of Literature*, 199.

38. Trilling, *Of This Time, of That Place*, 3–4.

39. Trilling, *The Last Decade*, 230.

40. Lionel Trilling, *Matthew Arnold* (New York, 1939), 194. On Bourne and Dewey, see Bender, *New York Intellect*, 242–45, 310–14.

41. Wellek, *History of Modern Criticism*, 6:139.

42. Denis Donoghue, "Trilling, Mind, and Society," *Sewanee Review* 86 (1978): 167.

43. Lionel Trilling et al., "*Sincerity and Authenticity*: A Symposium," *Salmagundi* 41 (Spring 1978): 109.

44. Trilling, *Speaking of Literature*, 109.

45. Lionel Trilling, "Four Decades of American Prose," *Nation* (7 November 1942): 483.

46. Donoghue, "Trilling, Mind, and Society," 169.

47. Trilling, *Liberal Imagination*, xi–xiii.

48. Ibid., 53, 289.

49. Ibid, 7.

50. Ibid., 96.

51. Webster, *Republic of Letters*, 253.

52. The Machiavelli I have in mind is the one brilliantly interpreted by Isaiah Berlin in his *Against the Current* (New York, 1980), 25–79.

53. Joseph Frank, in "Lionel Trilling and the Conservative Imagination," suggested this. Trilling's active involvement in radical politics seems to have been limited to about one year's membership in the National Committee for the Defense of Political Prisoners. He publicly opposed the Communist party in 1934, signing an Open Letter in the *New Masses* protesting the CP attack on a rally by the American Socialist party that honored Austrian Socialist workers killed by the Dollfus regime. He rapidly lost interest in practical politics and by 1937 had defined himself as a critic of Stalinist influence in literature and culture. See Krupnick, *Lionel Trilling and the Fate of Criticism* (Evanston, Ill., 1986), 42.

54. Leo Marx sighted this tendency rather early in Trilling's career. See Leo Marx, "Mr. Eliot, Mr. Trilling, and Huckleberry Finn," *American Scholar* 22 (1952–53): 423–40.

55. Trilling, *The Last Decade*, 237.

56. Trilling, *Opposing Self*, 103.

57. Ibid., 163–64; Trilling, *The Last Decade*, 6–9.

58. Trilling, *Beyond Culture*, 83.

59. Frank, "Conservative Imagination," 44–46.

60. See Lionel Trilling, "Art, Will, and Necessity," in his *The Last Decade*, 129–47, esp. 141.

61. Trilling, *Speaking of Literature*, 119.

62. Trilling, *Liberal Imagination*, 254, 205, 206.

63. Quentin Anderson, *The Imperial Self* (New York, 1971).

64. Henry Nash Smith, *Virgin Land* (Cambridge, Mass., 1950); R.W.B. Lewis, *The American Adam* (Chicago, 1955); Leo Marx, *The Machine in the Garden* (New York, 1964). Though it is not properly classified with these books, one might also mention here—for its contrast with Trilling—F. O. Matthiessen's *American Renaissance* (New York, 1941).

65. Trilling, *Liberal Imagination*, ix.

66. Delmore Schwartz, "The Duchess' Red Shoes," *Partisan Review* 20 (1953): 63–64.

67. Trilling, *Liberal Imagination*, 89. See also William Philips, "The Intellectuals' Tradition," *Partisan Review* 8 (1941): 481–90.

68. Trilling, *A Gathering*, 70, 76. As early as 1939, he had suggested that there was evidence of numerical and qualitative growth in this class. Trilling, *Speaking of Literature*, 121.

69. Trilling, *A Gathering*, 67.

70. Ibid., 103.

71. R. P. Blackmur, "The Politics of Human Power," in his *The Lion and the Honeycomb* (New York, 1955), 32, 33.

72. Trilling, *Beyond Culture*, 3–30. One also might read his essay on Jane Austen, written in 1974 and not completed at his death, as a commentary at least in part on this growing uncertainty about the consensus that bound him to his audience. This essay is printed in Trilling's *The Last Decade*, 204–25.

73. Houston, A. Baker, Jr., *Modernism and the Harlem Renaissance* (Chicago, 1987), 5–7. A similar issue is suggested, though without direct reference to Trilling, in Barbara Johnson's "Thresholds of Difference: Structures of Address in Zora Neale Hurston," in her *A World of Difference* (Baltimore, 1987), 172–83.

74. Lawrence Levine, comment in discussion of this paper at the symposium, "The Criticism of American Culture," Washington, D.C., 15–16 June 1989.

75. See Thomas Bender, "Making History Whole Again," *New York Times Book Review* (6 October 1985): 1, 42–43; idem, "Wholes and Parts: The Need for Synthesis in American History, *Journal of American History* 73 (1986): 120–36, and the subsequent "forum" of commentary and response in ibid., 74 (1987): 107–30.

76. See Thomas Bender, "New York in Theory," in Leslie Berlowitz, Denis Donoghue, and Louis Menand, eds., *America in Theory* (New York, 1988), 61–62.

8. Academic Knowledge and Political Democracy in the Age of the University

1. Hannah Arendt, "Truth and Politics," in Peter Laslett and W. C. Runciman, eds., *Philosophy, Politics, and Society*, 3d series (Oxford, 1967), 104–33.

2. On Florence and its university, see Gene Brucker, "Renaissance Florence: Who Needs a University?" in Bender, *University and the City*, 47–58.

3. The gender issues were noted by J.G.A. Pocock in the book that did so much to make American historians aware of the whole civic world. See his *The Machiavellian Moment: Florentine Political Thought and the Atlantic Republican Tradition* (Princeton, 1975), 37. Hannah Pitkin addressed the issue directly in her *Fortune Is a Woman: Gender and Politics in the Thought of Niccolo Machiavelli* (Berkeley, 1984).

4. See Quentin Skinner, *The Foundations of Modern Political Thought*, 2 vols. (Cambridge, 1978), vol. 1. See also Jerrold Seigel, *Rhetoric and Philosophy in Renaissance Humanism* (Princeton, 1968). The ideal of the educated man tracks the line of political thought, moving north from Italy to the Anglo-American world, that is delineated by Pocock in *The Machiavellian Moment*.

5. Skinner, *Foundations of Modern Political Thought*, 1:88. See also Daniel Walker Howe, "Classical Education and Political Culture in Nineteenth Century America," Intellectual History Group, *Newsletter*, no. 5 (1983): 9–14.

6. On the historiographical career of republicanism, see Daniel Rodgers, "Republicanism: The Career of a Concept," *Journal of American History*, forthcoming.

7. Carol Blum spoke to this issue in her *Rousseau and the Republic of Virtue* (Ithaca, N.Y., 1986). The most penetrating account of Rousseau's thought is that of Judith Shklar. She showed that there was great complexity to this thought, but she too seemed to argue that his point was to urge upon incipient moderns an impossible choice, one he knew was impossible even as he urged it. But such was his courage and insight. By doing what he did, he penetrated the heart of the problem of modern identity, morality, and politics. See Shklar, *Men and Citizens: A Study of Rousseau's Social Theory* (Cambridge, 1969).

8. See the enormously illuminating work by Kenneth Cmiel, *Democratic Eloquence: The Fight over Popular Speech in Nineteenth-Century America* (New York, 1990).

9. Columbia College, *Outline of a Plan for the Instruction of Graduate Classes . . . and for the Creation of a School of Preparation for the Civil Service* (New York, 1880), 4, 11.

10. See John Higham, "Herbert Baxter Adams and the Study of Local History," *American Historical Review* 89 (1984): 1225–39. For something of the public service, even "social work" ethos at Johns Hopkins in the 1880s, see Marvin Gettleman, *An Elusive Presence: John H. Finley and His America* (Chicago, 1979), bk. 2. The University of Chicago, which was founded in 1891 (a bit later), may have been modern from the beginning—hence its early distinctiveness in training women as social activists in its graduate social science program. Ellen Fitzpatrick gave a good account of the Chicago women but without inquiring into this question of the possibly modern institutional values at the university. See her *Endless Crusade: Women Social Scientists and Progressive Reform* (New York, 1990).

11. Bender, *New York Intellect*, 277–78

12. See Richard Hofstadter, "The Revolution in Higher Education," in Arthur M. Schlesinger, Jr., and Morton White, eds., *Paths of American Thought* (Boston, 1963), 269–90.

13. Kuklick, *Rise of American Philosophy*.

14. Thomas Bender, *History and Public Culture* (Baltimore, forthcoming). Some of this understanding of the danger of nostalgia is reflected in chap. 6 of this book, the most recently written of the essays.

15. What I am saying here bears a superficial resemblance to Michel Foucault's idea of a "specific" intellectual. I think what follows will reveal that his and my concepts are quite different. On Foucault's statement on this matter, see Colin Gordon, ed. *Power/Knowledge: Selected Interviews and Other Writings of Michel Foucault* (New York, 1980), chap. 6.

16. Lest I be misunderstood, let me say directly that the shift I am here outlining is not a move from critical distance to accepting embrace. Rather it is a change in

the terms of judgment, adopting a more modern sense of self and public, and this implies a change in the angle of critical judgment. And this makes the framing of the problem of academic intellect in a democratic America different but still a problem.

17. See Richard Rorty, *Philosophy and the Mirror of Nature* (Princeton, 1979); more recently, Rorty, *The Consequences of Pragmatism* (Minneapolis, 1982); and Rorty, "The Priority of Democracy to Philosophy," in Merrill D. Peterson and Robert C. Vaughn, eds. *The Virginia Statute for Religious Freedom* (New York, 1988), 257–82. Others who have explored this same issue from related positions (though resisting some of Rorty's extremes) are James T. Kloppenberg, *Uncertain Victory*, and Robert Westbrook, *John Dewey and Democracy* (Ithaca, N.Y., 1991). For my own caveat regarding Rorty's Dewey, in which I follow Westbrook, see my "Social Science, Objectivity, and Pragmatism," *Annals of Scholarship*, special issue on "Reconstructing Objectivity" (forthcoming).

18. I owe my understanding of this point to Louise Stevenson's essay, "Preparing for Public Life," in Bender, *University and the City*, 150–77. My sense of the issue has been reinforced by Fitzpatrick, *Endless Crusade*, though she does not raise this order of question.

19. Others who participated in this movement were more radical than Seligman. One thinks in this regard, most obviously, of Richard Ely at Johns Hopkins, who collaborated with Seligman in founding the AEA. The point holds for the whole spectrum of historical economists.

20. "The Single Tax Debate," *Journal of Social Science*, 27 (1890): 44, 85.

21. This point was made effectively by Furner, *Advocacy and Objectivity*, and more comprehensively by Ross, *Origins of American Social Science*.

22. See John R. Commons et al., "Discussion of the President's Address," *Publications of the American Economic Association*, 3d series, 1 (1900): 62–88, quotation on 83; E.R.A. Seligman et al., "Discussion of the President's Address," *Economic Studies* 4 (1899): 110–112.

23. See Croly, "A School of Social Research," 167; Mitchell, *Two Lives*, 340. See also Bender, *New York Intellect*, 300–302.

24. See Bender, *New York Intellect*, 312–13.

25. James T. Kloppenberg, "Independent Intellectuals and Democratic Theory in America, 1880–1920," paper presented to the Hungarian-American Historians Conference, Princeton, New Jersey, April 1985.

26. Recent accounts of the Dewey-Lippmann debate include Bender, *New York Intellect*, 245, 312–16; Westbrook, *John Dewey and Democracy*, chap. 9; and Christopher Lasch, *The True and Only Heaven* (New York, 1991), 363–68. See also James W. Carey, *Communication as Culture: Essays on Media and Society* (Boston, 1988), esp. chaps. 1-3.

27. See the rather curious statement in Lasch, *The True and Only Heaven*, 556.

28. John Dewey, *The Public and Its Problems*, (Athens, Ohio, 1954); orig. ed. 1927), 168, 184.

29. Immanuel Kant, "What Is Enlightenment?" in Hans Reiss, ed., *Kant's Political Writings* (Cambridge, 1970), 54–60.

30. See Jürgen Habermas, *The Structural Transformation of the Public Sphere*, trans. Thomas Burger (Cambridge, Mass., 1989); idem, *The Philosophical Discourse of Modernity*, trans. Frederick Lawrence (Cambridge, Mass., 1982). See also Martin Jay's recent review of the latter book, a review that takes the occasion to speak more generally about current issues in Habermas's work, in *History and Theory* 28 (1989): 94–113.

31. John Dewey, "Philosophy and Democracy," in JoAnn Boydston, ed., *The Middle Works, 1899–1924*, 14 vols. (Carbondale, Ill., 1982), 11:41–53. More generally, see Kloppenberg's interpretation of Dewey in his *Uncertain Victory*.

32. Dewey, "Philosophy and Democracy," 52.

33. Ibid., 50.

34. See Rorty, *Philosophy and the Mirror of Nature*; Rorty, *The Consequences of Pragmatism*; Rorty, "The Priority of Democracy to Philosophy"; and Westbrook, *John Dewey and Democracy*, 362, 539–42.

35. From a rather different philosophical perspective, this sense of objectivity is proposed by Thomas Nagel in *A View from Nowhere* (New York, 1986).

36. John Dewey, *Experience and Nature* (1925), in JoAnn Boydston, ed., *The Later Works* (Carbondale, Ill., 1981), 1:99.

Epilogue

1. Richard Rorty, "Intellectuals in Politics," *Dissent* (Fall 1991): 483–90. Within my own field of American culture studies, I note another provocative essay, also just come to hand: Steven Watts, "The Idiocy of American Studies: Post-Structuralism, Language, and Politics in The Age of Self-Fulfillment," *American Quarterly* 43 (1991): 625–60. Russell Jacoby, *The Last Intellectuals: American Culture in the Age of Academe* (New York, 1987), is a careless, ill-conceived, and perhaps even irresponsible book, but the wide discussion that surrounded its publication reveals the emerging worry about a possible academic withdrawal into careerism and irrelevance.

For a different perspective, one that shows the promise and difficulties of a Deweyan intellectual in public, one that does not make a careerism charge, and one that writes from a perspective philosophically close to my own, see the exceptionally insightful recent essay by Ross Posnock, "The Politics of Pragmatism and the Fortunes of the Public Intellectual," *American Literary History* 3 (1991): 566–87.

2. See Daniel Bell, *The Coming of Post-Industrial Society* (New York, 1973); idem, *The Reforming of General Education* (New York, 1966); idem, *The Winding Passage* (Cambridge, Mass., 1980), chap. 8.

3. Michael Walzer, *The Company of Critics* (New York, 1988), esp. 10–28, 229–38.

4. Herbert Croly, *The Promise of American Life* (New York, 1965), 447.

5. See Carl E. Schorske, "Science as Vocation in Burckhardt's Basel," in Bender, *University and the City*, 206.

6. Dewey, *The Public and Its Problems*, 211–19. Alexis de Tocqueville made much the same point about the importance of the give and take in known communities. See Alexis de Tocqueville, *Democracy in America*, ed. Thomas Bender (New York, 1982), esp. 47–71, 399–402, 414–18.

Index

Designed by Christopher Harris, Summer Hill Books

Composed by EPS Group Inc.
in Meridien text and display

Printed by BookCrafters on 50 lb. BookText Natural